Assessing Culturally Inform(Parenting in Social Work

This book explores how social workers incorporate issues of culture when evaluating the parenting competence of Black, Asian, and Minority Ethnic (BAME) parents and highlights the gap in how social workers assess safe parenting in BAME families.

Drawing on a study that combined a phenomenological research philosophy with frame analysis, the book explores how culturally informed parenting is construed by social workers and BAME parents. It argues that effective assessment of the parenting competence of BAME parents is predicated on understanding how culture frames perspectives of what constitutes competent parenting. Throughout the eight chapters, the book moves the debate within the literature away from the universality of parenting concepts to a focus on a deeper understanding of culture. It highlights the influence that culture has on the way that BAME parents socialise their children, as well as how parents and social workers conceptualise safe parenting. The result is useful insights into the cultural context of parenting.

The book will be of interest to all scholars and students of social work, childhood studies, sociology, and social policy, as well as social work professionals more broadly.

Davis Kiima is Senior Social Worker at Bexley Council, UK. He has a PhD in social work and social policy from the University of York, UK.

Routledge Advances in Social Work

Assessing Culturally Informed Parenting in Social Work

Davis Kiima

Routledge
Taylor & Francis Group

LONDON AND NEW YORK

First published 2021
by Routledge
2 Park Square, Milton Park, Abingdon, Oxon OX14 4RN

and by Routledge
52 Vanderbilt Avenue, New York, NY 10017

Routledge is an imprint of the Taylor & Francis Group, an informa business

© 2021 Davis Kiima

British Library Cataloguing-in-Publication Data
A catalogue record for this book is available from the British Library

Library of Congress Cataloging-in-Publication Data
Names: Kiima, Davis, author.
Title: Assessing culturally informed parenting in social work / Davis Kiima.
Description: New York : Routledge, 2021. | Series: Routledge advances in social work | Includes bibliographical references and index.
Identifiers: LCCN 2020039879 (print) | LCCN 2020039880 (ebook) | ISBN 9780367543839 (hardback) | ISBN 9781003089049 (ebook)
Subjects: LCSH: Social service. | Parenting—Social aspects. | Multiculturalism. | Intercultural communication.
Classification: LCC HV40 .K443 2021 (print) | LCC HV40 (ebook) | DDC 362.82/53—dc23
LC record available at https://lccn.loc.gov/2020039879
LC ebook record available at https://lccn.loc.gov/2020039880

ISBN: 978-0-367-54383-9 (hbk)
ISBN: 978-0-367-54385-3 (pbk)
ISBN: 978-1-003-08904-9 (ebk)

Typeset in Times New Roman
by Apex CoVantage, LLC

Contents

1   Introduction

Social workers, academics, and policy makers in the United Kingdom (UK) have long grappled with understanding why Black, Asian, and Minority Ethnic (BAME) children are disproportionally represented in safeguarding statistics. Although regional figures do not cohere, national data indicate that they are over-represented. The literature proposes myriad explanations for this. Some say that it is the result of factors such as poverty (Gupta and Blewett, 2008; Saar-Heiman and Gupta, 2019), education (Race Disparity Audit, 2017), racism (Kriz and Skivenes, 2010; McGregor-Smith, 2017), immigration (Berrie and Mendes, 2011), and culture (Featherstone et al, 2014, Bradshaw, 2016; Berrie and Mendes, 2011), as well as how social workers communicate with families (Koprowska, 2014).

Despite the myriad explanations, consensus is that no single factor can independently explain the disproportionality. Comprehending it is further complicated by the aftermath of events such as the London Bombings of 7 July 2005, the UK's exit from the European Union (EU) in 2019, the coronavirus pandemic in 2020, and the resurgent Black Lives Matter campaigns of 2020. The wake of such events often emphasises the unequal distribution of social power and contributes to the stigmatising experiences of BAME families. According to some BAME parents, how professionals respond following such events can inadvertently perpetuate social stigma.

In this book, I argue that the disproportional representation of BAME children in safeguarding statistics is associated with how culturally informed parenting is assessed. This is not to suggest that other socioeconomic factors have no credence. The point I make is that social workers who interpret the influence of socioeconomic factors outside BAME families' cultural contexts are likely to misunderstand parenting practices and draw inaccurate conclusions about children's safety. Equally, social workers who are oblivious about how their own worldview and cultural backgrounds impact their practice are susceptible to inflexibility when assessing culturally informed parenting.

The notion that inaccurate evaluations of BAME children's safety within their families contribute to disproportional representation is well documented within the literature. This book, therefore, seeks to achieve three main goals: first, to add a voice to a growing body of literature, which recognises that BAME parents have less social power compared to their White counterparts; second, to highlight how assessing social workers inadvertently stymie opportunities for BAME children to remain in the care of their birth families; and third, to explore how to enhance social workers' abilities to interpret the meanings of the different parenting practices that they encounter when assessing BAME families.

The impetus for this book was derived from a doctoral research that interviewed 80 participants about their experiences of being assessed or assessing parenting. The participants were made up of 40 BAME parents and 40 social workers from rural and urban settings in England. Whilst the findings reflected what is already known, that is, that culture influences the parenting practices of many Black and minority ethnic parents, it also highlighted a complex polarisation in how BAME parents and social workers draw on cultural artefacts to interpret safety in parenting contexts.

On the one hand, BAME parents argued that it is through culturally informed parenting that they structure themselves to function effectively within society in which their ethnicity can negatively impact on their life chances. They expressed this in terms of being complaint and not challenging professionals, in the hope of reducing perceived negative outcomes from assessments. On the other hand, social workers felt that some BAME parents use culture as a smoke screen to hide abuse. The BAME parents who took part in the study did not seem to recognise that they had a stake in assessments.

Equally, social workers felt unable to safely question parenting practices that could not be rejected through reasoned debate, often because they are imbued with transcendental qualities, yet endanger children's safety if left unchallenged, for example, socialisation practices based on rites of passage (e.g. female circumcision, gender roles within families, marriage, 'family honour').

Culture can create social conventions that cause BAME parents and social workers to respond differently to the same event. For example, a social worker could interpret the socialisation goal of ensuring that children always do what their elders tell them as indicating that a BAME parent has failed to promote their child or children's independence. This and similar scenarios highlight the dichotomy between culturally informed parenting and social workers' ideals about how children should be socialised. The result is often conflictual interaction that can contribute to inaccurate conclusions about the safety of BAME children in their birth families, and thus add to disproportionality.

There is, therefore, a need for assessing social workers to approach evaluations of safe parenting with the awareness that culture contributes to how BAME parents conceptualise risk, agency, and relatedness. Parenting within multicultural contexts adds complexity to how these aspects interrelate to form competence. This calls for an intersectional way of working with BAME families that considers their stigmatising experiences, as well as the power dynamics between assessors and parents.

The most challenging aim of this book is unpicking how assessing social workers inadvertently stymie opportunities for BAME children to remain in the care of their birth families. The difficulty is, in part, because addressing such a topic inevitably involves questioning practice structures. For example, the narratives of most participants who took part in the study that informed the insights in this book suggest that professional bias features heavily in assessment. A significant number of social workers felt that some BAME families use culture as a smoke screen to hide abuse. Conversely, BAME parents that social workers used perceived safeguarding concerns to block their effective participation in decisions that would affect them and their children.

For many BAME parents, professional bias against culturally informed parenting inadvertently created systemic disadvantage. This was reflected in the narratives of parents who felt that decisions against them were based on scant and misinterpreted evidence. The challenge is that social workers must draw on their professional knowledge when making judgements about what constitutes unsafe parenting. If their knowledge is based on Western culture, they risk perpetuating bias against parenting practices that do not align to Western ideals about how children develop. Yet, it is also well established within the literature that children develop via multiple, culturally specific pathways that are substantially different from Western patterns.

Some argue that for far too long interest in understanding culturally informed parenting has only been tokenistic (see Katz et al, 2007; Anastas, 2010; Sawrikar, 2017). But, as cultural diversity in the UK increases (Drinkwater and Robinson, 2011; Race Disparity Audit, 2017; ONS, 2020), it is incumbent on social workers to develop confidence in interpreting culturally informed parenting. Nevertheless, building interpretive skills should not just rest on individual social workers. The profession must embrace the responsibility of developing social workers' confidence in assessing parenting in BAME families. Only then can it move beyond rhetoric to implementing training and practice that enhance social workers' abilities to effectively assess BAME children's safety in their birth homes.

As Anastas (2010) contends, social work education and practice must take on all the dimensions of difference to understand the intersectionality that BAME parents enact. This requires social workers to be curious and open to alternative worldviews, as a way of approaching diversity and oppression issues when assessing parenting. It also compels social workers to expressly define families' cultural values and beliefs when evaluating children's safety. Assessments that limit cultural considerations to describing racial heritage, language, and artefacts undermine the importance of culture in parenting. Furthermore, it risks leaving BAME children vulnerable to abuse and neglect either from family perpetrators or from the safeguarding system.

Analysis of serious case reviews involving BAME children reveals that social workers' consideration of cultural beliefs on children's lives is still inadequate (Bernard and Harris, 2016). Enhancing social workers' abilities to interpret culturally informed parenting can help address this and, in the process, reduce the disproportional representation of BAME children in safeguarding statistics.

Prevalence of disproportionality

The literature on the disproportional representation of BAME children in welfare statistics does not cohere. Therefore, seeking to understand it based only on existing data can be challenging. But the totality of scholarships on disproportionality provides some insight. A close look at national demographic statistics provides a good background from which to begin understanding the prevalence of disproportional representation of BAME children in safeguarding statistics.

The 2011 census data indicate that 86% of the UK's population identify themselves as 'White' and 14% ethnic minorities. Of the 'White' population, 80.5% described themselves as 'White-British', 0.9% as 'White-Irish', 0.1% as 'White Gypsy/Traveller', and 4.4% as 'White other'. Asian/Asian British population make up the largest minority ethnic group, at 7.5%. This is followed by the Black African/Black Caribbean/Black Other who make up 3.3% of the population. The mixed/multiple ethnic group make up 2.2%. The remaining 1% of the population described themselves as 'Other ethnic group' and consisted of Arabs or 'other' ethnic group (ONS, 2012).

In terms of welfare statistics, Owen and Statham's (2009) study remains the most comprehensive and influential scholarship on the prevalence of BAME children within the 'looked after', 'child in need', and 'child protection' populations in England. However, there has been further scholarships in this area (e.g. Chimba et al, 2012; Middleton and DeSoysa, 2016; Bywaters et al, 2017). Bywaters et al's (2017) study, for example, analysed 8,000 children in care across 18 local authority areas in England. They found broadly similar patterns of disproportionality to Owen and Stratham's study. For example, both studies showed that children of mixed ethnic backgrounds were overrepresented whilst Asian children were underrepresented.

According to figures from the local government association, there are now 78,150 children in local authority care. This represents a rise of 28% in the last ten years (www.localgov.uk) and is up from 75,370 in 2018. The population of looked-after children is still predominantly White, as children of White heritage make up 75%. BAME children make up the remaining 25%, with children of mixed ethnicity making up 9%, Black or Black British 7%, Asian or Asian British 5%, and other ethnic groups making up 3%. This is despite people from BAME backgrounds only making up 14% of the UK population (Lammy, 2017).

The challenge with seeking to draw conclusions about disproportionality based purely on the statistics is that even with the most up-to-date census data, the ethnicity of some children is not recorded (ONS, 2012). What seems clear, however, is that in the last ten years, there has been a steady increase in the number of BAME children entering local authority care or who are deemed to need protection (Drinkwater and Robinson, 2011; Chan, 2012). National statistics over the same period indicate that the UK population grew to 66.4 million people and that the percentage of people from BAME backgrounds increased while the White-British population decreased (ONS, 2019).

As cultural diversity within the national population increases and BAME children continue to be disproportionally represented in safeguarding statistics, it is essential for social workers to develop cross-cultural competence in their interventions with families. Achieving effective cross-cultural competence in assessing safe parenting is not without challenges. Historically, the profession has adopted either a cultural deficit or a relativist approach to interventions. Both approaches have significant limitations and are explored in Chapter 3.

Defining key terms

Black, Asian, and Minority Ethnic (BAME)

There is no official definition for the term 'Black, Asian, and Minority Ethnic'. In the UK, it is commonly used to describe people of non-White descent. The term does not infer that people of non-White descent are homogenous. Rather, it is used as a concept that enables researchers, policy makers, and health and social care professionals to group people who do not define themselves as being White-British. For purposes of the discussions in this book, I use the term to refer to people who are not of White-European descent. Nevertheless, the discussions here also relate to parents who are socialising their children in communities where they are considered to form part of the ethnic minority. As such, the ideas shared here can be applied to parenting in mainland Europe, North America, and Australia.

Culture

One of the most exciting explorations of a definition for the term 'culture' is by American anthropologists Alfred Kroeber and Clyde Kluckhohn. In their book, *Culture: A Critical Review of Concepts and Definitions* (Kroeber and Kluckhohn, 1952), they argued that the concept of culture is related to how a group of people think about the world. They espoused the view that different nations operate with different categories, assumptions, and moralities, which cause them to interpret the world differently. Geertz (1973) advances a similar conceptualisation by defining culture as the way of life of a group of people, including their material artefacts. This conceptualisation of culture is seen as the traditional view.

Proponents of the traditional view of culture assert that when people think and feel differently about phenomena, they are simply drawing on different assumptions and using different categories to make sense of and find meaning in the world they inhabit. This is a fascinating starting point in seeking to understand culturally informed parenting.

In modern parlance, the term 'culture' is often interchangeably used with ethnicity or used together to mean the same thing. As Coliendo and McIlwain (2022) observe, it is an aspect of identity that is salient for some than others. While some view it as long established, others perceive it as a dynamic social construction. In any event, the term causes controversy because it can also be used for social stratification, which some commentators (e.g. Berreman, 1981; Jones, 1997; Fenton, 1999; Gillborn and Mirza, 2000; Maalouf, 2000; Ellison, 2005) see as perpetuating social inequality along the lines of race, kinship, age, class, and gender.

Berreman (1981), for example, explained that culture can be conceptualised as having a dichotic relation with race. He asserted that this dichotomy is based on the difference that racial stratification is rooted in the physical and cultural characteristics defined by outside groups, while culture is based on the cultural characteristics that an ethnic group defines for itself. In his view, both are ascribed at birth.

One way of interpreting Berreman's (1981) point is to reason that contrasting culture with race can be problematic because racial characteristics defined by the outside group often carry inaccuracies and stereotypes. But, even if in-group classification is normally more accurate, they are not without practice challenges. Cultural classifications can still be used by outside groups to stereotype entire communities in ways that are oversimplified and that view race as being a static cultural process. Consequently, there is a lack of consensus on how to define culture and ethnicity.

Nevertheless, there is some agreement over what the main features of culture should include. These are highlighted by Hutchinson and Smith (1996, 1996), Phoenix and Husain (2007), and Coakley (2012) as:

- Shared historical memories including events and commemorations (e.g. independence, heroes, and battles).
- Elements of a common culture that are not necessarily specific but include aspects such as religion, language, customs, and artefacts.
- Common ancestry in terms of notions of origin in time and place that give the group a sense of kinship.
- Common name to identify and link a community to a common homeland and give a sense of solidarity.

According to Swindler, culture is best understood as the publicly available symbolic forms through which people experience and express meaning (Swindler, 2008, p. 273), that is, that culture is experienced and expressed through vehicles such as ceremonies, art forms, beliefs, language, and dress. She refers to these vehicles as a tool-kit that people use to solve different kinds of problems, and argues that culture's causal influence is that it gives people persistent ways of ordering action by providing components that are used to construct strategies of action. In other words, people from the same cultural heritage deem culturally defined ways of doing things or perceiving the world as settled and requiring no further debate.

The attributes of cultural scripts are socially constructed, dynamic, and shape the behaviour and attitudes of BAME parents. For purposes of the discussions in this book, I use the term to refer to the shared identity or identities of a group of people based on common traits, customs, values, and patterns of behaviour that are derived from their beliefs and experiences. This conceptualisation goes beyond the narrow focus of race and ethnicity and makes it possible to understand, for example, why the parenting approaches of third-generation Black British or Asian British parents might be broadly similar to their White counterparts and distinctly different from first- and second-generation BAME parents.

Race

Definitions of race characterise it as being biologically determined. In other words, race is broadly defined in terms of physical features such as skin colour and geographical origin. Historic categorisations and definitions of the term race raise controversy in modern expressions and understanding of race. For example, nineteenth-century attempts to construct a universally accepted definition of the term attached great importance to physical attributes such as skin colour as well as moral and intellectual judgement.

As Walton and Caliendo (2011) note, it became widely accepted that some physical attributes were reflective of fundamental differences between groups and that some groups were inherently superior to others (p. 4). This approach to identifying races continued throughout the nineteenth century and into the twentieth century. For example, basing their study on population genetics, Herrnstein and Murray (1994) conducted a study on intelligence and concluded that genes and environment are associated with race differences. The controversy of defining race along biological attributes is that historically, such classifications have been used to disadvantage some groups by legitimising oppression (Hinginbotham, 1996). However, the terms ethnicity and race are still often used interchangeably to refer to a combination of skin colour, geographical origin, and behavioural attributes.

Ethnicity

Although seemingly straightforward, the term ethnicity is subject to several interpretations and is often interchangeably used with other terms such as race, tradition, and culture. These interpretations are socially constructed and continually redefined or modified over time. According to Professor Ignatieff, a historian and an academic, it is the plasticity of ethnicity that makes it an essential characteristic of human identity (Ignatieff, 1998). But, whilst ethnicity overlaps with concepts such as race, culture, and tradition, it is important to draw distinctions between them, as we seek to understand how culture influences parenting.

Anthropologists Hutchinson and Smith (1996) trace the origins of the term 'ethnicity' to ancient Greece where the Greek equivalent '*ethnos*' was used to refer to tribe, race, people, or band. The term is said to have first appeared in the Oxford English Dictionary in 1953. According to Jenkins (2008), in its most basic form, the English translation has retained the original Greek meaning, that is, a group of human beings living and acting together. Cashmore (2004) conceptualised ethnicity by referring to it as "*coherence and solidarity within a group of people who are, at least latently aware of having common origins*" (p. 142). A similar view is expressed by Caliendo and McIlwain (2011), who explain ethnicity as a concept that helps define individual and collective identities by "*reminding us and telling others of who we are, what we do, how we live and what we value*" (p. xxii).

In his book on the challenge of third-world development, Professor Howard Handelman, a political science academic at the University of Wisconsin-Milwaukee, in the United States (USA), draws on the Greek origins of the term to clarify the concept of ethnicity. He stresses that ethnicity is predicated on social interactions within human communities and goes on to suggest four levels of incorporation: the ethnic category, the ethnic network, the ethnic association, and the ethnic community (Handelman, 1996). According to Professor Handelman, the ethnic category is the lowest level of social interactions and only serves to establish perceived differences and boundaries between groups. At the ethnic network level, the community interacts to distribute resources among its members. The ethnic association level is the point at which the members possess common interests and engage in political organisation to express their interests. At the highest level, the ethnic community, the community occupies a permanent territory and operates in a clear political system.

The limitation of Professor Handelman's conceptualisation is in its focus on economic and political ambitions as key drivers to group formation. Consequently, his explanation of the ethnic community level fails to recognise that ethnic groups live within a broader community of other groups rather than as nation states. This is important when seeking to understand how ethnicity influences the parenting practices of Black and minority ethnic parents living in the UK. Schermerhorn's (1996) conceptualisation offers some insight. He defines ethnicity as a collective group of individuals within a larger society that derive their identity from real or putative ancestry, a shared history, or cultural artefacts.

In terms of seeking to understand culturally informed parenting, the key point to be drawn from Schermerhorn's conceptualisation is the shared history. According to Schermerhorn, ethnic groups use their shared history to reinforce what it means to be a member of the group. In the context of understanding parenting, this means that parents from the same ethnic group socialise their children in broadly similar ways that reinforce group identity. For example, as Fontes (2002) points out, what children need to learn and the best ways of teaching them about it are passed down as cultural knowledge from one generation to another. In terms of this study, whilst Professor Handleman's conceptualisation of ethnicity might help us understand conflict within nation states, Schermerhorn's conceptualisation offers an arguably more relevant explanation of how culture and ethnicity influence parenting practices.

That said, the social–economic environment within which parenting occurs also impacts on parents' behaviour (Featherstone, 2014; Gupta et al, 2016). Gupta and colleagues point out that factors such as poverty can limit parents' ability to purchase basic items such as food. Equally, families that experience racial discrimination and disrespect can become wary of 'outsiders' and develop parenting strategies aimed at protecting themselves and their children. In this regard, Professor Handleman's conceptualisation is important in helping us understand how economic and political factors contribute to the development of culturally defined parenting scripts. Handleman and Shemmerhorn's conceptualisations also point to the need for parenting competence assessment processes that adopt a multi-dimensional approach to analysing the interaction of Black and minority ethnic parents' individual, relational, and social factors.

Parenting

Parenting means different things to different people and defining it is not straightforward or easily defined. Some writers prefer to place emphasis on the activities that parents perform (e.g. Morrison, 1978; Hoghughi and Long, 2004; Watson and Skinner, 2004; Lee et al, 2014), while others (e.g. Brooks, 1987; Hays, 1996; Smith, 2010; Golombok, 2014) conceptualise the definition of parenting based on the process or state and responsibility of being a parent. When assessing parenting, social workers place great emphasis on how parents' behaviour and approaches to socialising their children impact the children's development.

Although the literature reflects diverse definitions of parenting, studies tend to be gender biased. Feminist writers argue that most definitions approach parenting from a patriarchal ideal that excludes men from the parenting role. This, they argue, creates social imbalance by suggesting that the quality of parenting is associated with the gender that takes responsibility for socialising a child. They point out that parenting is a gender-neutral term and advocates for feminist consciousness when constructing its definition. In their view, this would help deconstruct perceptions that associate gender identity with most parenting definitions (see Chodorow, 1978; Zimmerman, 2002).

In this book, I adopt a definition of parenting based on Watson and Skinner's (2004) conceptualisation. That is, that although parenting roles are usually conducted by biological parents, that is, birth mothers and/or fathers of children, parenting also refers to other contexts, such as the care and/or guidance provided by extended family members, legal guardians, and foster or adoptive parents. It involves a range of practices or events that encompass how parents socialise children and is influenced by a range of ecological factors, including culture.

Parenting practices

There is no accepted definition for the term *parenting practice*, within the literature. However, it is understood in relation to how parents socialise their children. For example, some refer to parenting practices as consisting of the regular activities that parents perform with their children, such as storytelling or reading a book to improve a child's learning and setting boundaries to guide children and strategies used to discipline and reward children (see Spera, 2005; Roopnarine et al, 2014; Teti et al, 2017).

According to Roopnarine et al (2014), parenting practices reflect cultural socialisations in that they are based on how parents balance the multiple dimensions of family life within unique social, physical, and cultural circumstances. These circumstances include the influence of factors such as social class, culture, poverty, the child's temperament, the parents' own history, neighbourhood, the community, and the era in which the child is born (Waylen and Stewart-Brown, 2008; Kellett and Apps, 2009).

In this book, I define parenting practices as the regular and varied range of activities that parents adopt to socialise their children. They include but are not limited to how parents discipline and reward their children, the physical care they give, the messages they reinforce about the world, and the behaviour they model.

Parenting styles

Definitions of parenting styles, within parenting literature, draw heavily on Diana Baumrind's (1967, 1991) conceptualisation to describe variations in the way that parents control and socialise their children. Such definitions tend to focus on two main points. The first is that parenting must be understood in terms of issues of nurturing, communication, expectations of maturity, and control. Second, that Baumrind's typologies describe 'normal' parenting and cannot be used to understand parenting that is abusive or neglectful.

Additionally, definitions on parenting styles suggest that there is a causal link between the strategies that parents use to socialise children and children's behaviour. But, whilst establishing causality is difficult (O'Connor and Scott, 2007; Benson and Marshall, 2009), research indicates that parenting styles can have an impact on children's behaviour that carries on into their adulthood.

In their definition of parenting styles, Darling and Steinberg (1993) seek to distinguish styles from practices. They define parenting style in terms of the constellation of the values and attitudes that parents communicate to children, which, when taken together, create the climate in which parents' behaviour is expressed (Darling and Steinberg, 1993, p. 488). They distinguish styles from practices by suggesting that parenting practices are context-specific interactions, whilst parenting styles are the dominant strategies that parents use to socialise their children.

Consensus within the literature is that parenting styles are the psychological constructs that represent the standard strategies that parents use to socialise their children (Spera, 2005; Golombok, 2014; Bryne et al, 2014). The parenting styles discussions within this study are based on this definition as it refers to the overall pattern of actions and behaviour of parents, rather than specific tasks.

Parenting competence

Definitions of parenting competence are open to debate within the literature. This is partly because there is no universal agreement on a definition of parenting or how children should be socialised. Furthermore, the theoretical and empirical foundations that inform discussions of parenting competence are heavily based on Western constructions of parenting. Indeed, much of the debate tends to centre on identifying which components of parenting to consider and what tools to use when evaluating competence (see, e.g. Teti and Candelania, 2002; O'Connor and Scott, 2007).

Whilst there is evidence to suggest that some components of parenting (e.g. the goal of ensuring safety) are universally accepted, linking the quality of the parent–child relationship to children's outcomes is neither simple nor direct (O'Connor and Scott, 2017). What emerges from the literature is that the context within which parenting activities are conducted plays a crucial role not only in understanding the meaning of parenting practices but also in understanding their effect on a range of outcomes for children. This suggests that parenting competence is socially constructed and, as Teti and Candelania (2002) propose, can only be defined with reference to the socialisation outcomes desired by a group of people.

In this book, parenting competence is referred to in terms of parents' abilities to socialise children towards achieving the expectations and outcomes of a specific social group. I conceptualised as a social construction that is determined by cultural values. In terms of the discussions contained here, this definition allows for critical exploration of the varied constructions of parenting competence expressed by BAME parents and social workers.

Safe parenting

Safe parenting is a concept that is associated with statutory social work. There is no universally accepted definition for safe parenting, but conceptualisations within the literature suggest that it involves parents' ability to keep children safe from harm. Safe parenting and parenting competence are closely related concepts in that they focus attention on how parents show and prioritise children's development. When assessing parenting, social workers evaluate both concepts in terms of identifying attributes that demonstrate that a parent can provide enduring care for a child within a specific setting. These attributes are summarised in the assessment triangle espoused in the framework for the assessment of children in need and their families (Department of Health, 2000).

Defining what constitutes safe parenting also involves consideration of the extent to which parents can positively adapt to their children's changing needs and circumstances. As White (2005) points out, safe parenting is context driven and predicated on factors such as culture, socioeconomic circumstances, and family support systems.

Culturally informed parenting

Culturally informed parenting is another concept of parenting for which there is no agreed definition within the literature. In this book, I use the term to refer to the intersection between culture and parenting. It is about recognising that cultures are characterised and distinguished from each other by deeply rooted and acknowledged ideas about how to socialise children to function as members of the culture. The shared beliefs help parents to organise their children's development around the group's culturally acceptable values (Bornstein and Lansford, 2010; Bornstein et al, 2018). In other words, central to the concept of culturally informed parenting is the expectation that people with the same racial and ethnic heritage parent in unique and broadly similar ways, to promote the effective transmission of their cultural values.

The discussions in this book offer nuanced understanding of culturally informed parenting by drawing attention to the circumstances and influences imposed by BAME parents' cultures. As Bornstein et al (2018) note, virtually all aspects of parenting are informed by culture. This issue is that the variations that exist within and across BAME families are often difficult to divide. What adds to the complication is that each BAME family lives within a broader community and alongside people from other cultural backgrounds. Understanding culturally informed parenting, therefore, entails considering the contexts within which BAME parents socialise their children, before seeking to assess whether their parenting falls below the level that might be considered 'good enough'.

Linking parenting practices, styles, and competence to safe parenting

Parenting research suggests that there is at least an association between the way children are socialised and the outcomes they achieve throughout their lifespan. In general, the specific actions that parents perform (practices) and the dominant strategies they employ (styles) when socialising children play an important role in determining children's developmental outcomes. Conversely, research also shows that children's responses to parenting practices and parenting styles vary significantly (see Darling and Steinberg, 1993; Leug et al, 1998; Darling et al, 2006; Fletcher et al, 2008).

Parenting styles research, especially in relation to children's education attainments, suggests that variability in how children respond to the different 'styles' is associated with ethnic and cultural background (Shaffer et al, 2009; Bornstein, 2013a). It is within cultural contexts that parenting competence is determined (Bornstein, 2013a). This, in part, is associated with the fact that parents seek to socialise children to develop competences that prepare them to function effectively within their communities and as members of a distinct cultural and ethnic group.

The link between parenting practices, parenting styles, and parenting competence is perhaps best conceptualised as an interrelated context. That is, that parenting practices are moderated by the parents' dominant style and aim to influence children's behaviour so that it is congruent with cultural expectations. The extent to which parents achieve the socialisation goals is measured against cultural expectations, to determine parenting competence.

Structure and content of the book

Following this introductory chapter, the rest of the book is organised into a further seven chapters summarised as follows:

Chapter 2: Parenting. This chapter contextualises what is already known about the role that parenting plays in shaping children's outcomes. The discussion within this chapter provides an introductory base upon which later chapters are built and traces the evolvement of Western parenting practices to conceptualisations initially shaped by religious beliefs. Additionally, the review critically explores how current knowledge relates to the parenting practices of Black and minority ethnic parents.

Chapter 3: This chapter looks more closely at how culture influences parenting. The discussions in this chapter highlight the challenges of identifying the true effects that culture has on parenting. It also explores how factors such as poverty, racism, stereotypes, bias, and White privilege affect BAME families. The central premise of this chapter is that culture frames passionately held beliefs about parenting and is associated with the variability that complicates evaluation of parenting. This is linked to the fact that parenting is a ubiquitous individual characteristic.

Chapter 4: This chapter critiques the policy context within which parenting evaluations are conducted. It explores key policy changes and how they address issues of culture in assessments. The discussions in this chapter highlight the wider social and cultural changes influencing policies in the UK. Alongside this, the chapter discusses policy approaches that explicitly encourage cultural considerations in evaluations of parenting. The chapter also provides a thematic overview of relevant empirical.

Chapter 5: This chapter presents the epistemology, theoretical perspective, and methodology adopted in the study from which this book draws its insights. It explains why frame analysis and phenomenology were preferred to other approaches of empirical enquiry. It includes a description of how participants were recruited and discusses the relevant ethical considerations to the study including how ethical challenges encountered during the study were managed.

Chapter 6: This is the first of the findings chapters, and it presents the findings from 15 qualitative interviews with Black and minority ethnic parents. It presents participants' narratives about how they parent and sets out their conceptualisations of parenting competence. Participants' narratives are presented in themes. The purpose of this is to categorise their perspectives to aid analysis.

Chapter 7: This is the second findings chapter. It presents the findings from 15 interviews with social workers. The chapter highlights the different dimensions of parenting espoused by social workers and presents them as themes. The purpose of this is to set out what participants consider to be the defining characteristics of 'good' parenting as well as their perspectives of parenting competence. Additionally, the presentation aims to provide the starting point for in-depth analysis in the discussion chapter.

Chapter 8: This chapter builds on the findings chapters by moving from detailed reporting of participants' narratives to interpreting and discussing what the findings mean. The chapter explores how BAME parents and social workers construe and negotiate safe parenting. These constructions are juxtaposed in the context of the themes that explain how culture frames ideas about parenting.

Chapter 9: This chapter reviews and provides a reflective evaluation of culturally informed parenting. It commences by presenting an overview of the discussions and then summarises the existing evidence base, methodology, and findings. The purpose of this is to contextualise the conclusions. As a way of concluding the discussions contained in this book, the chapter evaluates the credibility, originality, and usefulness of the research from which the ideas presented are drawn. It also makes recommendations about how to effectively evaluate culturally informed parenting.

2   Parenting

Although parenting is done in private, it is a ubiquitous individual characteristic that intersects with other ecological factors. Parenting literature suggests that the features of acceptable parenting should include providing a safe environment, being able to express positive emotions to a child, being child centred when socialising children, and providing routines. It is for this reason that modern parenting approaches place great emphasis on parents' abilities to enable children to socialise within multifaceted ecological frameworks (see Barn, 2002; Shaffer et al, 2009).

Consensus is that at the core of most parenting practices is the desire to protect, nourish, nurture, educate, and socialise children competently. But the parenting standards that should form the minimum expectations for delivering positive outcomes for children continue to be a matter of debate. Therefore, although useful to consider, the features suggested in parenting literature are, at best, a good starting point. They do not transcend cultural influences on parenting.

Early conceptualisations of parenting concluded that the most basic role of parents is to secure the safety and wellbeing of children. What constitutes safe parenting is socially constructed and continually evolving. This makes it challenging for social workers to assess culturally informed parenting. Furthermore, the multiple contexts within which children are socialised can affect the quality of parenting that they receive and restrict the options through which parents socialise them. For example, financial pressure and social isolation can lead to a single mother expecting her 11-year-old daughter to be responsible for her 4-year-old sibling while the mother goes to work.

Additionally, parents will perpetuate the parenting practices of previous generations within their birth lineage. For instance, by influencing views about when children are old enough to contribute to family functioning. This remains relevant today, as great emphasis is placed on ensuring that children are safe within their families and develop across various domains (see Smith and Farrington, 2004; Luthar, 2006; Masten et al, 2006).

The limitation of modern approaches is that they tend to be informed by research that proposes a bewildering amount of theories and opinions about the 'best' way to parent. This poses more questions than answers about what constitutes safe parenting. Indeed, debates about minimum parenting standards are intensified by the fact that most parenting studies have tended to focus on understanding difference rather than the universality of parenting. It is therefore useful to start an exploration of parenting by considering how our understanding of parenting has evolved through history.

A historical context of parenting

Parents socialise their children according to parenting patterns that tend to be consistent across generations (Quah, 2004; Serbin and Karp, 2004; Belsky and Jaffe, 2006; Shaffer et al, 2009). Although each generation of parents will differ from the preceding one in terms of their approaches to parenting, the nature and pace of change are subtle and heavily moderated by culture. According to Shaffer et al's (2009) study on intergenerational continuity in parenting quality, the mediating role of culture is that it shapes parenting.

Quah's (2004) study highlighted similar findings but added that intergenerational continuity does not preclude the fact that successful parenting is also influenced by children's temperaments as well as other ecological factors such as social class, acculturation, formal education, changing gender roles and family structures, legislation and policy, financial ability, and the geographical neighbourhood in which parenting takes place. What can be inferred from Shaffer et al's (2009) study, and other parenting literature, is that views about what constitutes acceptable parenting practices have undergone several paradigm shifts over the years.

In seventh-century Britain, for example, children were thought of as property, and it was deemed acceptable for parents to treat their children with little or no regard for their vulnerability or welfare (Steinmetz, 1987; DeMause, 1974; Hoghughi and Long, 2004). The parenting practices of the time were largely influenced by religious teachings that human nature, reflected in children, was totally depraved. Therefore, society charged parents with the responsibility of taming what was perceived as children's evil dispositions to control unrestricted passions (DeMause, 1974).

Steinmetz (1987) explains this parenting paradigm by citing Aristotle's remark, in response to the widespread infanticide of the time. He likened the parent–child relationship to that between a master and a slave in that until children became adults, they belonged to their parents, so that parents' actions towards them could not be deemed to be just or unjust (pp. 293–295). This perception that the role of parenting was to tame children's unrestricted passions began to shift following John Locke's (1693) studies.

Locke's findings highlighted how childhood experiences impacted on development. Locke defined identity as a continuum of consciousness and postulated that children were born without innate ideas and that their knowledge was determined by their experiences of the world around them. His studies led him to advocate that the focus of parenting activities needed to shift towards developing children's physical habits in the first instance as this would ensure their overall development. Locke's findings were later modified by Jean-Jacques Rousseau (1762), who took a view consistent with permissive parenting and proposed that early education should be derived from children's interactions with the world.

By postulating that human nature is good, or at least neutral, Locke and Rousseau's studies introduced the notion that children's behaviour could be shaped through parenting activities. They held the view that human nature was not, as hitherto believed, intrinsically evil and that children reflected society's influence on them. This led to a shift from parenting practices that typically instilled fear, shamed children, and used physical chastisement (DeMause, 1974; Keniston, 1977) to practices that aimed to ensure that children were socialised with the 'right' competences. This approach continued into the early eighteenth century, as parents were concerned with self-control and orderly developments.

Along with industrialisation, the mid-eighteenth century brought in another shift in parenting practices. Historians believe that although industrialisation extended the use of children as a means of cheap labour, their vulnerability meant that they held the same amount of societal attention relative to their times as they do today (Hawes, 1985; Heywood, 2001; Schön and Silvén, 2007). Citing Aries (1962), Hawes (1985) postulates that the progress ushered in by industrialisation improved the importance of children within Western societies and acted as the precursor to modern parenting approaches. This is echoed by Hoghughi and Long (2004) as well as Schön and Silvén (2007), who suggest that public interest in the welfare of children increased as Britain developed and her structures formalised. They explain that the growing prosperity increased public interest in the welfare of children, and the public began to recognise that parental care was deficient for some children.

Public interest in children's welfare led to regional and national campaigns to stop cruelty to children, more notably, the Liverpool Society for the Prevention of Cruelty to Children and the London Society for the Prevention of Cruelty to Children. Some (e.g. Flegel, 2007; Ferguson, 2011; Rogowski, 2015) suggest that the founding of the London Society for the Prevention of Cruelty to Children, which later renamed the National Society for the Prevention of Cruelty to Children (NSPCC) in July 1884, was arguably the single most significant factor in influencing the development of legislation to protect children from abuse and neglect, in England. The NSPCC conceptualising cruelty to children as a pathology and focused campaigns on educating the public on the nature of cruelty, thus shaping public discourse.

With the public beginning to view cruelty to children as a crime (Flegel, 2007), child abuse became a subject of social and legal concern. In 1889, campaigns against cruelty to children succeeded in influencing parliament to pass England's first ever legislation to protect children – the Prevention of Cruelty to Children Act (1889). Through this Act, cruelty to children became a criminal offence. Chapter 4 provides a more detailed discussion of the importance of the Prevention of Cruelty to Children Act (1889) in the development of child safeguarding policy and social work practice.

By the twentieth century, widespread child abuse and deficiencies in biological parents had given rise to public view that the state had a responsibility to intervene and protect children who were experiencing poor parenting (Watson and Skinner, 2004). The political philosophy of the twentieth century was that parents have their children 'in trust' and could not do with them what they chose. Through legislation and practice policies, the UK began to recognise that children should be free from abuse and receive culturally assigned minimum levels of care and developmental opportunities (Hoghughi and Long, 2004).

In terms of research, early twentieth-century parenting studies considered issues such as childhood abnormalities and poor family histories within the context of poverty, ill health, and delinquency. However, it was the emergency of empirical child psychiatry and psychology that gave focus to parenting research (Watson and Skinner, 2004; Shaffer, 2008). Freud's emphasis on the central role of early specialisation of children on their adjustments later in life was arguably the most significant early pointer to the importance of parenting.

Freud's ideas are said to have influenced the work of Erikson (1963), who formulated the psychosocial theory as a framework for understanding lifespan development. Although not as central in providing an understanding of how parenting influences children's outcomes, Erikson's ideas had profound influence among professionals and academics concerned with children's development. He introduced the notion that individuals' ability to change was dependent on how they dealt with the trajectories in their lives. Thus, professionals' intervention strategies were aimed at helping families to negotiate their trajectories better.

In Hoghughi and Long's (2004) review of parenting literature, they noted that, after the Second World War, parenting studies gained momentum in the UK. For example, John Bowlby's (1951) research into the effects of removing children from their parents highlighted the importance of maternal love to the wellbeing of children. His focus on the complexity of the parent–child interaction and the consequent attachment intrigued practitioners' and academics' interest in parenting processes and outcomes for children.

The growing interest in parenting research then resulted in a series of influential contributions that include Winnicott's (1965) *good enough parenting*, modified by Adcock and White (1985); Skinner (1953)'s *behaviour modification theory*; Piaget (1955)'s *cognitive development*; Bowlby (1951)'s *attachment theory*, later modified by Ainsworth et al (1978)'s *attachment and strange situation*; Maslow (1943)'s *hierarchy of needs*; Bronfenbrenne (1979)'s *ecological systems theory*; Baumrind (1967)'s *parenting styles*; Chess and Thomas (1999)'s studies on children's temperament, and Rutter's (1985, 1999) work on *vulnerability and resilience*. This list is not exhaustive, but it is not within the scope of this book to discuss each contribution in detail. Hoghughi and Long (2004) provide a comprehensive discussion on how the aforementioned contributions have illuminated our understanding of parenting and its impact on children's behavioural outcomes and prospects.

More recently, researchers have questioned the belief that parenting is the most important factor in shaping children's development. Harris (1998), for example, famously postulated that children's personalities are shaped by the experiences they have away from the family home and that parents have little or no influence over long-term development. She argued that children, as opposed to parents, socialise children, and any similarities between parents and their children are due to shared genes and culture. Her findings challenge conventional understanding of the role of parenting within the social context. In the context of the focus of this research, Harris's perspective could explain some of the conflicts that some Black and minority ethnic parents interviewed for this study said they had with their children.

Whilst Harris does not seek to minimise the role of parenting in determining children's outcomes, she argues that parents' influence on emotional and behavioural development is perhaps less than we imagine it to be and suggests that peers exert more influence than parents. Harris (1998) uses the development of language amongst children of immigrants to illustrate her point. Drawing on the example of her Russian landlords' family, she observed that the children of immigrants learn the language of their home countries with ease but speak the language of the host country with the accent of their peers rather than their parents. This, she argues, is because children identify with their classmates and their playmates rather than their parents and thus modify their behaviour to fit with the peer group (Harris, 1998).

Studies on risk behaviour in children and adolescents (e.g. Gardner and Steinberg, 2005; Prinstein and Dodge, 2008; Brechwald and Prinstein, 2011) express similar views to Harris by suggesting that the relationships that children have with their peers exert enormous influence on their lives through friendships that help them to adjust to school or contribute to later-life problems through bullying and/or rejection. While Harris' observations do not deal with children who have experienced social care intervention, her work highlights some of the conflicts between BAME parents and their children. BAME parents report that they experience conflict when socialising their children to conform to the cultural values that the family aspire to.

The social context of parenting

In Western communities, society's understanding of parenting and children's development is significantly influenced by research contributions, especially in relation to modern parenting practices. This is often disseminated through books and manuals that offer parenting advice. At a macro level, the recommendations made by researchers inform policies designed to support parents to overcome social challenges and enhance their parenting skills. Conversely, several studies have shown that the social contexts in which families operate affect the quality of parenting that children receive.

Social circumstances such as financial pressures, poor support networks, societal trends, and family composition restrict the options through which parents socialise their children and make it difficult for them to focus on the task of parenting (Utting and Pugh, 2004). The Sure Start centres are an example of policy-driven support programmes aimed at helping parents navigate through the wide range of parenting approaches. But, for most Black and minority ethnic parents, acculturation processes, family transitions, and the impact of racial and ethnic socialisation are added environmental factors that have significant influences on parenting.

Bronfenbrenner's (1979) concept of ecological systems theory provides an important framework for understanding how the factors highlighted earlier affect parenting in general. He proposed that ecological factors interact within a hierarchy that describes pathways of influence in four interdependent systems: 1. the macro system, which consists of socio-cultural influences; 2. the exo system, which consists of community influences; 3. the micro system, which consists of family influences and 4. the ontogenic system, which accounts for temperaments. The complexity with which the systems interact with each other makes it necessary for us to understand how factors in one level of the system are associated with other levels. For example, how social and economic factors interact to influence the parenting practices of Black and minority ethnic parents.

Social challenges tend to be associated with financial challenges. Rodgers and Pryor (1998) describe the interconnectedness of social and financial implications by highlighting the psychological distress associated with divorce and how it influences children's outcome. Divorce creates difficult social situations that affect parental nurturance by placing considerable pressure on the parent to adopt practices that they believe will help them cope better in their circumstances. Such practices may include imposing strict, age-inappropriate, and inflexible rules, roles, and responsibilities upon their children (see Farrington, 2002). Findings from other studies (e.g. Caldwell and Bradley, 1984; Tripp and Cockett, 1998; Barn, 2002) echo this view, albeit there seems to be more focus on economic rather than social factors. Utting and Pugh's (2004) review offers a detailed discussion of the role that research has played in shaping the social context of parenting.

Overall, parenting advice often cites research concerned with children's physical, emotional, and, in recent years, early brain development. The implicit message, which is one on which my work colleagues and I (I am still a practicing social worker) base our advice, is that parents who understand their children's development are more likely to provide age-appropriate parenting, regardless of cultural and ethnic background. My observation, from professional experience, is that parents tend to tailor their practices based on what they have been told is going on at different stages of their children's development. But, from a research point of view, the most helpful way of understanding the social context of parenting is to draw from the interpretation of *parenting styles* and attachment. These frameworks offer insight into how parents 'do parenting' and how parenting influences children's developmental outcomes.

Parenting styles

Diana Baumrind's (1967) *parenting styles* framework is arguably the best known and perhaps most referenced theory on understanding the strategies that parents adopt when socialising their children. She posited that parents fall in one of three parenting categories: 1. the authoritarian parenting – parents whose style is to prioritise strict conformity to rules with little dialogue between the parent and the child; 2. the authoritative parenting – parents whose style is more child centred so that the parents explain rules and guide the children without being demanding, and 3. indulgent parenting – parents whose style is to be heavily involved with their children but allow them to do whatever they want (Baumrind, 1967). Maccoby and Martin (1983) expanded Baumrind's theory to include a fourth category: neglectful parenting – parents whose style is emotionally detached as they tend to disregard their children and focus on other interests.

As a framework for understanding parenting practices, *parenting styles* have been tested and validated by various researchers over the years (e.g. Lamborn et al, 1991; Farrington, 2002; O'Connor and Scott, 2007). Lamborn et al's (1991) research on patterns of competence and adjustment among adolescents offers a comprehensive illustration of how *parenting styles* impact on children's outcomes. They studied the families of over 4,000 children aged between 14- and 18-year-olds to test the impact of parenting styles on adolescent's outcomes. The families were categorised along the four prototypical parenting styles identified by Baumrind (1967) and Maccoby and Martin (1983). Their categorisation was based on how the children rated their parents in respect to acceptance/involvement and strictness/supervision.

Apart from confirming the *parenting styles* framework, Lamborn et al's (1991) study showed that parenting influences children's outcomes. The findings were that adolescents who rated their parents as authoritative scored highest on measures of psychosocial competence but lowest on measures of psychological and behavioural dysfunction, while adolescents who rated their parents as neglectful scored highest on psychological and behavioural dysfunction and lowest on measures of psychosocial competence. Adolescents who rated their parents as authoritarian scored reasonably well on measures indexing obedience and conformity to the parents' standards but had relatively poor self-conception compared to their counterparts. In contrast, adolescents from indulgent families evidenced a strong sense of self-confidence but reported a higher frequency of substance abuse and behavioural challenges.

Although Diana Baumrind's *parenting styles* framework had primarily been used to explain how parenting influenced children's outcomes during early and middle childhood, Lamborn and colleagues' study demonstrated that the effects of parenting styles were consistent across different age and ethnic groups. However, the universal applicability of the findings has been called into question with researchers such as Steinberg et al (1992) arguing that the results are mainly consistent with White middle-class and, to a lesser degree, ethnic minority middle-class families. Garcia-Coll et al (1995) add to the parenting styles debate by postulating that the parenting practices and beliefs of middle-class American and European parents are part of normative parenting behaviour in those communities (American and European communities) and cannot be used to suggest universal applicability.

Additionally, research that has identified differences in outcomes associated with gender or race (e.g. Weiss and Schwarz, 1996; McLoyd et al, 2000; Brody and Flor, 1998) challenges the notion that there is a universal relationship between parenting styles and children's outcomes. Interestingly, Lamborn et al's (1991) study also found some variations associated with ethnicity and culture. In their study, authoritarian parenting did not appear to be associated with good educational outcomes in African American children but was beneficial to achievement-orientated Asian American children. Nevertheless, rather than disprove the efficacy of parenting styles, these studies show that, in the main, there is merit and applicability to the framework. What is perhaps clear is that caution needs to be exercised when interpreting and generalising results from parenting research.

Studies on various parenting practices and their effects on children provide consistent evidence that parenting practices are robust indicators of children's outcomes. Knowledge about *parenting styles*, for example, indicates that the way parents interact and become involved in their children's daily lives influences developmental outcomes (see Demo and Cox, 2000; Dornbusch et al, 1987; Leung et al, 1998; Radziszewska et al, 1996; Aquilino and Supple, 2001). Conversely, Shaffer et al's (2009) study on intergenerational continuity highlights the significance that parents' own experience of being parented plays in shaping the *parenting styles* they adopt when socialising their own children. That is, that the repertoire of skills and coping strategies that parents learn from their own childhood experience informs their parenting practice.

Much of the debate around parenting styles has tended to focus on the links between dysfunctional parenting and children's behavioural challenges. However, longitudinal studies highlight the positive ways in which *parenting style* enables parents in otherwise adverse circumstances to contribute to their children's well-being and achievement (Utting and Pugh, 2004). Nevertheless, it remains the case, as Belsky (1984) observed, that competent parenting is the *parenting style* that socialises a child to develop the competences required to effectively deal with the ecological variables that they will encounter within their community (p. 251).

Attachment theory

Like *parenting styles*, attachment theory illuminates our understanding of the nature and importance of the parent–child relationship. The concept of attachment was pioneered by Bowlby's (1951) observations of children in institutions. Borrowing from ethology, control systems theory, object relations theory, and cognitive psychology, Bowlby described four infant behavioural systems: 1. the exploratory system, in which the child explores their world; 2. the affiliate system, in which the child learns to be with others; 3. the fear or wariness system, in which the child learns about danger and how to stay safe, and 4. the attachment system, in which the child seeks proximity to their attachment figure in order to feel safe.

Bowlby saw the attachment system as being the most crucial of the four systems in developing a child's personality and interaction with their world. He postulated that through behaviour such as crying, clinging, and seeking proximity to their caregivers, children expressed separation anxieties designed to get them back to a position of safety. His theory highlights the psychological and developmental significance of secure attachments and gives useful insights into the social context of parenting.

According to Bowlby, attachment is predicated on the child seeking visual or psychological reassurance from their caregiver. It is only when the child is sure that the caregiver is nearby, accessible, and attentive that he or she will feel loved, secure, and confident. Through attachment, cognitive representations of relationships are established and carried forward to influence several areas of an individual's psychosocial functioning (Shaffer et al, 2009, p. 129). Indeed, according to Shaffer et al (2009), attachment histories are causally related to intergenerational continuity and discontinuity in parenting practices. Their study found that the nature of attachment forms the basis upon which parents either seek to replicate or redress their own experiences of being parented.

In the early stages of attachment theory, its theorists recommended the highest levels of maternal devotion as the ideal parenting situation for children's development. Parenting was therefore based on mothers taking on the bulk of childcare responsibilities. We now know that the primary attachment figure does not have to be the mother or any specific member of the family but that attachment bonds between children and both or either parent, friends, and the wider community can affect children's outcomes (see Rutter, 1985). When the attachment bond is developed from an early age and is secure, then the child is more likely to exhibit social competence in forming and maintaining relationships as well as exercising resilience to adversity in later life (see Berscheid and Regan, 2005; Masten and Shaffer, 2006; Burt et al, 2008). However, empirical evidence highlights that there are cultural differences in the way that children appraise the accessibility of their attachment figure and regulate their responses to threat.

The differences in how children appraise their parents' accessibility were articulated by Mary Ainsworth and her colleagues who, through a laboratory paradigm for studying child–parent attachments, developed a technique that they referred to as the strange situation. They put parents and their 12-month-old children in a laboratory and systematically separated and reunited them. Their studies found that 60% of the children behaved in the way that Bowlby described as normative, that is, became distressed when the parents left the room and actively sought parental comfort on the parents' return – Ainsworth and her colleagues referred to this as secure attachment; 20% were distressed from the onset and were not easily soothed even after the reunification – anxious-resistant attachment; the remaining 20% did not appear too distressed about the separation and, on reunification, the children actively avoided seeking contact with their parent – avoidant attachment.

Apart from identifying and naming the different attachment patterns, Mary Ainsworth and her colleagues demonstrated that children's attachment patterns were correlated to the parent–child interaction during the first year of the child's life. In terms of understanding parenting, the studies provided empirical demonstration of how attachment behaviour is formed within safe and frightening social contexts. Children who appear secure in a strange situation tend to have parents who are sensitive to their needs, while anxious-resistant or avoidant children tend to have parents who are insensitive to their needs, neglectful in the care they provide, or inconsistent in responding to their children's needs. Ainsworth and Bell (1969) work was later modified by Mary Main and her colleagues, who added a fourth category of attachment: disorganised or disorientated attachment (Main and Solomon, 1986, 1990).

To illustrate disorganised attachment, Mary Main and her colleagues described a group of children who did not demonstrate a characteristic or predictable response to the strange situation. According to Main and her colleagues, these children typically had a history of being regularly exposed to neglect or abuse. The interpretation was that it is the caregiver's parenting practices and the dynamic and reciprocal nature of the relationship they have with the child that form the hierarchy, and based upon which more complex relationships are built. Main's work arguably gives the clearest link between parenting styles and attachment behaviour. In terms of the context of this research, it highlights the social context of parenting. That is, that human relationships are initially developed with the primary caregiver.

It is well documented that a variety of factors can influence the impact of secure attachment on later functioning. Studies that confirm the link between attachment security and early parental sensitivity and responsiveness (e.g. Srouge et al, 1992; Bartholomew and Shaver, 1998; Howe et al, 1999) have added to this knowledge. The consistent themes from research findings are that attachment transcends cultural boundaries and ethnic parenting practices; fulfils children's instinctual needs; is dependent on the reciprocity of the relationship between a parent and child; is hierarchical, enduring across the lifespan; and, when it is secure, predicts good psychosocial outcomes in later years (see Belsky et al, 1991; Greenberg et al, 1993; Howe et al, 1999).

The limitation to the cross-cultural applicability of the theory is that attachment behaviour is learned, that is, children learn how to behave in a manner that allows them to successfully adapt to the cultural norms around them. For example, Mary Ainsworth's (1967) studies of the Baganda tribe in Uganda revealed a difference in observable attachment behaviour between American children and the children in the Ugandan tribe, that is, while the American children hugged and kissed their attachment figure on return, the Ugandan children clapped. These salient differences reflect children's conditioning to parents' expected behaviour rather than intuitive responses. It therefore follows that if the culture-specific meaning of the behaviour is not known, the validity of the interpretations is open to debate.

Culture in parenting

A review of the literature suggests that the influence of culture often transcends social class differences and shapes parents' views around issues such as gender roles, discipline regimes, hierarchy of power within the family, and perceptions about when children are deemed to be ready to contribute to family functioning (Waylen and Stewart-Brown, 2008; Chuang and Tamis-LeMonda, 2009). It is such views that then influence how parents socialise their children as they seek to promote competences that make them recognisable members of a cultural or social group.

There is consensus within the literature that culture is a significant component of the social phenomena that influence parenting. This is because ideals about competent parenting and social competence in children are shaped through exposure to shared identity, lifestyle, and ancestry (see Barn, 2002; Quah, 2004). Being exposed to a shared way of life influences the relationships between parents and their children in ways that are more profound than the sharing of common goals. For example, when it comes to areas such as ensuring children's health and language competence, it is not uncommon for parents who share the same culture to socialise their children differently (Super and Harkness, 1997; Jambunathan et al, 2000).

Our current understanding of culturally informed parenting scripts remains, at best, speculative. As Allen et al (2008) point out, quite often professionals make assumptions about the parenting of BAME families. This is reflected in some professionals seeing certain cultures as being nurturing, egalitarian, and authoritative, while their colleagues might see the same family as being authoritarian and permissive. The challenge is that differences in parenting practices, within and across cultures, are defined by the variety of ecological prescriptions that influence biological and social parenting.

Roopnarine and Gielen (2005), in their review of parenting literature, postulate that explanations of universal patterns of parenting practices are often grounded in thin databases. They question whether, in the face of increasing globalisation, BAME parents can continue to hold on to practices established from their cultural backgrounds. Increased social diversity, they argue, contributes to some of the misguided and controversial academic criticism about the merit of culturally informed parenting in producing positive outcomes for children (p. 4). Sigle-Rushton and McLanahan (2000) raised the same point and highlighted the need to embrace insight from perspectives that are not necessarily based on empirical research but add to our understanding of culturally informed parenting.

Culture is a constant attribute of every community, irrespective of their relative size when compared with other communities within the country. Therefore, studies that focus on the socially constructed dichotomy between "White majority" and "ethnic minorities" offer limited perspectives on the dynamics of ethnic and cultural influences on parenting. Today's families may be immersed in global consciousness, but cultural variations still set them apart and continue to influence how they socialise their children. Understanding how cultural attributes influence parenting can help improve how culturally informed parenting is assessed.

Parenting literature suggests that research on parenting practices has not always been inclusive. Indeed, much of the criticism levelled at modern parenting approaches is that the recommendations are derived from research based on theories arrived at by studying predominantly White middle-class families (e.g. Steinberg et al, 1992). That said, it must also be acknowledged that there are an increasing number of studies that focus on the ethnic and cultural aspects of family (e.g. Arnett, 2002; Comunian and Gielen, 2001; Booth, 2002; Alder and Gielen, 2003; Spicer, 2010), to add contextual nuance to parenting and in some instances confirm universal aspects.

We know, for example, that the parenting practices of immigrant BAME families are likely to be influenced by their social environment as well as the complexity of acculturation (Barn, 2002; Allen et al, 2008; Kriz and Skivenes, 2010). In their study, Kriz and Skivenes (2010) found that as migrants settle into new neighbourhoods, the children often adopt the values of the majority ethnic group quicker than their parents. The ensuing conflicts between parents and children then force parents to adjust their cultural values and parenting practices (Barn, 2002). These adaptations potentially lead to more authoritarian parenting than is used in their countries of origin (Allen et al, 2008).

Quah's (2004) study of the parenting styles of Singapore families also makes a welcome contribution to our contextual understanding of parenting in ethnic minority families. Her study highlighted the pervasiveness with which ethnicity and culture shape individuals' identities and their subjective perceptions of the world around them. She found that parents from different ethnic backgrounds differed significantly in their parenting styles due to the pervasive influence of ethnicity and culture.

Much of what Quah uncovers, such as the benefits of authoritative parenting and how the expectations that parents have for their children influence their parenting practices, confirms what is already known. However, her findings emphasise the point that the values, beliefs, and customs associated with parents' ethnic and cultural group identities significantly influence parenting practices. A more detailed discussion of how ethnicity and culture influence parenting will be provided in Chapter 8. However, it is pertinent to point out that the implication of Quah's and other filial studies is that policy makers must address the variety of ecological factors that influence parenting when drawing up national policies.

Child development

It is widely accepted that cultural variations can dramatically influence socialisation patterns and thus children's development. This is because it is in the context of culture that parents communicate with and understand their world. Indeed, cultural artefacts such as dress, language, behaviour, traditions, beliefs, and values influence parents' perceptions of children's development. Citing Whiting and Child (1953), Bornstein (2013c) advances the view that cultural variation in parenting is an integral reason why individuals from different cultures are often so different from one another (p. 3). Bornstein (2013c) illustrates the point by positing that culture and ethnicity influence children's development in the same way that they influence the language that children eventually speak.

Bornstein's position appears to address child development from the point of cognitive development. But children's development encompasses physical, emotional, social, intellectual, and language development. Much of the literature on child development is greatly influenced by three main theories: Piaget, Psychoanalysis, and Learning theory, which describe child development in terms of linear or sequential stage processes that are similar for all humans.

This study does not seek to explore the different theories of child development. Rather, the reason for including a brief section on child development in this first literature review chapter is twofold. First, it is to acknowledge the ubiquity of understanding children's development within parenting literature. Second, it is to set the stage for later discussions about the influence that culture and ethnicity have on Black and minority ethnic parents' understanding of children's development.

Parenting in a policy context

Child welfare policy in the UK continues to see children as being vulnerable, at least until their middle childhood. As a result, parenting (quality and practice) is seen as the starting point for indicating whether a child is at risk or that there are protective factors present when predicting children's development and behavioural outcomes (Collins et al, 2000; Luthar, 2006). But child welfare policies are also based on the idea that children's natural families are the best place for them to grow. Thus, policy and legislation make it clear that the state and other institutions should intervene only in cases of need or crisis.

Historically, feminists' criticism of child welfare policies was that they were rooted in a patriarchy understanding of family. However, demographic changes in family dynamics and structures have resulted in policies being amended to consider the diversity of family forms. For example, social trends such as increased divorce rates and the raise in single parenthood have resulted in an increase in the number of single mothers accessing welfare benefits to help support their children. According to Davies (1998) between 1981 and 1988, there was an 86% rise in the number of single parents receiving welfare benefits. This, along with concerns about the welfare of children, culminated in the Children Act (1989), aimed at redefining parental responsibility.

Nevertheless, parenting policies are still based on the notion that parenting is causally related to children's outcomes and that 'good' parenting mediates the effects of a family's environment. Policy makers continue to view families as economic agents that also serve important functions in relation to social integration and order. Therefore, rather than have policies that are specifically oriented to parenting, the UK incorporated policies that support families, intentionally or otherwise, within several pieces of legislation (Holden et al, 2011). The support is spread across sectors such as social security, education provision, employment, taxation, and health care, with the aim of locating individuals and families closer to the market.

Combining the social and economic aspects of parenting makes policies complex and somewhat unstable. For example, although New Labour's Sure Start schemes offered locally available child- and family-centred support to parents, it also had overtones of employment concerns as the employability of parents on benefits became one of its core targets. In some ways, this continued the

Conservative's child support system philosophy. Ushered in by the Child Support Act (1991), the child support system sought to place the cost of looking after children squarely on parents' shoulders. Researchers and academics (e.g. Craig et al, 1996; Van Drenth et al, 1999; Bradshaw et al, 1999; Jenkinson, 2001) argue that the benefits of such policies have been sporadic.

Jenkinson (2001), for instance, posits that Child Support maintenance has had a disproportionate effect on the poorest children and often results in acrimonious relationships between parents who have previously had amicable arrangements. According to Van Drenth et al (1999), the controversy of the Child Support Act (1991) is that it can reduce a father's second family to welfare dependency. A similar view is espoused by Bradshaw et al (1999) following their study of 600 non-resident fathers in the UK. They found that absent father felt stigmatised by policies that failed to recognise the entwined nature of fathers' financial obligations with their social and emotional bonds with children.

Additionally, commentators argue that the adversarial nature of family policies fails to achieve the intended benefits for children. Family-friendly policies aim to reduce poverty and encourage parents' involvement in their children's lives (Hayes and Williams, 1999). This purpose is lost when policy initiatives such as Sure Start schemes and the Child Support Agency emphasise the elements of social order and control by targeting poor parents rather than helping parents who need parenting support. The control element is also evident in the judicial nature of 'Parenting Orders' and 'Parenting Contracts', through which Courts and local authorities, respectively, can require parents to attend parenting classes if their children's behaviour is deemed to be anti-social.

That said, it is also important to acknowledge that government legislation has been instrumental in strengthening family relationships and furthering 'good parenting' through policies that focus on improving parenting skills and facilitating parents' presence in children's lives. For example, drawing on research evidence that children benefit from parents being at home, the Employment Act (2002) recognised parents' care-giving responsibilities and enabled them to take time out to raise their children. This improved parents' work–life balance by ushering in options for flexible working and maternity and paternity leave. As a result, parents can combine work commitments and looking after their children without losing out financially.

Furthermore, investment in parenting support services such as conflict resolution, relationship counselling, and early years help ensure that parents have access to professional help throughout their children's life spans. In the main, access to professional support equips parents with effective parenting strategies. The down side is that it has the potential of undermining authoritative parenting and shifting the power balance from parents to professionals by questioning parents' abilities to correct their own errors.

The political and public debates that followed the youth riots in the summer of 2011 are an example of how the power balance can quickly shift from parents to professionals. In response to the riots, the government unveiled proposals to get involved in the way parents bring up their children. The proposed interventions

will offer intensive and persistent support to entire families through family intervention projects (FIPs). These interventions are the key to unlocking positive
social change through community-wide parenting.

Politicised parenting support is not a new phenomenon in the UK's policy
framework. In fact, according to Winter (2011), David Cameron's proposed FIPs
are largely built on ideas introduced by the Labour government. FIP workers will
give families practical assistance such as help to access support that is already
crafted along, education, care and wellbeing of children, financial support to
families with children, family functioning, parental employment, and the work–
family balance. This reflects New Labour's Every Child Matters (2003) agendas,
which signalled the beginning of policy focus on the interface between parenting
and children's outcomes.

Parenting policies have always emphasised the preference for children to
remain cared for within their own birth families, except in situations where they
are likely to be exposed to severe harm. Indeed, the role that parents play in promoting good outcomes for children is at the heart of legislation such as Children
Acts (1989 and 2004), which oblige local authorities to support families in their
parenting tasks. The emphasis is that parents should ensure that their children's
moral, physical, and emotional wellbeing are promoted. However, with increased
scientific knowledge about parenting, policy focus has shifted to prevention and
early intervention.

Moran et al (2004) attribute the focus on prevention and early intervention
to three key developments in policy makers' thinking: 1. research evidence was
showing that the risk factors responsible for children developing poor outcomes
were clear and the outcomes could be predicated at an early stage; 2. addressing
the issues early would benefit families as well as the community, and 3. many
families who were in need were not being reached by social services (p. 14).

But, as I have already mentioned, despite the prescriptive nature of support and
policy guidelines, parenting is influenced by a variety of ecological factors. These
factors must be understood within the contexts in which they interact because
some of them are salient and affect families in different ways (Williams and Soydan, 2005; Liabo, 2005; Welbourne, 2002). As Moran et al (2004) put it, *"within
any society, parents start off from different places and will encounter different
sets of circumstances that will help or hinder them as they progress through the
parenting life course"* (p. 21).

Legislation and policies contribute to the way parenting is done by seeking to
ensure that children receive a minimum standard of care from their parents. This
is done by equipping parents who are deemed to be struggling in their parenting
tasks with the skills to function within societal ideals of 'good parenting'. The
limitation is that most support initiatives only address the factors that affect parenting at the family and individual levels of Bronfenbrenner's ecological model,
yet research shows that the root causes of most parenting challenges are in the
macro- and exo-systems described in Bronfenbrenner's (1979) ecological model.
These factors include, albeit not exhaustively, poverty, inadequate education,

social exclusion, poor housing, and degraded physical environments (Moran et al, 2004).

The likelihood is that beyond ecological factors, parents' temperaments (perhaps best reflected in parenting style), and children's temperaments, Black and minority ethnic parents base their parenting practices on cultural constructions. The result is that social workers and policy makers are constantly presented with recommendations from parenting studies that proposed a bewildering amount of theories and opinions about the 'best' way to parent. Therefore, applying even-handedness to the assessment of parenting competence is a complex task that requires social workers to be reflexive and aware of how factors such as ethnicity and culture (among a variety of other factors) shape parenting practices.

Considering the earlier discussion, it can be argued that support which concentrates on improving parent–child interactions, enhancing parents' knowledge of child development, and bolstering relationships between familial partnerships fails to provide lasting solutions. Moran et al (2004) note that although there is much discourse about holistic services, it is perhaps unrealistic to expect intervention to be able to offer ecologically comprehensive support. At best, most services will be aware of the ecology of parenting and child development, have a clear idea of the systems level at which their own interventions are targeted, and refer parents to other agencies that provide aspects of support that fit families' unmet needs at specific ecological levels.

3 Culture

Studies on cross-cultural parenting suggest that all aspects of children's development and parents' socialisation practices are informed by culture (see, e.g. Bernard and Gupta, 2006; Page and Whitting, 2007; Chimba et al, 2012; Bywaters et al, 2016; Dominelli, 2017; Bornstein, 2019). It frames passionately held beliefs about how children should be socialised, as well as influences how parents organise their families, engage with issues such as power relations (e.g. between parents; between parents and children; as well as between parents and assessing social workers), and engage in economic activities as they attempt to maintain key aspects of their cultural traditions. This is not to suggest that culture is the only determinant of parenting. Rather, by understanding how it influences parenting, we can focus on identifying commonalities within different cultures and, in the process, contribute to the way that culturally informed parenting is assessed.

Historically, social work has adopted either a cultural deficit or relativist perspective when working with BAME families. Both approaches have limitations. A cultural deficit perspective can contribute to assessing social workers regarding BAME families' beliefs and practices as harmful or deficient. This can then lead to interventions that are intrusive or disproportional. Conversely, a relativist perspective can result in assessing social workers viewing all cultural beliefs and practices, including potentially harmful ones, as equally valid. This can lead to interventions that are weak or tentative. Given the context of disproportional representation of BAME children in safeguarding statistics, there is an urgent need to understand not only how culture influences parenting but also how to effectively evaluate culturally informed parenting.

Why culture matters

Culture is a significant component of the social phenomena that influence parenting.

It provides group strategies for collecting, organising, and interpreting the social world so that even if the social contexts change, socialisation goals remain relatively unchanged. But, despite several cultural competence frameworks being proposed in social work practice and academia, there is no consensus on how culturally informed parenting should be assessed. This increases the likelihood of ethnocentric assessments of BAME parents. Additionally, reliance on findings from Eurocentric studies of parenting carries the risk of inadvertently promoting Western ideals of socialising children as the normative standard for safe parenting. This makes it necessary for social workers to have nuanced understanding of culturally informed practice.

The challenge is that BAME parents are not a homogenous group nor are they shaped by one aspect of their identity. Their identity is shaped by the intersectionality of a combination of characteristics that include religion, disability, geographical location, education, family setup, poverty, and migration history (see Modood and May, 2001; Barlow et al, 2004; Keller et al, 2005; Barn, 2006a; Phoenix and Pattynama, 2006; Carra et al, 2013). This can have the effect of changing the way that BAME parents perceive themselves.

Conversely, how BAME parents perceive themselves can influence how they are treated by others. This can create tensions that run through the realities of common experiences among people from the same ethnic background and can produce variations and nuances that are hard to divide. For example, individuals from the same ethnic group are likely to experience issues such as poverty or racism differently, based on aspects such as age, gender, level of education, or neighbourhood.

Consequently, there are broad patterns of difference in the way BAME parents approach parenting: not just across different BAME groups, but also within the same group. The variations make it unrealistic to explore issues in relation to all BAME parents. On the other hand, focusing on differences between BAME groups does not address current trends in social demographics, especially those that are a result of mixed relationships (McLoyd et al, 2000; Phoenix and Husain, 2007).

Culture is not just a historically formed social construct. Rather, it is perhaps best seen as a "*modern transformation of ancient memories and recent mobilisations of authentic and artificial group feelings*" (Brubaker, 1996, p. 15). So, although there is general information about ethnic groups (see Hewlett et al, 1998; Fenton, 1999; Ellison, 2005), it is often not sufficiently detailed or nuanced as to inform decisions about how best to evaluate culturally informed parenting. Therefore, it is important to identify commonalities that can enhance how culturally informed parenting is evaluated.

Furthermore, much of the research on the parenting practices of BAME parents in Western cultures is based on studies in America (e.g. Garcia-Coll et al, 1995; Roopnarine et al, 2005; Berry et al, 2006). Their history, for example, in the case of Latino children or Jewish immigrants, does not map particularly well onto the British situation. Given increasing diversity in the UK's population, as well as current trends in globalisation and migration, there is a need to enhance social workers' abilities to interpret culturally informed parenting, especially if doing so can help address issues of disproportionality within welfare statistics. Enhancing social workers' interpretive abilities widens their awareness of a range of cultural parenting scripts.

Theories of understanding culture

Culture has long been regarded as the central base for organising society. Early conceptualisations of culture focused on sociobiological factors and linked culture to genetics. Further intellectual developments in the understanding of culture proposed different conceptualisations. For example, materialists linked culture to a desire for possession and physical comfort, and rational choice theorists advanced a utilitarian perspective that conceptualised culture as a set of moral and ethical choices aimed at benefiting the majority in society.

Much of what we know about culture is derived from conceptualisations that were based on studying culture in undifferentiated Western societies. However, Western societies are now diverse. This makes it necessary to understand why BAME parents socialise their children in ways that are different from the wider society in which they live. Therefore, social workers must go beyond simply linking culture to identity. This entails increasing their awareness of alternative conceptualisations of child development.

This book does not offer an exhaustive exploration of conceptualisations of culture and their underpinnings. The focus here is on summarising how theories of culture help us to understand how parenting behaviour is formed and sustained. Smesler (1988) provides a helpful synthesis of the history of culture. He pointed out that the idea of culture is multifaceted and part of the fabric of stratification and domination in many European societies (Smesler, 1988, p. 4). Despite several conceptualisations, culture remains a significant tool for understanding behaviour.

Primordial theory and parenting

Originally coined by Edward Shils in the 1950s, primordialism was later developed by Clifford Geertz, Joshau Fishman and Pierre Van den Berghe (Smith, 1998). It explains culture as:

1 An ascribed identity inherited from ancestry.
2 Because of an inherited ancestry, the members of a cultural group have the same geographical demarcation.
3 Shared ancestry and geographical demarcation also mean that culture is static, that is, one cannot change one's ancestry or geographical origin.

Primordialism places emphasis on the view that culture is determined by biological origins and argues that it is sustained by primordial bonds (Van den Berghe, 1981; Geertz, 1996) that often mean that people from the same cultural group hold similar notions about aspects such as gender, sexuality, and race.

Within the primordial paradigm, there are two perspectives that are relevant for the considerations in this book: the first is the *culturalist* perspective, which places emphasis on the importance of a common culture in determining membership to any given ethnic group. This perspective espouses the view that even in the absence of common ancestry, ethnic identity is determined by common culture, that is, where the group shares a common language, a religion, and norms. The implication here is that groups of people from the same country can be categorised as sharing the same cultural identity even if they do not have the same biological bonds. The common language, customs, and beliefs, and, quite often, a common religion, often mean that they socialise their children in similar ways. This has been shown to ring true in studies that explore how BAME groups socialise their children (see, e.g. Phinney and Chavira, 1995; Stewart and Bond, 2002).

The second perspective of primordialism emphasises the importance of socio-biological factors. Proponents of this perspective (e.g. Van den Berghe, 1981; Smith, 1996) argue that ethnic affiliation is rooted in the nuclear family and is an extension of kinship. Consequently, cultural identity develops and persists because of the ancestral bond that families from the same ethnic background share. The inference to be drawn from this perspective is that parents from the same ethnic group will broadly parent in similar ways because they seek to socialise their children according to the shared ties, memories, and identities they hold about their ancestry. Indeed, some (e.g. Cornell and Hartmann, 1998; Chandra and Wilkinson, 2008; Bayer, 2009) have suggested that primordialism explains social behaviour better because cultural identities persist even in societies where the ethnic group is the minority.

Both perspectives of primordialism advance explanations that suggest that culture is based on the sentimental attachment that individuals have to their ancestry. But, while culture requires some form of common origin, the theory does not explain why individual perceptions of cultural identity change or why new identities are formed. Critics of primordialism assert that this position is untenable because it has limited empirical support (Eller and Coughlan, 1993; Brubaker, 1996). Eller and Coughlan (1993) go on to point out that cultural groups are not socially passive unchanging entities; they are shaped by economic and scientific changes. Eller and Coughan's view is reflected in early studies of parenting within BAME groups, which highlight the influence of socioeconomic factors on parenting (see, e.g. Rutter et al, 1975; Garcia-Coll et al, 1995; McLoyd et al, 2000; Cox and Cox, 2000).

What the aforementioned studies suggest is that common ancestry is important insofar as it tells us about families' backgrounds. But this does not imply that common origins are the sole determinants of cultural affiliation. In terms of understanding culturally informed parenting, this goes some way in explaining the differences in how BAME parents socialise their children. It does not explain how to determine safe parenting within BAME families. The constructionist school of thought takes a different focus by advancing the argument that culture is a socially constructed and flexible phenomenon.

Constructionist theory and parenting

In addition to the arguments that culture is socially constructed and dynamic, the constructionist theory asserts that culture is determined by reaction to changing social environments. This view is widely known to have first been advanced by Max Weber, who argued that historical and social circumstances coalesce to form a group marker that differentiates communities (Stone, 2003) but that shared belief in common descent does not of itself constitute a group. Although he does not offer an analysis on why physical and cultural differences are used to mobilise collective action within groups from the same ethnic background, the constructionist school of thought offers several perspectives. Yancey et al (1976), for example, proposed what they referred to as an '*emergent ethnicity*' perspective. Their perspective suggests that culture is shaped by structural conditions strongly associated with the industrial revolution.

In their conceptualisation of culture, Yancey and his colleagues propose that as industries developed, groups of individuals with different occupational skills were drawn together along the lines of similarity in lifestyles, work relationships, class interests, and transportation needs. This perspective downplays the impact of cultural heritage in favour of structural conditioning as an explanation for similarities in the practices and behaviours of people from the same ethnic backgrounds. The premise of their argument is that culture is the product of social integration. This is a helpful conceptualisation when working with BAME parents because it suggests that culture emerges when information about parenting is transmitted through social learning mechanisms.

A constructionist understanding of culture enables social workers to approach interventions with the mind-set of empowering BAME parents. The problem with this approach is that culture is not static and cultural groups are not always integrated. Instead, culture has changeable rules, the boundaries of which are recognised by the members of the group. These boundaries differ from one ethnic group to another. For example, in Uganda, my country of origin, cultural, and ethnic identity is reflected within geographical regions occupied by several tribes that have subtle differences that distinguish one tribal unit from another. To the outsider, the tribes are similar and socially integrated. But, within the tribes, there are overt cultural differences that influence how behaviour is sanctioned and rewarded different through parenting.

The tribe of my ancestry, the Bakonjo, for example, consists of the Bamba and Bafumbira. These groups share the same language, cultural identity, and similar customs. However, there are important cultural differences. Whilst both are patriarchal, the Bafumbira see girls as fully mature and ready for marriage at the age of 12 years, while the Bamba see them as part of the family workforce to be held on to for the right bride price. It would therefore be simplistic to suggest that geographical and social integration are the critical factors in sustaining cultural diversity. This is because overt institutional forms do not constitute the cultural features that definitively distinguish an ethnic group. Rather, overt forms are determined by aspects of ecological as well as transmitted culture.

A helpful way of reconciling these differences is to approach the influence of culture on parenting by taking Fredrick Barth's argument that culture:

> ... *entails social processes of exclusion and incorporation whereby discrete categories are maintained despite changing participation and membership*

in the course of individual life stories [. . .] The features which are taken into
account are not the sum of the objective differences but only those which the
actors themselves regard as significant.

(Barth, 1969, pp. 10, 14)

In terms of assessing culturally informed parenting, this allows social workers
to focus on the values that BAME parents hold to be important when socialising
their children.

Sarna (1978) proposes another constructivist theory: one of *ethnicisation*. Basing his study on immigrants in America, he contrasted the fragmented nature
of immigrant groups arriving in America to the social and cultural unities they
formed years later and proposed that culture is created from ascription and adversity. He argued that culture is ascribed to groups by outsiders such as government
departments, religious organisations, the media, and other immigrants. His view
was that culture is created through the adversity that members of a group face as
they confront prejudice, racism, and discrimination. The adversity forces them to
unite and create group identity and solidarity. The limitation of this perspective
is that in locating cultural identity to the larger society, it gives more credence to
the effects of outside forces and understates the active role of ethnic groups in
shaping their identities.

Instrumentalist theory and parenting

Like constructionist theory, instrumentalism gives credence to outside forces.
At the core of instrumentalist theory is the notion that things that do not mani-
fest in physical form or are not observed cannot reveal anything about what is
observable. Instrumentalists argue that it is not possible to make meaningful
assertions about things such as culture that cannot be observed. This is because
non-observable objects are neither true nor false (Schiffman, 1998; Okasha,
2002) and can only acquire meaning by being associated with what can be
observed (Torretti, 1999; Okasha, 2002). Therefore, they argue, culture is neither inherent in human nature nor intrinsically valuable (see Schelling, 1963;
Collier and Hoeffler, 2004).

Basing their ideas on cultural conflict, instrumentalist commentators such as
Bates (1983), Fearon and Laitin (1996), and Chandra (2004) posit that culture
simply masks economic or political interests and should be understood as a tool
for gaining political power or drawing resources from the state. Fearon and Laitin
(1996), for example, suggest that cultural groups are merely information networks
in which group members police each other. They assert that culture is not derived
from an intense form of group attachment; rather, it is best conceptualised as a
communication and information device. The implication is that cultural groups'
reasons for doing things are motivated by the economic or political ambitions of
the leaders within the group. The issue with this perspective is that it glosses over
the fact that people live in a world of meaning. It is in the context of a world of
meaning that parents seek to socialise their children.

For social workers assessing culturally informed parenting, understanding BAME parents' worlds of meaning implies considering socialisation strategies within cultural contexts. Professor Judith Suissa, an academic in philosophy and education, eloquently discusses the influence of instrumentalism in her article on notions of 'good' parenting. According to Professor Suissa, instrumentalist ideals are implicit in scientific accounts of parenting that see parents as responsible for creating a certain kind of child. But, she cautions, the scientific language of measurable outcomes can obscure the process of parenting. She explains that instrumentalist approaches to parenting posit 'outcomes' or goals such as 'wellbeing' and 'resilience' as empirically measurable, yet they are neither neutral nor empirically measurable. Instead, *"they are reactions to the kind of values, beliefs and ethical commitments that form part of parents' ongoing interactions with their children"* (Suissa, 2014, p. 121).

Collectivist and individualist cultures

Parenting literature suggests that culturally informed parenting is best understood in terms of interconnectedness within communities. The concept proposes that it is the level of interconnectedness within a cultural group that determines how individuals will respond to social situations (Herman and Kempen, 1998; Held et al, 1999). Interconnectedness is espoused as the extent to which individuals are intricately linked to produce cultural conformity and acceptance (Gilmore, 1990; McPhee et al, 1996; Triandis, 2001; Fenton, 2003). According to Fenton (2003), interconnectedness pervades cultures and influences behaviour in ways that define communities.

Community interconnectedness is typically divided into two categories: collectivist and individualist. Collectivist cultures, such as those of the participant parents who took part in the study from which this book draws its insight, are described as strong connections. This helps perpetuate cultural values and norms within individual families to form complex group identity. Collective cultures emphasise interdependence, family, and collective group goals above individual needs or achievements.

Conversely, individualist cultures such as those of Western countries, including the UK, are described as loosely connected. They emphasise independence and personal achievements over collective group interests and in the process foster a strong sense of competition (Triandis, 2001; Huff and Kelley, 2003). This, in part, can be associated with individuals typically assessing the benefits of continuing relationships with others.

There are other, no less valid, theories and models of conceptualising culture that focus on the construction of culture through aggregate behaviour and group members' cognition (e.g. acculturation). The theories I have summarised here are an attempt to highlight the complexity of understanding culture, rather than to deny the value and contribution of other conceptualisations. Indeed, cultural identity processes unfold simultaneously. The acculturation process, for example, helps us recognise that cultural formation is bidimensional (Berry, 2005). That is, on the one hand, it is through institutions, rituals, socialisation practices, and the modelling of interactions that culture influences individuals' behaviour. Equally, culture is constructed, perpetuated, and modified by the actions of and beliefs of individuals.

Overall analysis of the different schools of thought leads to the conclusion that culture is an elusive and relative concept. For example, instrumentalists and constructionists' conceptualisations of culture as the construct of power, authority, legitimisation, and dominion suggest that it carries an adversarial tone. As Henry and Cabot (1996) observe, it involves passions, emotions, imaginations, memories, and ways of perceiving the world that are passed on in ways that "*are so thick with life that they lie beyond the power of consciousness, let alone of verbal and analytic reasoning*" (p. xvii). These different conceptualisations of culture offer a way of beginning to understand how to assess culturally informed parenting.

The link between culture and parenting

The myriad explanations of how culture shapes behaviour make it necessary to establish a clear understanding of the link between culture and parenting. For example, parenting studies suggest that the variability in parenting practices within and across ethnic groups is associated with the relative importance that parents attach to an independent or interdependent cultural framework (Harwood et al, 2002; Greenfield et al, 2003). Within the independent framework, parenting practices focus on fostering emotional independence, while an interdependent cultural framework emphasises the fundamental connectedness of human beings to each other (Fergus and Zimmerman, 2005). The reality, as Leyendecker et al (2005) observe, is that both frameworks coexist in all ethnic communities and overlap, albeit with differing emphasis.

Although studies on culture have contributed substantially to our understanding of the parenting practices of BAME parents, they tend to give the impression that there is little variation in the way all cultures parent infants. Where differences are highlighted (e.g. LeVine, 1994; Hewlett et al, 1998), the findings tend to be based on short studies and therefore preclude evaluations of the ways in which context might influence parent–child interactions with other cultures, as well as within their own cultures. Hewlett et al's (1998) study of the parenting practices of the Aka and Ngandu tribes of the Central African Republic found that although the Aka and Ngandu share the same ethnic and cultural belief systems and are regularly exposed to each other, they had distinct parenting approaches.

Looking specifically at how the tribes in Hwelette and colleagues' study approach the parenting of children aged 3 to 10 months, the results showed that while the Aka responded to children's distress by soothing their children, the Ngandu left the children to cry. The researchers suggest that the differences in the parenting approach might be explained in terms of the hazards within the community. The researchers explained that there were more hazards within the hunter–gatherer Aka tribe compared to the farming Ngandu tribe. However, this does not fully explain why parenting behaviour remains relatively unaltered even when hazards no longer exist.

Cross-cultural studies of parenting (e.g. Dixon et al, 1981; Super et al, 2007; Carra et al, 2013) suggest that parenting is linked to distinct cultural goals. For example, most Western cultures seek to promote independence and autonomy, whereas BAME cultures seek to promote group-oriented tendencies. The result is parenting practices that vary significantly even within cultures. Such a view is whether parenting practices are influenced by cultural ideology or, as some researchers (e.g. LeVine, 1994, Keller et al, 2005) have suggested, by practical necessity.

There is some convergence within the literature that because of the relatively high intergenerational tendency towards patriarchy and gender bias within BAME cultures, they tend to approach parenting in ways that are similar whilst being distinctly different from Western parenting approaches where the tendency is towards gender egalitarianism. That said, the literature also highlights the empirical complexity of any purported causal link between culture and parenting practices. This means that consideration must be given to the fact that parenting is also influenced by multiple factors including poverty, education, community resources, and social policy. As communities integrate, the socialisation contexts change and affect parenting.

Understanding parenting in the context of integration requires a comparative aspect to cultural considerations. For example, by comparing BAME parents and social workers' conceptualisations of parenting, we can begin to explore whether evaluations of culturally informed parenting need to take a different approach. This book draws on the findings of a study that provides that comparative aspect. The caution is that the dearth of research in this area calls for a cautious approach when making generalisations about findings. Parents all over the world hold specific beliefs about how children develop (Richman et al, 1992; Littlechild, 2012; Greenfield and Cocking, 2014) and how they should be socialised to become competent members of the communities within which they live.

Cross-cultural studies of BAME parenting in WEIRD communities need to be complemented by studies in other parts of the world. Keller et al's (2005) study of parenting among West African Nso and Northern German women offers helpful insights. Drawing from a sample of 46 Northern German women and 39 West African women, Keller and her colleagues observed 10 Nso and 10 German women. They found that for both sets of women, parenting was associated with cultural goals and reflected the conscious nature of parenting as a shared cultural activity. The implication is that evaluating BAME parenting with the standards of Western cultures ignores the different realities and value systems that influence how BAME parents socialise their children the way they do.

Similar findings are espoused from studies of parenting in India (Kurtz, 1992; Saraswathi and Pai, 1997; Jambunathan and Counselman, 2002; Tuli, 2012; Raj and Raval, 2013), Pakistan (Zaman, 2014; Batool and Mumtaz, 2015), Poland (Dwairy and Achoui, 2010; Kmita, 2015), and China (Chao, 2000; Chen et al, 2010). Keller et al (2005) espouse this as *"shared cultural common-sense conceptions that demonstrate that parenting goals and practices are deliberate moral judgements of a particular society at a particular moment in history"* (p. 179).

In general terms, our understanding of parenting behaviour can be traced back to the development of contextual and ecological theories such as Bronfenbrenner's (1979) Ecological Theory and Developmental Contextualism (Gottlieb, 1998; Lerner, 1998; Thelen and Smith, 1998). These theories explained how internal characteristics such as personality, health status, developmental stage, and temperament interact with external influence such as parenting, neighbourhood, and other societal factors to shape human behaviour. Based on a systems approach, the ecological theory and developmental contextualism represent our earliest understanding of the influence that culture has on parenting.

The ecological construction places culture in the outer concentric circles of influence. This suggests that culture only has an indirect influence on parenting. However, the dynamic interactions between parents and their social–cultural contexts mean that as they engage with the values and beliefs associated with their culture, it becomes a personal construct that has a proximal rather than a distant influence on their parenting. As Suissa (2014) asserts, parenting should not be reduced to an instrumentalist discourse on outcomes. It involves constantly evaluating how one prepares their child for the social–cultural environment in which they live and comprises a moral aspect that should be considered when evaluating safe parenting.

The moral aspect of parenting implies that although social change has significantly altered the social ecology of the UK, the core concepts sustaining many BAME family systems have not changed significantly. Interdependence and collectivist ideals are still the main tenets of many BAME family systems (Sarna, 1978; Keller et al, 2005). This is not to suggest that BAME parents do not adjust their parenting approaches. Indeed, studies of the parenting practices of migrant families in Western cultures advance the point that the confrontations and translations between Western and minority ethnic cultural practices produce new parenting strategies that are qualitatively different from those found in the migrants' original communities and the host communities (see Cohen, 1969, 1974; Murray et al, 2001; Leyendecker et al, 2005; Quintana et al, 2006).

Culture and parenting styles

Diana Baumrind's parenting styles is one of the most used and most robust approach to studying how parents influence their children's social competence and development. There is continued debate about the universal applicability of parenting styles. A common criticism is that the parenting practices of White middle-class parents are actively promoted as normative parenting behaviour. This criticism is reflected in some studies that have been conducted on parenting styles in different ethnicities. For example, authoritative parenting, which is seen as the most successful and ideal style of parenting, was found to be most common in White, two-parent middle-class families of European descent but did not appear to produce the same outcomes for African and Asian children (Gonzales et al, 1996; Weiss and Schwarz, 1996; Darling, 1999).

Parenting style categories have been used in much of the research on parenting, including parenting in minority ethnic families. This has generated interesting debates. For example, in her study of Chinese American and European American parents, Chao (1994) argues that parenting styles can be inaccurate and ethnocentric when explaining the values that are important to ethnic minority parents. Lindahl and Malik (1999) draw distinctions between hierarchical and authoritarian parenting styles to express a similar view. They suggest that hierarchical parenting is a more useful concept when studying families where there are strong traditions of collectivist values. Stewart and Bond (2002) also weigh in on Choa's argument and suggest that parenting styles should be organised in dimensions and scales so that component parts such as warmth, responsiveness, and regulation can be measured to give a more relevant assessment of parenting within minority ethnic groups. The problem is that while there is agreement about the component parts that should be included, there is no consensus on how they should be organised.

Phoenix and Husain (2007) build on Stewart and Bond's suggestion further by pointing out that even then, scales can have similar names but be used in different ways and with different meanings. Uniformity is important because, as Whiteside-Mansell et al (2001) point out, unless there is compatibility *"what appears to be group differences could be a result of assessment tools not capturing the same construct across ethnic groups"* (p. 768). This also has implications for research in that the differences in findings may be associated with instruments measuring different constructs in the various groups studied rather than indicating variation based on the same constructs.

Debates about which dimensions of parenting should be considered when studying the parenting styles of parents from minority ethnic groups have also led to researcher drawing distinctions between parenting 'style' and parenting 'practice'. Darling and Steinberg (1993) argue that this is important if we are to begin with minority ethnic groups socialise their children. They go on to define parenting practices as the specific behaviours that parents use to socialise their children and parenting style as the emotional climate in which parents raise their children. Stewart and Bond (2002) share a similar view and suggest that distinguishing parenting practice from parenting styles makes it easier to research hitherto understudied minority ethnic groups.

In some ways, there are clear advantages to approaching the assessment of BAME with this distinction. Not least because, as Kotchick and Forehand (2002) point out, contextual factors play a key part in determining parenting. Additionally, research on parenting in Black and minority ethnic groups is sparse and, as Phoenix and Husain (2007) observe, not always as methodologically robust as studies of parenting of White ethnic groups. Nevertheless, both parenting styles and parenting practices are necessary when assessing parenting competence because it is through this combination that core belief systems can be identified.

Featherstone et al (2014) caution social workers about the risk of developing stereotypes about the parenting practices of Black and minority ethnic parents. Featherstone and colleagues suggest that social workers who fail to evaluate the social context of parenting perpetuate disadvantage by creating an atmosphere of defensive practice that disempowers families. They advocate for a practice approach that evaluates relational identities within social contexts when appraising parenting competence. Their position reflects the findings of studies that highlight variations about how different belief systems influence parenting styles within and across ethnic groups (see, e.g. Gonzales et al, 1996; Super and Harkness, 1997; Darling, 1999).

Researchers attribute differences in parenting styles to the goals, aspirations, and values that parents hold for their children (Stevenson et al, 1990; Darling and Steinberg, 1993; Wentzel, 1998; Peterson and Hann, 1999; Quah, 2004; Spera, 2005). For example, for a parent whose belief system prioritises behaviour over education, it will be much more important to them that the child behaves in a manner that they find acceptable, regardless of their educational achievements.

As aforementioned, although belief systems are at the core of parents' motivation when socialising their children, it is also important to bear in mind that parenting and parent–child relationships are constantly evolving. This adds to the complication of assessing parenting practices. Some commentators have suggested that with increased globalisation and migration, families across the world have similar expectations of children, that is, to develop the social competence and skills needed to successfully navigate through life within multicultural communities and to raise successful offspring (Roopnarine and Gielen, 2005). Consequently, parenting tendencies will universally range from autocratic methods of control and assertion of power to relaxed reciprocal parenting.

The impact of globalisation and migration is perhaps undeniable in certain cognitive and behavioural aspects of life such as in language development, but it does not hold true across all aspects of socialisation. Different ethnic groups attach different meanings to the same parenting behaviour. For example, Kotchick and Forehand (2002) explain that parenting practices that may appear to the outsider as being restrictive and lacking in maternal warmth towards children are necessary in dangerous and impoverished neighbourhoods. Similarly, a study by Brody et al (2002) found that authoritarian parenting style correlated to positive emotional, behavioural, educational, and social outcomes in African American children, but these outcomes were not reflected in children from White backgrounds.

Overall, the theories and concepts summarised earlier help conceptualise what makes one group of people different from another. The view adopted in this book is that ethnic identification and categories are socially constructed, vary widely, and ethnic group members have little control over their group membership. As such, there can be no universal or absolute metanarrative to explain how culture influences the parenting practices of BAME parents. This is because concepts and theories of culture have a narrow focus, which offers a limited understanding of how culture influences parenting. Therefore, the influence that culture has on the parenting practices of BAME parents is relative to each parent's perception and consideration.

Nuanced understanding of culturally informed parenting can only be achieved by identifying the characteristics that make BAME parents socialise their children in ways that are considered a deviation and majority group behaviour as the norm that is typical of a country. There is an implicit assumption within theories of culture that it is a neutral, empirical, and descriptive construct but parenting studies suggest that it is both conditioning and conditions. As BAME parents integrate within host countries, they acquire the beliefs and practices of host nations without necessarily discarding the beliefs of their original cultures. This bidimensional aspect to culture formation makes it difficult to understand the construction of parenting within BAME families.

Studies that have explored parenting practices in Africa suggest that parenting is linked to distinct cultural goals and that cultural parenting scripts are relatively stable, regardless of the settings. Conversely, studies on the parenting practices of BAME parents in Western cultures suggest that changes in the social contexts can contribute to rifts within families as new environments create situations in which what is taught in the family is incompatible with what is emphasised in the community (Amato and Fowler, 2002; Super et al, 2007; Carra et al, 2013). This bidimensional aspect to culture formation results in the creation of what Carra et al (2013) refer to as blended solutions in parenting strategies, for example, socialising children to achieve interdependent as well as dependent goals.

The inference that we can draw from the literature on culture and parenting is that differences in cultural expectations for the timing of developmental milestones are the catalyst for the attention that BAME parents give to socialisation approaches. The challenge for social workers evaluating safe parenting is that in the absence of a universally accepted standard of parenting. Given the gravity of the decisions for which social workers' assessments of parenting competence is used, there is a need for a social policy position that sets out the potentially relevant areas for determining acceptable standards of parenting.

4   Social policy

In the UK, the process of identifying whether parents are meeting their children's developmental needs safely is guided by child welfare legislation including the Children Act (HM Government, 1989; Children Act, 2004); Childcare Act (2006); Department of Health (1999a); HM Government (2006, 2010, 2013, 2015, 2017); Department of Health (2000); the United Nations Convention on the Rights of the Child (1989); the Human Rights Act (1998); HM Treasury (2003); Children and Young Persons Act (2008); and Children and Adoption Act (2008). This is not an exhaustive list of child safeguarding legislation. Indeed, safeguarding legislation and practice guidance in England is continually being amended and updated. The driving principle is that all children should be protected from harm, regardless of their race, gender, sexuality, language, religion, nationality, or social origin. This principle is embedded in child protection policy in England.

Understanding the policy context within which parenting is evaluated helps us appraise the effectiveness of parenting assessments. This is because police defines (or should) the conditions which constitute 'harmful' or 'unsafe' parenting and helps social workers to identify parenting that is harmful (Lennings, 2002; White, 2005; Choate, 2009; Parton, 2010; Crawford, 2011). Alongside safeguarding legislation, social workers are expected to develop evaluation skills through their professional training. Kellett and Apps' (2009) interview of 54 professionals from health, education, and social care found that knowledge of safeguarding legislation and assessment skills gained through training were the key components health and social care practitioners needed to effectively appraise parenting.

Similarly, Turney et al's (2011) scholarship, which reviewed social work-focused research published between 1999 and 2010, concluded that effective parenting assessments are predicated on the skills assessors gain through training. The skills enable them to identify parents' strengths and weaknesses across the six dimensions of parenting espoused by the framework for the assessment of children in need and their families, namely, basic care, ensuring safety, emotional warmth, stimulation, guidance and boundaries and stability (HM Government, 2013).

But there are complexities and tensions that exist when applying safeguarding policies to work with BAME families. For example, in their study of the effects of child protection interventions on BAME children, Chimba et al (2012) reviewed

41 case files and interviewed 8 families and 8 social workers. Their findings suggested that when evaluating culturally informed parenting, social workers are often ambivalent about which aspects of parenting to appraise. This results in significant inconsistencies as some interventions are disproportionally forceful and intrusive, while others are tentative or adequate. This may explain some of the disproportionality patterns seen in safeguarding statistics.

Bhatti-Sinclair (2011), herself a social work academic, expresses similar observations and suggests that there is a causal link between social workers' lack of knowledge about how to work with BAME families and the diminishing emphasis on learning about race and ethnicity in qualifying social work education and training courses over time. In her view, social work training and education need to incorporate learning about race and ethnicity to enhance practitioners' confidence about working with diversity. The burden for building interpretive skills rests not just on individual social workers but also on the social work profession. It is by embracing such responsibility that the profession can move beyond rhetoric to implementing practices that place greater emphasis on the efficacy of assessing culturally informed parenting.

As policy commentators (e.g. Cameron et al, 2007; Parton, 2010, 2014; Nadan et al, 2015) have argued, it is social policy that regulates how social workers respond to social and moral arrangements to protect individual rights, family privacy, and children's welfare. Safe parenting is framed by how policy defines child maltreatment. For example, child protection-oriented policies tend to conceive maltreatment as an act that requires services to respond to protect children, whereas service-oriented policies perceive maltreatment as a problem of family conflict or dysfunction that is triggered by social and psychological difficulties (Parton, 2014).

Social workers who approach assessment from a safeguarding mind-set tend to be more legalistic and adversarial, whereas those who take a family service-oriented approach offer a therapeutic response to family needs and therefore focus on assessing needs. Either approach is determined by organisational setting and culture, which is itself often a reflection of the political climate. For example, there is often intense political pressure following high-profile child deaths (e.g. Jasmin Beckford; Victoria Climbie; Peter Connelly). Drawing on my social work experience and anecdotal evidence from work colleagues, I observed that political pressure can influence decisions about local authority thresholds of concern and eligibility for support. The associated constraints on social worker's time contribute to poor staff morale and coalesce to negatively impact the quality and effectiveness of assessments.

In terms of research, studies into the efficacy of assessments have generally focused on issues of child welfare and taken their lead from the way in which policy constructs child maltreatment. Consequently, research tends to be divided into two main areas: studies that examine the process of assessment (e.g. Gibbons et al, 1995; Farmer and Owen, 1995; Cleaver and Freeman, 1995; Lennings, 2002; Taylor, 2006) and studies that examine the factors that influence assessment outcomes (e.g. Thoburn et al, 1995; Cleaver and Walker, 2004; Miller and Corby, 2006; Platt, 2006).

Whilst there is an increase in research converging around the effectiveness of social work assessments in general, the focus on aspects of culture in relation to assessment is underexplored. What can be drawn from existing empirical evidence is that professionals evaluating safe parenting are still uncertain about how to assess culturally informed parenting or indeed how best to work with BAME families (Laming, 2003; Barn et al, 2006; Stevenson, 2007; Dutt and Phillips, 2010).

Child abuse policy in England

The policy initiatives that shape social work with children and families can be traced back to the Prevention of Cruelty to Children Act (1889). This act allowed the state to intervene in family matters for the first time. It also gave the police and inspectors of the National Society for the Prevention of Cruelty to Children (NSPCC) powers to investigate suspected cruelty to children. Back then, the language used in child welfare policy and practice was 'cruelty to children'. Policy implementation focused on investigating and punishing caregivers for 'child cruelty' (Rogowski, 2015).

In 1894, the Prevention of Cruelty to Children Act (1889) was amended to recognise mental cruelty and allow children to give evidence in Court. Commentators (e.g. Ferguson, 2011) suggest that the Prevention of Cruelty to Children Act (1889), also known as the children's charter, was the precursor of professional social work practice. It marked the beginning of state intervention in the way that children are cared for within the family home. The children's charter and its amendment in 1894 gave courts power to override father's rights over their children and introduced the welfare of the child as a principal determining factor in making decisions about a child's welfare.

Legislation that followed the children's charter widened the areas in which the state could get involved in family matters. For example, the Children Act (1908) made sexual abuse within families a matter for the state rather than being an issue that was only dealt with by the clergy. It also introduced juvenile courts and the registration of foster parents.

The Children and Young People Act of 1932 broadened the powers of juvenile courts and introduced supervision orders for children who were deemed to be at risk. A year later, all child protection law was combined into a single piece of legislation. The key feature of safeguarding practice, between 1889 and 1945, was to prevent cruelty to children by prosecuting adults for the ill treatment of children. This focus gradually changed from punishing adults for child maltreatment to practice that was centred on interventions that sought to work with families to improve outcomes for children.

After the Second World War, local authority children's departments were formed and given greater responsibility for providing services to safeguard children's welfare under the auspices of the Children Act (1948). Until then, child welfare support was mainly provided by churches and voluntary organisations. The Children Act (1948) made it incumbent on local authorities to establish children's committees and appoint children's officers. This brought the concept of the child's wellbeing to the fore of practice and focused interventions on keeping children within their families.

The Children and Young Persons Act (1963) gave local authorities powers and duties to "*make available such advice, assistance and guidance as may promote the welfare of children by diminishing the need for receiving children into or keep them in care*" (Children and Young Persons Act, 1963, S.1). These duties were extended in the Children and Young Persons Act (1969), which bolstered the concepts of care and control by making it possible for courts to grant local authorities care orders for children who had committed criminal acts. Alongside this, the act introduced measures for local authorities to share parental responsibility with children's parents.

Between the 1960s and the early 1970s, the language used to describe child maltreatment in policy and practice had moved from 'cruelty to children' to 'battered child syndrome'. The term 'battered child syndrome' was coined by Henry Kemp and his colleagues, who described it as "*a clinical condition in young children who have received serious physical abuse*" (Kemp et al, 1962, cited in Krugman and Korbin, 2013, p. 23). The term came at a time when children's rights within the family setting were only beginning to be recognised. The work of Kemp and his colleagues was instrumental in increasing awareness of child abuse within the family home. It highlighted that child abuse was a regular and recurring aspect of family life and was not confined to individuals with psychiatric problems as was thought at the time.

In the 1970s, the term 'battered child syndrome' was replaced by non-accidental injury to children. At the same time, sexual and emotional abuse became recognised as separate forms of abuse to children. Identifying separate categories of abuse also coincided with increasing concern about the 'drift' in planning for children's permanence. This led to the Local Authority Social Services Act (1970). The act brought together the different areas of social work and consolidated local authority departments into social services departments.

The early 1970s was also a time in which there was a drive to achieve permanence for children in care. This stimulated the introduction of the Children Act (1975) and the Adoption Act (1976). The Children Act (1975) coincided with the implementation of area child protection committees, which had been established a year earlier, following the death of Maria Colwell. These committees were designed to coordinate local efforts to safeguard children at risk.

By the 1980s, 'child abuse' had become the generic terms used to describe neglect, physical, sexual, and emotional abuse of children. The 1980s was also a period characterised by a series of influential reports that examined the effectiveness of social services' interventions to protect children from harm. The most notable ones followed the child deaths of Jasmine Beckford in 1985 and Kimberly Carlile and Tyra Henry in 1987. These reports highlighted failures in partnership working between agencies and criticised social services for failing to effectively harmful environments and intervene to protect children from harm. The result was that social workers became wary of leaving children in potentially abusive environments.

In 1987, there was a wave of child sexual abuse diagnosis in Cleveland. This saw 121 children diagnosed by paediatricians as having been sexually abused. The children were removed from their family homes and placed in local authority care. The Cleveland (1988) report, which came after the children were placed in care, criticised social services and medical professionals for being over-zealous in diagnosing sexual abuse and intervening too hastily in the lives of families. Child welfare professionals were also blamed for failing to communicate amongst themselves and lacking proper understanding of each other's roles.

The communication failures highlighted in the Cleveland report led to new policies and legislation being framed around the concept of partnership working. For example, new area committees were formed and expected to draw representation from all local agencies that had a role in safeguarding children. Additionally, specific guidance for partnership working was published under the title *Working Together to Safeguard Children* (1991). This guidance set out how professionals should work together to safeguard children in accordance with relevant legislation. The guidance was revised in 2006, 2010, 2013, 2015, and 2018.

The Cleveland (1988) report also argued that by intervening too hastily in family life, professionals were abusing parents' rights. This finding contributed to a shift towards policies that emphasised the importance of children being looked after within their natural families. The focus on partnership working had the broad aim of ensuring that professionals assessing parenting consulted with each other as part of the assessment process. In some ways, this marked the beginning of the concept of holistic assessment as a means of improving the quality and reliability of assessments.

The Children Act (1989) came into effect three years after the Cleveland report. The act enshrined in law the right for children to be protected from abuse and exploitation and for inquiries to be made to ensure that their welfare is safeguarded. Parental rights were also built into the act to ensure that only a court could permanently sever contact between children and their parents, rather than this being the outcome of social work assessment. Area Child Protection Committees (ACPCs) continued to hold responsibility for investigating whether child protection procedures were correctly followed whenever a child death was suspected to have been caused by abuse.

The death of Victoria Climbie at the hands of her aunt and her aunt's male friend in 2000 led to the publication of the policy document, *Every Child Matters*. This followed an inquiry led by Lord Laming, which made more than 100 recommendations for change in the way that child safeguarding practice was carried out by local authorities. The inquiry highlighted the tendency of professionals assessing BAME families to make assumptions about culturally informed parenting that prevent them from conducting full assessments.

In terms of highlighting the importance of issues of culture and ethnicity, the inquiry pointed out that *cultural norms and modes of behaviour can vary considerably between communities and even between families so that it becomes meaningless to make generalisations about behavioural patterns* (Laming, 2003, p. 345). Although Section 1 (3)(d) of the Children Act (1989) had already provided for issues of culture to be addressed through the welfare checklist, Lord Laming's inquiry and the subsequent development of the Children Act (2004) was, arguably, the first time that policy explicitly acknowledged and confronted issues of culturally informed parenting.

Lord Laming's inquiry placed a responsibility on professionals to develop knowledge about different cultures to avoid potentially damaging the effectiveness of their assessments. But the main change in policy was that Area Child Protection Committees were then changed to Local Safeguarding Children's Boards (LSCBs) and given mandatory responsibility for child protection in their area. Further changes included incorporating the Child Protection Register into Child Protection Plans that specify the category of abuse or likely abuse that a child may suffer and how professionals will manage the plan.

The death of baby Peter Connelly in 2009 led to another inquiry into child protection practice. It was led by Professor Eileen Munro, who published her final report in 2011(Munro, 2011). While Professor Munro's inquiry was still in progress, the revised statutory guidance Working Together to Safeguard Children (2010) was released. When Professor Munro's report was finally published, it made 15 recommendations that concentrated on the need to shift focus from prescriptive social work practice towards assessments that focused on identifying the needs of the child.

Professor Munro's report continued the theme on the importance of effective assessments. But, like previous inquiries, it placed an expectation on social workers to address issues of culture in assessment, without being clear how this should be achieved. The message from the literature is that the relationship between culture and parenting is complex. Some have questioned whether there are legitimate concerns about culturally informed parenting (Allen et al, 2008; Kriz and Skivenes, 2010).

Social policy and safe parenting

Over the years, policy developments have oscillated between focusing on protecting children from harm and supporting families to achieve their preferred outcomes (Parton, 2014). Nevertheless, the overarching aim since 1948 has been to reinforce the paramount interests of the child. Current policies strike a balance between protecting children and supporting families. For example, both the *Framework for the Assessment of Children in Need and Their Families* (Department of Health, 1999b) and the *Working Together to Safeguard Children* direct social workers to identify the risk of harm to children but also support families to minimise identified risk.

More recently, policy developments have been driven by public outcry following high-profile child deaths. This has contributed to a gradual move towards increased bureaucratisation of assessment procedures, with the aim of standardising and managing practice (Broadhurst et al, 2010). Whilst emphasis is placed on supporting families, it has not meant that issues of abuse and harm no longer form part of assessments. Social workers are still expected to evaluate parenting in terms of whether it is abusive (s.47, The Children Act, 1989). Policy therefore provides a conceptual framework that helps professionals to determine the point at which to intervene in families' lives (HM Government, 2013).

As an assessment tool, for example, the *Framework for the Assessment of Children in Need, and Their Families*, draws on the ecological model to help social workers to identify families' strengths. The aim here is to help families meet children's needs by harnessing the resources that are within their unique environment. This method of intervening in families was underpinned by research that highlighted the importance of an inclusive approach to assessing families (see Jack and Jordan, 1999; Department of Health et al, 2000; Horwath, 2002; Ward and Rose, 2002; Jack and Gill, 2003; Aldgate et al, 2006). In fact, the framework was the main tool for assessment until new guidance was issued in the Working Together to Safeguard Children (2018) guidance document.

With emphasis on assessing children's needs rather than on processes, the Working Together to Safeguard children (2018) guidance streamlined prior guidance and provided clarity about social workers' responsibilities to children's safety. There is no longer a requirement for local authorities to use the assessment framework, but they must make clear what assessment tools they use in assessment. The guidance also maintains that safeguarding children is everyone's responsibility. Achieving effective collective responsibility is not without challenges.

Legislations, such as the Children Act (1989, 2004), direct assessments by defining when and at what level local authorities should intervene in family life. For example, the Children Act (1989) embeds the philosophy that the best place for a child is to be brought up in their natural family (Department of Health, 1999a). This implicitly directs local authorities to focus on identifying parents' strengths. The implication for practice is that greater emphasis is placed on supporting families' needs stay together. Such a focus helps social workers to avoid separating children from their families unless there is no possibility of securing adequate care within the child's natural family.

Conversely, working with families presents challenges that can impede engagement, hinder professional judgement, and limit actions. Brandon et al's (2008) analysis of serious case reviews between 2003 and 2005 found that social workers struggle to deal with the emotional impact of working with hostility from violent parents and disaffected adolescents. Equally, there are several tensions inherent in working with BAME parents. These, as Bernard and Gupta (2006) note, include reconciling different values and beliefs about children's development, empowering families to access community resources, and determining children's safety within families.

Intervention thresholds

Intervention thresholds offer the benefit of structuring decisions about when to intervene in families' lives and help moderate reliance on professional judgement alone. However, they are not without controversy. This is because there is considerable variability in how they are applied in different local authorities in the UK.

Some have argued that the overlap and interdependence between local authority priorities and social policy imperatives limit thresholds to selection criteria for determining which families should receive help. Platt and Turney (2014) reviewed threshold decisions in the UK and elsewhere and found that they varied based on factors such as the nature of safeguarding concerns reported, local authority policies and the organisational circumstances, the role of multiagency collaboration, and the decision making of front-line social workers and team managers.

In seeking to standardise assessments, social policy prescribes how social workers should assess families. However, as Dalzell and Sawyer (2011) put it, this has the potential to undermine practitioners' confidence and their ability to focus on families' individual circumstances. In the context of this book, the result is that the outcomes of assessments tend to recommend solutions that are not always forthcoming for BAME families or fail to meet their needs.

Barlow et al (2012) undertook a systematic review of conceptual frameworks and found that although there were clear benefits, there was a need for most of them to be piloted further and validated within a UK setting. The inference here is that conceptual tools are not necessarily effective in assessing all family situations. Their successful use with one group cannot be generalised to all social groups. Similarly, studies of the Integrated Children's System suggest that practitioners found it to be too prescriptive and repetitive to the extent that it was incongruent with the practice they aspired to (Bell et al, 2007).

Although no longer relevant, the Integrated Children's System, for example, generated debate about increased micromanagement (Bell, 2007; White et al, 2010). Initially heralded as a tool to modernise and unify hitherto disjointed processes, the Integrated Children's System drew fierce criticism about its efficacy. Hill and Shaw (2011) suggested that it resulted in the loss of the 'human' aspect from assessments. The loss of the 'human' aspect that they refer to contextualises the views expressed by the respondents in Bell and colleague's study. That is, that processes can become prescriptive tick-box exercises that do not reflect families' circumstances.

The Integrated Children's System encouraged pre-mature categorisation and dangerously high case closures (Broadhurst et al, 2009; White et al, 2010). When Professor Sue White and her colleagues reviewed it in 2010, their findings were that it encouraged rigid performance management regimes and centrally prescribed practice models that disrupted the professional task. They explained this to be associated with social work managers focusing on process, which led to unhelpfully speedy categorisations and rigidity in recording. In terms of working with BAME families, such a process would limit professionals' abilities to identify the impact of the underlying issues that affect some BAME parents (e.g. poverty, racism, language difficulties, acculturation experiences).

Focussing on processes hinders effective communication between social workers and BAME parents and in turn affects the efficacy of parenting assessments. Poor communication can contribute to BAME parents being treated as homogenous group (Owen and Farmer, 1996; Dominelli, 2002a; Laming, 2003; Barn, 2006b, Stevenson, 2007; Selwy et al, 2010; Chimba et al, 2012). As Dominelli

(2002a) pointed out, this can lead to professionals losing sight of the fact that culture is only one dimension of identity. The danger here is that they are then likely to perpetuate oppressive practice by not engaging appropriately with the racialised nature of social relationships.

Intervention thresholds are also influenced by resource constraints. This impacts social workers' abilities to analyse vast and often conflicting information gathered for assessment and contributes to assessment becoming prescribed (Bell et al, 2007; Broadhurst et al, 2009; Helm, 2010; Munro, 2011). Intervention threshold, therefore, becomes the process through which local authorities manage their resources. For example, by seeking to create a standardised interpretation of safe parenting, yet parenting practices vary from family to family. Additionally, there is no legal definition of what a minimum standard of safe parenting should be.

In the absence of a clear legal definition, research offers what seems to be a generally accepted standard of safe parenting. That is, that the minimum expectation should be based on Winnicott's (1973) concept of '*good enough*' parenting. While the concept of '*good enough*' is itself not contested, the standard of what '*good enough*' parenting looks like varies widely. Several factors influence how it is defined. According to Kellet and Apps (2009), they include assessors' personal and professional experience influence. The problem is that quite often, parents and the professionals have different views about what is 'good enough'.

One example is the importance of children being respectful and obedient in some BAME families. Parents who hold strong views about socialising their children to respect and obey adults in their families can often find themselves at polar ends of discussions with social workers who see their approach as limiting children's independence.

Another illustration of the challenges associated with defining 'good enough' relates to the use of physical chastisement. Heilmann et al's (2015) study reviewed international longitudinal research on the impact of physical punishment on children, and their findings suggest that perceptions about the effectiveness of physical chastisement to discipline children have changed, partly as a result of changes in the law, but also because research continues to show that it can be harmful to children's health and development. Professionals who approach assessments without pre-conceived ideas about the use of physical chastisement are more likely to communicate the message identified by Heilmann and colleagues, as a way of educating families rather than making recommendations that families may find patronising and punitive.

Policy and legislation, therefore, play an important role in helping practitioners to evaluate parenting within the confines of what is acceptable in law. Whilst there is criticism about attempts to standardise assessments, evidence suggests that despite the wide range of parenting practices within communities, the concept of 'good enough' parenting is helpful in identifying aspects of parenting that reflect safe and acceptable care for children within the boundaries of legislation (Kellett and Apps, 2009). These aspects of 'good enough' parenting include parents being able to meet their children's health and developmental needs, putting their children's needs first, providing routine and consistent care, and acknowledging problems and engaging with support services.

Social policy and diversity

Child protection policy acknowledges the diverse needs that families have, as well as the diversity within the families that make up of the UK's population. For example, the threshold criteria contained in the HM Government (1989) emphasises the need to consider a family's cultural background and their expressed views and preferences. The issue is that safeguarding policies in the UK reflect the overall culture and values of British society and how the society responds to issues of child maltreatment (Beishon et al, 1998; Hetherington, 2006; Cameron et al, 2007; Broadhurst et al, 2009). With increasing diversity in the UK's population, it is not surprising that many BAME parents find the values and parenting norms that underpin the way children are raised in Britain to be different from those of their own cultures (Chimba et al, 2012).

Whilst standardising assessment processes can offer the benefit of transparency, the challenge is that reconciling policy with varied parenting practices is complex often because family circumstances are ambiguous and BAME parents tend to be suspicious of social workers' intentions. There is a growing body of scholarships that suggest that some of the distrust stems from BAME families experiencing more pronounced disadvantages when engaging with public organisations.

Safeguarding policy may have sought to create transparency and inclusivity through standardised assessments; the unintended consequence is that the criteria for assessing safe parenting tend to view culturally informed parenting as unsafe. In some cases, the focus on thresholds for intervention can lead to assessment of BAME parenting being based on social workers' 'fixed' ideas rather than on evidence (Brandon et al, 2009; Farmer and Lutman, 2012). This can lead to either missing safeguarding concerns as thresholds for determining decisive action become difficult to identify (Daniel et al, 2011) or intervening disproportionally.

The picture is far more complex than it appears. For example, studies show that thresholds are based on factors such as the information contained in a referral, organisational resources, and assessors' skills (Biehal, 2005; Brandon et al, 2008; Sheppard, 2009). Because they have limited resources, local authorities set high thresholds and in the process fail to identify families with significant need. These tend to be families where there are concerns about neglect and emotional abuse (Farmer et al, 2008; Brandon et al, 2009; Ward et al, 2010), which also reflect why many BAME children are referred to social services (Chimba et al, 2012).

Thresholds can disadvantage BAME families by creating practice situations in which support is not forthcoming until families' needs or problems are entrenched. This is not an area of policy that has much scholarship. However, there is some suggestion from research that BAME families may benefit from timely assessment and early intervention (Barnado's, 2011; Royston and Rodrigues, 2013). My criticism is that such recommendations tend to be about signposting BAME families to access community resources where they are signposted back to social services.

The dearth of research that specifically addresses how policy affects assessment of BAME parents means that the issues highlighted earlier remain controversial in practice and in academic circles. Further research is therefore needed to inform our understanding of assessing culturally informed parenting.

Systemic issues

Debates about the success or otherwise of multiculturalism highlight some of the challenges involved in working with diversity. While some commentators (e.g. Huntington, 1993; Beishon et al, 1998) highlight anxieties about the extent to which different ethnic groups follow paths that create strong minority ethnic identities, Parekh (2000) suggests that multiculturalism has succeeded in integrating diverse populations. The challenge for social workers assessing culturally informed parenting is that BAME families that maintain strong ethnic identities often separate and alienate themselves from the wider society, making them hard to reach (Doherty et al, 2004). As Nandi and Platt (2013) put it, there is little empirical evidence to suggest that maintaining strong cultural distinctiveness necessarily challenges national consensus.

Another systemic issue relates to how some professionals perceived BAME families. Beishon et al (1998) suggested that professionals sometimes see the lack of help-seeking behaviour from BAME families as suggesting that they are resistant to the perceived values of UK liberalism. Such perceptions limit social workers' abilities to appropriately engage with diversity. Social workers whose views are rooted in universalism ignore the influence of culture on social relations and the importance of diversity among the clients they work with. This can lead to assessments that do not accurately interpret culturally informed parenting.

Understanding safe parenting goes beyond interpreting a lack of help-seeking behaviour or the implications of maintaining ethnic distinctiveness. We know, for example, that retaining some form of positive personal identity whilst also holding multiple identities at different levels of abstraction is good for individuals' psychological wellbeing (Nandi and Platt, 2013). Furthermore, identities are not necessarily binary or oppositional. The challenge, as Broadhurst et al (2009) argue, is that child welfare policy is based on Western constructions of parenting. Evaluating culturally informed parenting without seeking to understand how culture influences parenting in BAME families risks perpetuating oppressive practice.

Policy has not fully addressed issues of culture within parenting. This, in part, contributes to some of the controversies associated with assessing BAME parents. For example, some BAME families report that their parenting is often misunderstood, and they are left feeling that decisions favour their White counterparts whose parenting approaches are advance as the benchmark for what is acceptable (Kiima, 2017). This brings the issue of privilege to the fore, along with the complexities associated with seeking to understand inequalities within society.

Kendall (2012) refers to privilege as an issue that is difficult to identify and articulate constructively but is visible to those to whom privilege is denied.

For many BAME parents, privilege carries connotations of institutional racism. They report their experiences to be that public structures prioritise meeting the needs of their White counterparts, often to the exclusion or disadvantage of BAME families (Kiima, 2017). Peggy McIntosh, a renown American researcher, whose paper on White privilege and male privilege is widely referenced, viewed privilege as "an invisible package of unearned assets" (McIntosh, 1988). It involves conferring benefits and advantages to dominant groups in society, based on a variety of sociodemographic traits, whilst also supporting structural barriers to other groups. Whilst studies suggest that this is often perpetuated unconsciously, there is convergence towards the idea that privilege is fuelled by racial bias (e.g. Wildman and Davis, 1997; Chimba et al, 2012; Azzopardi and McNeil, 2016).

According to Wildman and Davis (1997), privilege is an institutional issue because social benefits are conferred on people who by race resemble those who dominate powerful institutional positions. Wildman and Davis assert that in an intricate system, privilege can have the effect of neutralising or ignoring issues of race and culture. In social work, this can take the form of professionals failing to evaluate the power dynamics in their relationships with BAME families or not recognising how social systems of oppression marginalise the families they work with. Professor Lena Dominelli, a social work academic, advances an important point when she states that culture is a contested and troubling category. It forms an aspect of identity which can become the basis of oppression.

Culture plays a significant role in influencing the parenting practices of many BAME parents, but not all BAME parents seek to follow cultural scripts to socialise their children. Therefore, social workers who base assessments on assumptions about BAME groups can inadvertently perpetuate stereotypes about cultural differences by viewing culture based on observable characteristics. This can lead to assessments that emphasise difference from the mainstream rather than focusing on identifying families' needs.

There are limitations within the literature too. Much of what is written on culture and parenting assumes a traditional view. That is, one that sees BAME parenting as being influenced by cultures that have been brought to a new country (Dutt and Phillips, 2010). This can lead to reductionism and unhelpful generalisations or unexamined assumptions. For example, some argue that the process of migration will end in assimilation, in which case parents hold similar views as the majority population. Others take culturally pluralist positions in which parents fail to understand professionals' welfare concerns. As such, determining safe parenting continues to be problematic in practice (Dalzell and Sawyer, 2007; Helm, 2010; White et al, 2010; Brown et al, 2011; Platt, 2011).

There is some clarity about how risk is conceptualised (Parton, 2010, 2014) and the role of professionals in identifying what causes harm to children (Laming, 2009; Broadhurst et al, 2010; Munro, 2011). However, what constitutes acceptable parenting is still contested. This makes assessing multifaceted and sometimes contradictory parenting scripts especially difficult (Turney et al, 2011). The result, as Crawford (2011), Turney et al (2011), and Reupert et al (2015) observe, is uncertainty in gathering the appropriate information to help formulate evidence-based assessments.

Obtaining the right information is an integral first step in seeking to understand culturally informed parenting and drawing conclusions about parents' abilities (Munro, 2008; Broadhurst et al, 2009; Holland, 2010). Policy attaches great importance to including children's voices in the information gathering. However, research indicates that social workers face difficulties in making and maintaining relationships with children. The reasons for this are varied and include children being concerned about the consequences of their disclosures – both to themselves and to their parents. This is not necessarily unique to BAME families. Studies show that the fear of alienating themselves from their local communities and support networks can mean that children are reluctant to disclose abuse (Barn, 2006a; Chimba et al, 2012). It is therefore for social workers to have the appropriate strategies and resources to respond to the needs of BAME children.

Chimba et al's (2012) study, which highlights professionals' lack of confidence when assessing BAME families, found that families from outside the UK had a significant lack of knowledge about the role of social services. In their interviews with parents, they found that many BAME parents had no prior knowledge of social services. The implication for practice is that there is a need to build relationships and convey positive images about engaging with social services. Without positive relationships, BAME parents are less likely to understand social care's concerns.

Chimba and his colleagues cite an example in which a family was expected to turn up for a conference without being given prior information about its purpose. Their reticence was interpreted as a lack of engagement. Other studies have shown that in some instances, BAME families are reluctant to engage with services due to strong cultural expectations to care for children without external agency support or simply a desire to keep family life private. As Chimba et al (2012) observe, for some BAME families, distrust can be fuelled by fears arising from their experience with the immigration system or an instinctive distrust of the state that is based on experiences from their countries of origin.

What we can infer from the literature is that assessing culturally informed parenting is complex, partly because culture intersects with a range of personal and environmental factors, including poverty (Gupta et al, 2016), acculturation (Chao, 2000; Kriz and Skivenes, 2010), and education (Cleaver and Unell, 2011), to influence how BAME parents socialise their children but also because effective assessments are dependent on individual social workers' skills and the resources that policy avails them. This contributes to disparities in assessment, and some argue that the issue is one for social work training to address rather than to the assessment system (see, e.g. Bhatti-Sinclair, 2011; Chimba et al, 2012).

5   A detailed study/research

This book draws its insights from a study that interviewed 80 participants about their experiences of parenting assessments. The participants were made up of 40 BAME parents and 40 social workers. Data were collected between 2011 and 2013. All the parents had previously been assessed by a social worker. They were recruited from five inner-city community organisations. The organisations were approached because they provided support to parents who had social services involvement, including whose children had been placed in local authority care.

The broad aim of the study was to understand how issues of culture are addressed in parenting competence assessments. The subject was approached from three main prongs: the first was to understand how culture frames the parenting practices of BAME parents; the second was to understand how BAME parents and social workers conceptualise parenting competence; and the third was to establish the link between the way that BAME parents and social workers conceptualise safe parenting.

The methodology for the study was designed with the aforementioned process in mind and focused on gathering qualitative data. The broad research question was refined after reviewing the literature about how BAME parents socialise their children. This was done alongside a critique of literature that addresses child welfare policy in England and Wales. The questions that emerged from review are detailed later and reflect the gaps in the literature:

- How is parenting in BAME families understood in the UK context?
- Does the parenting assessment process effectively evaluate the parenting competence of BAME parents?
- Is there a link between social workers' expectations of BAME parents and the competences that BAME parents seek to promote?

I started off by acknowledging that parenting practices are determined by numerous factors (see Bronfenbrenner, 1979; Belsky, 1984; Belsky and Jaffe, 2006). I was also aware participants' narratives would inextricably bind feelings with actual experience.

The qualitative design facilitated this in two key ways: first, in capturing aspects of cultural influence, as well as the words, emotions, feelings, and expectations that both sets of participants used to express their perspectives of parenting and of parenting assessment processes, and second, in understanding how BAME parents and social workers conceptualise safe parenting.

This made it easy to incorporate information from the literature review into the interview discussions. For example, asking whether parents should be firm (e.g. Baumrind, 1968; Maccoby and Martin, 1983) or permissive (e.g. Shumow et al, 1998; Talbot, 2009; Foulk, 2007) or whether they should prioritise personality or character (Shaffer, 2008) when socialising their children. Participants' responses enabled me to juxtapose how BAME parents and social workers perceive culturally informed parenting. The other consideration related to transference and counter transference.

Consequently, I chose to use frame analysis and a phenomenological research philosophy. After deliberating over whether to use the Biographic-Narrative Interpretive Method (BNIM), or Ethnography, I felt that frame analysis and phenomenology were congruent with the aims of the study as they allow for subjective interconnection between the participants and the researcher (Creswell, 2009). Frame analysis was chosen as the theoretic approach for analysing the findings because I was also interested in capturing a comparative aspect to the way that parents and social workers conceptualise safe parenting.

Research design

At the start of the project, I had hoped to find opportunities to compare the effect of culture within the participant groups. I felt that this would offer the potential of establishing whether parenting across distinct BAME groups can be explained by the same causes. The intention was to compare variables and develop classifications as suggested by Ditch et al (1995), whose view is that this can lead to a better understanding of social phenomena. In this case, I envisaged that I would use the classifications to evaluate the interventions that social workers adopt to deal with culturally informed parenting scripts. However, the differences within the groups were too wide to offer opportunities for comparison.

Nevertheless, the consistent variable was that all the parents who took part in the study were first-generation immigrants. Their expressed views offer powerful insight into how parenting competence evaluations impact BAME parents. The research began with five focus groups, each consisting of eight BAME parents. Two of the focus groups were made up of parents from distinct backgrounds and three were made up of parents from various BAME backgrounds – mostly African and Caribbean. Of the two groups with parents from the similar background, one was made up of predominantly Indian and Pakistani parents and another was of parents predominantly from Poland. This was associated with the fact that the participants were recruited from third sector organisations that provide support to those distinct groups.

The focus groups were used as a preliminary stage of the study in that the topics generated from discussions were followed up in the one-to-one interviews. This made it possible to triangulate the findings. Morgan and Kreuger (1998) warn against such an approach as it can present challenges in separating individual views from group views. However, the themes that emerged from focus groups discussions were useful for exploring the degree of consensus outside expressed group views. Additionally, as Gibbs (1997) asserts, focus groups are a good way to draw upon participants' attitudes, reactions, and feelings in a way that is not always feasible using methods such as one-to-one interviews or questionnaire surveys.

Feminist commentators (e.g. Wilkinson, 1998; Green et al, 1993) express a similar argument and add that using focus groups addresses ethical concerns such as power dynamics and the imposition of meaning. Starting with focus groups, therefore, helped with identifying themes in a manner that balanced the power dynamics. The information gathered from the focus groups helped me to draw up the guidance prompts that I used during the one-to-one interviews.

During the focus groups, I explained the criteria I would use to select three participants for one-to-one interviews. For the parents, my selection was based on the plans in which their children were placed following assessment, as well as the duration of social care involvement. I explained what the different social care intervention plans meant. This ensured that the participants understood the parameters of the study. The participants selected for one-to-one interviews were those whose children were involved in the care system the longest, followed by parents whose children were made subject to child protection plans but remained home and, finally, the parents whose children were left at home and supported under Child in Need plans. This information was provided by the parents and I was not able to verify it. None of the parents had similar circumstances.

The sample of social workers was made up of participants who had experience of assessing BAME parents. Initially, I sought to recruit all social workers through local authorities. But I was only successful in securing partial permissions that resulted in very few social workers agreeing to take part. As a result, I asked those who attended to recommend colleagues that would agree to take part. I also asked my social worker friends and colleagues to take part and recommend their colleagues. The vignette that I drew up from my group discussions with the parents was used as a prompt in my group discussions with social workers.

I selected three social workers from each social work group to take part in the in-depth interviews. Selection was based on their direct experience of evaluating the parenting of BAME parents. Using this criterion, I selected the three social workers who had the most experience. The process is represented in the diagram on the page that follows:

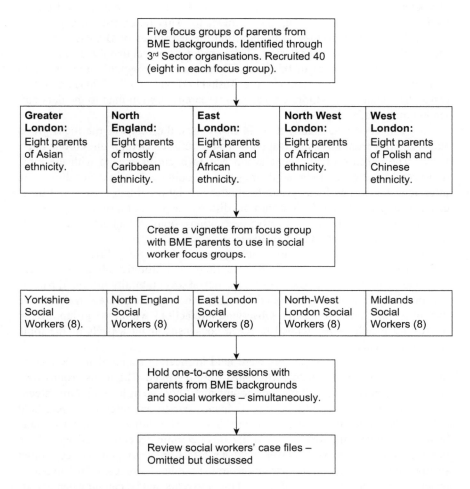

Figure 5.1 Research design diagram

Preliminary data collection results

Although the participants were not a homogenous group in terms of their cultural backgrounds, they shared the experience of having been involved in parenting competence evaluations, either as parents or as assessing social workers. This shared experience meant that they had something to share about the efficacy of parenting assessments.

The recruitment approach involved defining the inclusion criterion that participants were required to have to be able to answer the research questions then approaching organisations that work with people who met the pre-defined characteristics. Participants were then separated into five groups, based on the locations that were easier for me to travel to. This pragmatic approach narrowed the scope of discussion by omitting the narratives of BAME parents in the locations that were not selected. However, I did not feel that this significantly impacted on the findings of this study. Proponents of pragmatic approaches to choosing data collection methods (e.g. Tashakkori and Teddie, 2003) argue that researchers should give more credence to research question than to the data collection methods.

Data collection was mainly done in two stages: the first was the focus group stage, and it is from this stage that participants were selected for one-to-one interviews. The purpose of the focus group was to begin to engage with the topic under study and generate broad themes that I would explore in detail during the interview stages. The focus group facilitates this by providing a cost- and time-efficient way of gaining insight into the different aspects of a topic. My interest was to obtain participants' collective perceptions, opinion, beliefs, and attitudes towards parenting competence evaluations.

The focus group session with social workers had a slightly different focus. In addition to seeking to obtain their perceptions, and attitudes about assessment processes, I wanted to get a sense of how they assess culturally informed parenting. In the absence of viewing social work files, the vignette offered an alternative way of gaining practice insight. Observing interactions within the group offered interesting insight. They tended to reach consensus about aspects of the topic relatively quickly.

The focus groups with parents were held in meeting rooms that I booked at the organisations from which participants were recruited. The focus groups with social workers were held in meeting rooms that I booked at local children's centres. Because of the varied mix of participants, one-to-one interviews were held either in the community or at participants' homes. The choice of venue was made by the participants and was often a local café or community centre. All one-to-one interviews with social workers were held at a café. Care was taken to select a quiet section and ensure maximum privacy from the public. Participants' involvement in selecting the interview venues helped them to relax and be candid when narrating their lived experiences.

The vignette drawn up following the focus group discussions with parents was only used as the starting point of discussions in the focus groups with social workers. The vignette gave a referral scenario that required social workers to assess a fictitious family depicting characteristics that BAME parents had said were important to them, for example, the importance of discipline, religion, and cultural artefacts. The purpose of the vignette was to obtain a broad understanding of social workers' perspectives on parenting competence evaluations.

The vignette generated extensive discussions within the social worker focus groups. Despite the 'eclectic' mix of social workers, the groups generally gave the same responses in terms of identified themes. Initially, I saw social workers as primarily from the 'culture' of social work but realised that the range of backgrounds they represented was a distinctive, unusual, and valuable feature of the study. The mix included social workers of White-British, African, American, Indian, Scandinavian, and Australian cultural backgrounds. Indeed, during the one-to-one interviews, their narratives included some illustrations from their own cultural and ethnic backgrounds.

Missing voices

There were two key absences from the one-to-one stages. The first is that although there were some men in the BAME parents focus group stages, none of them took part in the one-to-one interviews. The second absence was that in one of the focus groups, there were parents of Chinese heritage, but they were not represented in the interviews. The absence of BAME fathers from the interviews is a limitation in that their voices are missing. Similarly, the voices of Chinese parents are missing.

At the focus group stage, I had expected to interview four fathers, along with the mothers, as a single unit. When the mother's attended on their own, gave the following reasons for why the fathers didn't attend: three of the fathers were at work and had not been able to get time off and one had stayed home to look after the children.

In hindsight, it would have perhaps been better to interview couples separately so that fathers' voices could be separated from the mothers' voices. In fact, a focus on father's voices is potentially an area to explore in future research.

The absence of Chinese parents from the one-to-one interviews is a missed opportunity. The Chinese parents who attended the focus group sessions did not meet the selection criteria for the one-to-one interviews. Although their parenting competence had been evaluated by a social worker, their children had only been made subject to Child in Need plans for 3 months. Because they were the only ethnic group that was not represented in the interview stages, including them would have given a wider sample of perspectives. However, I only realised this missed opportunity after the study was completed.

That said, I also recognise that increasing the demographic heterogeneity of the study would not have necessarily enhanced the quality or effectiveness of the study. The integrity and authenticity of the study were not undermined, as the inclusion criteria were clearly defined, and participants selected accordingly.

The other missing voices were those of BAME adults who had previously been removed from their parents' care. Their reflections would have added nuance to understanding the efficacy of parenting competence evaluations. This is another area of consideration in future research.

Rationale for the methodology

The choice of methodology and the methods used for this project were influenced by the need to capture participants' experiences and feelings about parenting assessments. Alongside this, I was mindful that my beliefs and experiences could be implicated in the study. A phenomenological approach offered a way to bring my beliefs to the foreground and question them in light of new evidence.

Gaps in the literature

The research focus was refined following a review of the literature, which high-lighted gaps in three main aspects of knowledge concerning assessing parenting. First, while there is consensus that culture is a significant component of the social phenomena that influence the parenting BAME families (Barn, 2006b; Lloyd and Rafferty, 2006; Williams and Churchill, 2006; White, 2005; Moon and Ivins, 2004), little has been written on this topic in the UK. Within the UK context, studies of BAME parenting tend to focus on the structures, disadvantage, and discrimination experienced by BAME families (see Butt and Mirza, 1996; Barn, 2002; Chahal and Ullah, 2004; Barn, 2006b; Bebbington and Beecham, 2003; Owen and Statham, 2009).

Second, there is a dearth of research on the effectiveness within which cultur-ally informed parenting is appraised. Studies on the effectiveness of parenting assessments tend to focus on evaluating either the processes that professionals use to evaluate parenting competence (see White, 2005; Cleaver et al, 2007; Dan-iel et al, 2009) or the skills and competence needed to ensure that professionals are able to consistently identify whether a child's functioning and developmental needs are being met (see Reder et al, 2003; Budd, 2005; Cleaver et al, 2011). Consequently, findings from such studies report on the variability of the quality of assessment reports (e.g. Budd et al, 2001; Conley, 2003).

The third aspect relates to the absence of an assessment tool that can help enhance social workers' abilities to assess culturally informed parenting. This would offer an objective way of deciding the relative weight to ascribe to various dimensions of parenting practices within BAME families. There is considerable debate about the need for culturally sensitive parenting assessments, but little is known about how culture affects assessment processes. Some commentators have therefore advocated for a practical guide that helps professionals to be sensitive to the influences that culture has on parenting, while also retaining a sense of individual uniqueness for each case (see Dutt and Phillips, 2000; Becher and Husain, 2003).

The gaps highlighted earlier suggest that there is a need to enhance the effective-ness with which social workers assess culturally informed parenting. This would entail improving social workers' understanding of the nature and value of the contributions that culturally informed parenting makes towards maximising the cognitive, behavioural, and emotional development of BAME children. The gaps led me to refine the original research question from *How do culture and ethnicity considerations influence social workers' decisions when intervening with families from Black and Minority Ethnic backgrounds?* to *How are cultural considerations incorporated in evaluations of the parenting competence of BAME parents.*

Researcher subjectivity

Adopting a phenomenological research philosophy helped me to find equilibrium in the inter-subjective connectedness between myself and the research partici-pants. According to Giorgi (1994), researchers taking a phenomenological stance should explain their subjectivity rather than eliminate it from the research. In my case, being a first-generation African, a parent, and a practicing social worker meant that my subjectivity was implicated as I identified and empathised with the participants.

Perks and Thomson (2006) suggest that seeking to eliminate researcher subjectivity can result in bias that distorts historical accounts. Being aware of pre-existing beliefs and bringing them to the foreground help to later separate out what belongs to the researcher rather than the researched (Giorgi, 1994; Halling et al, 2006; Finlay, 2009).

Choosing an inductive approach

I began the study from the premise that BAME parents influence their children as members of distinct communities. The access they have to resources and networks that reinforce culturally informed parenting practices causes them to socialise their children in, broadly, similar ways (e.g. Dutt and Phillips, 2000; Becher and Husain, 2003; Akilapa and Simkiss, 2012). This premise dictated the need to focus on obtaining fresh, complex, and rich descriptions of participants' lived experiences.

The decision to focus on understanding the meaning of complex data through the development of summary themes made it necessary to take an inductive approach. This provided a structure for condensing extensive and varied raw data to allow for reflective analysis of participants' experiences. For example, I was able to add nuanced understanding of culturally informed parenting by allowing findings to emerge from recurring, dominant, or significant themes inherent in the raw data. Achieving this required me to have a degree of flexibility in data collection, whilst also paying close attention to the contexts of participants' experiences.

The alternative would have been to have used a deductive research approach. This would have entailed testing a pre-set hypothesis. But my intention was to rely on qualitative data and allow themes to evolve rather than to test pre-existing theory. Therefore, the deductive approach was not deemed to be appropriate. Additionally, I had envisaged that there would be enough variety within individual narratives to warrant an inductive approach as being a better way of exploring participants' experiences. I was aware that the complexities involved in trying to understand the effectiveness of assessment processes would require me to consider the trade-off between detail and generality. I opted for the inductive approach.

Shaw (2011) argues that researchers risk losing the subtle secondary meanings derived from narrative contexts and private accounts of common past experiences if they subject studies to the restraints imposed by deductive methodologies. A deductive approach would have been suitable if my motive was to conduct an explanatory or evaluative study that relied on quantitative data. Although there are some quasi quantitative aspects in this study (e.g. quantifying the frequency with which themes appear within the data set), the dominant approach is qualitative.

A qualitative methods approach to phenomenological analysis

To gain accurate understanding of participants' experiences, I needed to use a methodology that foregrounded detail over breadth. The qualitative methods approach enabled me to obtain insights into narratives in a way that would not have been accessible using a quantitative methodology. Marshall (1996) explains a focus on detail as *"aiming to provide illumination and understanding of complex psychosocial issues"* (p. 522). A similar view is espoused by Hill (2012). In his article about helping children after sexual abuse, Hill advances the argument that by going beyond association, qualitative methods help us to understand the complex dynamics involved in social phenomena and can be used to get to causality.

By adopting a qualitative approach, I was able to explore multiple aspects of meaning across a web of interrelated participant narratives. I used participants' words to report their views of participants and then analysed the findings by identifying, coding, and categorising the patterns emerging from the data. Throughout this process, I addressed three unifying questions as I kept focused on qualitative epistemology and ontology: 1. what was my role; 2. what was reality; and 3. what was knowledge?

My responses to the earlier questions formed the basis of the philosophical stance I took; that is, that the nature of reality is one of inter-subjectively constructed meaning. Therefore, I acknowledged from the onset that my subjectivity would be implicated by the fact that I am a Black man and a social worker. Indeed, this was implicated in moments when I identified and empathised with participants as a way of demonstrating that I understood what they were expressing from their frames of reference. For example, participants would give a narrative and follow it up with the rhetorical question *"you know what I mean?"* as if to suggest that I should have had similar experiences because I share characteristics of their background. Cottle expresses it thus:

> *"For a method as fundamental as visiting with people, listening, speaking and allowing conversations to proceed as they will, means that one's own life is implicated in the life of another person and one's own feelings are evoked by the language, history and accounts of this other person".*
>
> (Cottle, 1972, p. xvi)

As Fraser (2004) asserts, it is the plurality of truths that makes qualitative methods useful for offering explanations for causality and association in outcomes studies. Reality, therefore, is subjective, socially, and individually constructed. It is also experienced internally and externally, value laden, and meaningful (Smith, 2004; Levitt et al, 2006). Some critics have argued that by focusing on meaning, the interpretive nature of qualitative research excludes participants' actual involvement in the material world (Giddens, 1993). My own view is that the strength of qualitative inquiries is associated with the fact that participants' narratives include a rich description of their actions, thoughts, and feelings. This provides useful insights for understanding social phenomena.

Differences in the conceptualisation of meaning are to be expected because not all populations are homogenous. For example, although the BAME parents and social workers recruited for this study met specific inclusion criteria, they all had individual conceptualisations of safe parenting and the evaluation process. Analysing their experiences allowed me to embrace and explore the complexity and richness of culturally informed parenting scripts. This complexity is determined by people's access to resources that facilitate the development of valued competences and customary theories of behaviour (Ogbu, 1981)

Given that there is now greater emphasis on using evidence-based practice in social work, practitioners can rely on qualitative studies such as this one to provide nuanced understanding of complex practice domains (Howard et al, 2003; Jenson, 2005; Adams et al, 2009; Shaw, 2011).

A social constructivist approach

Having made the decision to prioritise detail over generality, I opted for a research design that was intrinsic to the phenomenological philosophy. As a philosophy that explores human subjectivity systematically, phenomenology represents a social constructivist model of interpreting the meaning of lived experience (Spiegelberg, 1982). I started the study from the constructivist position that each participant had a unique and valid experience of parenting assessments. From this perspective, participants' individual narratives were construed as human experience that can be transformed and projected as reality (Van Manen, 2007).

According to Bateson (1972), the limitation of a social constructivist approach is that it does not prescribe a linear notion of causality for the explanation of social reality. However, my focus was not to prove causality. As Krauss (2005) observes, multiple constructions of reality can coexist and are imbued with knowledge creating power. Therefore, in the process of interpreting and searching for meaning, I shifted back and forth between focusing on individually constructed models of reality (from the one-to-one interviews) and how participants interacted with one another (during focus groups) to construct, modify, and maintain what their society holds to be true, real, and meaningful (Freedman and Combs, 1996).

Constructivist commentators contend that collating individual and group meaning is necessary because reality is socially constructed, and individuals' perspectives are historically and culturally specific (White and Epston, 1990; Howe, 1992; Burr, 1995; Monk et al, 1997; Rapmund and Moore, 2000). This debate within social constructivist literature had a significant influence on my thinking in terms of how to interpret participants' narratives. For example, I heeded Rapmund and Moore's (2000) caution against allowing the power of singular accounts to further silence and marginalise those whose stories fail to fit. As such, although I took the view that all lived experience has equal validity, I analysed and interpreted individual narratives as instances of the construction of meaning rather than encode each narrative as a complete construction of reality.

It is the inclusion and emphasis on multiple realities and personal stories (Wheeldon and Åhlberg, 2012) that make social constructivist theory relevant to this study. This is not to advance the case that it is better than other theories. My point is that it was appropriate for this study. Social constructivist theory has been widely used in studies that have sought to understand the lived experiences of parents (e.g. Barn, 2002, 2006a; Hill, 2006; Bebbington and Beecham, 2003; Thoburn et al, 2005; Asmussen and Weizel, 2010; Chimba et al, 212). That said, it appears to be scarcely used in evaluative studies.

Given that appraising the efficacy of parenting evaluations was a fundamental component of this study, I set out the contexts and concepts of effectiveness. My approach was to consider efficacy from the perspectives of participants. Using the social constructivist theory represented a dynamic and pragmatic approach, in part, because it is *"not wedded to the assumption that there is one research method to be preferred for its potential to illuminate and demonstrate social work effectiveness"* (Cheetham et al, 1992, p. 8).

The dynamism of social constructivist theory was used to understand experience and evaluate effectiveness from the variety of participants' perspectives and assumptions, whilst at the same time striking a balance through reference to wider social and policy contexts. This approach enabled me to acknowledge participants' expressed views about how parenting competence evaluations can be improved and the constraints imposed by policy.

Parton (2003) advocates for dynamism in research by advancing the argument that in an era where claims to knowledge have become subject to doubt, constructivist perspectives that recognise the importance of fluid and artistic forms of creating knowledge may prove productive in informing practice. This creativity is illustrated in Barn (2006a) who used a social constructivist approach to good effect in drawing our attention to how migration, ethnicity, socioeconomic circumstances, multiculturalism, and racism shape the complex lives and needs of minority ethnic families.

Likewise, the topic of this study meant that I had to be aware that participants' lived experiences would involve the influence of complex intangible issues such as poverty, social networks, diversity, relationships, and community. This meant that philosophies that espouse notions of linear causality were not ideal for capturing the complexities of the participants' lives (Schön, 1987). At their worst, philosophies of linear causality can be culturally oppressive. Thus, I chose a fluid approach which would allow for the evaluation of effectiveness that was flexible enough to assess whether interventions had been successful in terms of objectives achieved, but also give a view about whether objectives were 'either trivial, inappropriate or misconceived' (Cheetham et al, 1992, p. 10).

The influence of theory

While seeking to balance the trade-off between complexity and generality, I selected research methods that were grounded in a phenomenological research philosophy. Phenomenology has a significant influence on qualitative methods (Crabtree and Miller, 1999; Cohen et al, 2000) in that as a research process, it facilitates direct investigation and description of phenomena as they are consciously experienced. This focus is congruent with the purpose of this study, which aims to explore and understand how Black and minority ethnic parents and social workers experience parenting capacity assessments.

A lot has been written about phenomenology but, within the literature, there is much debate and disagreement about what it means or what constitutes phenomenological research (see Moustakas, 1994; Moran, 2000). In the debates that abound, phenomenology is conceptualised as a philosophy, a research method, and an overarching perspective from which qualitative research is sourced. This is mainly because there are distinct schools of phenomenological thought which, as Moran (2000) observes, are *"extraordinarily diverse in their interests; their interpretation of the central issues of phenomenology and their application of what they understand to be phenomenological methods"* (p. 3). Despite their diversity, phenomenological schools of thought agree that the embodiment of experiential meanings is integral to phenomenological research (Moustakas, 1994).

I chose an explicitly Heideggerian approach and therefore consider the methodological underpinnings of this study to be interpretive and hermeneutic, rather than following Husserl's more descriptive and eidetic methods (Moran and Mooney, 2002). The Heideggerian hermeneutic approach focuses on interpreting lived experience as revealed through participants' consciousness. Heidegger (2000) was concerned with the question of *Being* and advanced the argument that it is through accessing lived experience that researchers can gain understanding of the meanings and perceptions of participants' worlds. This is achieved by using the hermeneutic circle to enable the researcher's understanding of the connection between theory, data, and participants' lived experience (Ezzy, 2002).

Heidegger's analysis of *Being* was influential in guiding my choice of research philosophy. To explain the uniqueness of human beings, Heidegger (2000) posits that although we exist as individuals, we do so within a social context. He argued that it is therefore erroneous to objectify and separate individuals from their experience (Heidegger, 2000, p. 80). Cohn (2002) expounds this by explaining it as the interconnectedness and interdependence of human relationships.

Another key element of Heideggerian phenomenology that influenced me was the concept of temporality. Heidegger also views *Being* as essentially temporal in that individuals are shaped by the past, present, and future of their personal and social contexts. This means that when exploring lived experience, researchers must consider the historical and temporal nature of social contexts. For example, Creasy and Trikha (2004) conducted studies that showed that minority ethnic families often encounter cultural conflicts when attempting to reconcile their heritage and traditions with the English traditions and ways of life.

The focus on experiential meaning was congruent with what I sought to achieve through this study. This is because when I was working in a London social work team, between 2008 and 2010, my practice observations led me to question how minority ethnic parents experience the parenting capacity assessment process. I noted then that except in cases where there was extreme domestic violence, cruelty to children, or severe parental mental health, social workers often seemed uneasy about making intervention decisions with Black and ethnic minority families. The social workers were keen to ensure that their decisions were not seen to be oppressive. But social workers also found issues of ethnicity and culture particularly challenging to deal with in cases where there were concerns of possible neglect or emotional abuse.

In the absence of accessible research, the tendency was to be guided by anecdotal information from colleagues of similar backgrounds to the families. The challenge for social workers was in undertaking an assessment of parenting capacity that also considered ecological factors in an environment of diverse belief systems. My observations were that social workers often focused practice decisions on narrow interpretations of single issues, for example, physical punishment (Children Act, 2004, s.58). This can itself be oppressive.

Following my review of the literature, I identified that the voices of Black and minority ethnic parents were underrepresented in parenting literature in the UK (see parenting chapter). This gap in knowledge strengthened my commitment to the topic and my preference to use participants' narratives, whilst also considering that the narratives of lived experiences may be made up of influences that were not necessarily part of the mainstream society.

At the analysis stage, my expansive reading around phenomenology, as well as my practice and personal experience with the topic of parenting competence evaluations proved beneficial in how I interpreted participants' narratives. For example, social work experience as well as being a first-generation African immigrant made me aware that parenting practices are often a reflection of broader familial, social, temporal, and cultural contexts. Therefore, I tapped into this knowledge during analysis. This is consistent with Heideggerian phenomenology that argues against the notion that researchers ought to bracket out all prior experiences and emotions by reducing their understanding to an objective opinion. This attention to praxis and reflexivity is congruent with a social constructivist approach (Patton, 2002) and with the qualitative design of this study.

Overall, the phenomenological approach enabled me to engage with participants' experiences through the personal, social and cultural influences that shape their views. This also offered the benefit of ensuring that I did not lose the detail by only valuing generalisation across participant groups. In other words, I was open to the notion that what was unique about a specific participant's experience was potentially all that mattered. Bogdan and Taylor (1975) explain it as follows:

> *"When we reduce people to statistical aggregates, we lose sight of the subjective nature of human behaviour".*

(pp. 4–5)

Frame analysis

My main reason for choosing frame analysis was because of its potential to link behaviour to participants' reception and production processes. In other words, it helps us understand the social construction of reality. Frame analysis is attributed to the work of Erving Goffman (1974) and further developed by Ritchie and

Spencer (Ritchie and Spencer, 1994), cited in Bryman and Burgess (1994). It is conceptualised as socially produced structures that individuals use to select, organise, interpret, and make sense of complex reality (Schön and Rein, 1994, p. 32). Goffman conceptualised frames as being mental structures through which people make sense of their world. However, he also warns that understanding how people make sense of their worlds is not a perfect process because individuals can draw from several frames to construct meaning.

Entman (1993) expresses a similar view and suggests that the insights that can be drawn from narratives of complex reality can easily be lost because communication often lacks disciplinary status. He proposes that the use of frame analysis helps us identify how framing influences thinking by *"illuminating the precise way in which influence over a human consciousness is exerted by the transfer of information"* (p. 51). Entman's explanation that perspectives are 'framed' by prior knowledge resonated with my own view that participants' conceptualisations of parenting would not have developed in a vacuum. Rather, their perspectives would have been shaped through selection and salience, to emphasise specific discourse (Entman, 1993).

As an approach to analysing qualitative data, frame analysis allows for thematic and explanatory themes to be explored. Specific to this research, I saw the use of frame analysis as being an effective way of analysing conceptions of parenting competence by exploring why Black and minority ethnic parents say they parent the way they do and juxtaposing how parents and social workers conceptualise parenting competence. Because the focus of the study was on understanding how culture and ethnicity influence parenting practices and how social workers incorporate it in evaluations of parenting competence, using frames represented a helpful way of beginning to draw nuanced understanding of the topic.

According to Entman (1993), the frames (often referred to schemata) through which people make sense of their experience can be identified through what they say and are captured in the presence or indeed omission of certain key words, stereotyped images, stock phrases, or references made to sources of information. Thus, I analysed transcribed data to identify how BAME parents defined parenting and how they said their cultures and ethnicity influenced their parenting practices. Likewise, I used frame analysis to identify how social workers defined culture and ethnicity and how they said they incorporated their understanding of culture and ethnicity in evaluations of the parenting competence of Black and minority ethnic parents.

The narratives that participants gave of their experience contained clusters of judgements that reflected the frames from which the perception was drawn. For example, the mother who explained that her daughters needed to do more housework compared to her sons because *"it is the girls who will have responsibility for the family; and who wants to marry a woman who can't cook"* was analysed as drawing on a cultural frame about gender roles. Similarly, a social worker who suggests that Black and minority ethnic parents use culture and ethnicity *"as smoke screen to hide abuse"* analysed as drawing on the frame that culture and ethnicity are an excuse for poor parenting behaviour.

What became clear from using frame analysis was that the different views and perspectives that parents and social workers held about culturally informed parenting scripts fuelled mistrust and hindered attempts to work more closely together. This was key to understanding the challenges involved in evaluating parenting competence in a multi-ethnic community. From a frame analysis perspective, it could be argued that this is because in the process of selecting, highlighting and using highlighted elements of lived experience to construct their arguments about parenting and what influences parenting practices, parents, and social workers invoke different frames. For most BAME parents, their culture is the stock of commonly invoked frames, while social workers generally invoked frames from their individual cultures as well as their profession's cultures.

Alternative theories

In the preceding section, I provided a detailed discussion about how this study is influenced by a phenomenological philosophy and analysed using frame analysis. However, it is important to acknowledge that not only are there several theoretical orientations from which to conduct qualitative studies, I also considered using either Ethnography or BNIM for this study.

Ethnography could have been used for this study if participants' social settings were able to accommodate direct observation, communication, and interaction with those being studied and if there were sufficient opportunity for informal and formal interviews (Lofland, 1974). However, the cornerstone of ethnographic research, participant observation, entails extensive fieldwork that requires the researcher to actively form relationships with participants. Van Manen (1982) summarises ethnographic research as follows: *"The result of ethnographic inquiry is cultural description. It is, however, a description that can emerge only from a lengthy period of intimate study and residence in a given social setting"* (p. 103).

Van Manen adds emphasis to the requirement for the researcher to understand the language spoken in participants' social settings, participate first-hand in some of the activities that take place, and, most critically, do intensive work with a few informants drawn from the setting. This, as Moustakas (1994) observes, makes ethnography better suited for examining phenomena within specific group situations and is largely shaped and constrained by those situations. It can have the advantage of revealing nuances and subtleties within thick cultural and ethnic contexts.

However, the practicalities involved in identifying an ideal study group that is representative of a larger cultural population, as well as the requirement for prolonged contact in the social setting, are factors that I was unable to fit around my current professional commitments. Conversely, as I have already mentioned, I was not only interested in understanding shared perspectives, I also want to capture the heterogeneity that exists within participants' experiences.

A BNIM would have permitted studying facets of participants' experience that were not directly observable (Wengraf, 2002). This could have provided an intimate view of how Black and ethnic minority families experience parenting capacity assessments by allowing us to see parents in the contexts of their entire lives, from birth to the present. Using BNIM provides a cutting edge by which we can examine our most basic common-sense assumptions about the nature of reality. This could have helped the development of a fuller understanding of the stages and critical periods in the construction of participants' parenting practices. For example, using Wengraf's (2001) conceptualisation of semi-structured interviewing, I could have elicited a fuller understanding of ethnic minority parenting by asking questions about the points at which parents decided that their method of disciplining or setting boundaries was the most appropriate.

Given that narrative expressions tend to represent conscious concerns and unconscious cultural, societal, and individual processes and presumptions (Chamberlayne et al, 2002), BNIM would have facilitated my understanding of how participants' historically evolving internal and external worlds interact. This lends itself well to the psycho-dynamic and socio-dynamic approaches used in social work practice. Thus, the findings would have potentially provided a fully psychosocial understanding in which neither the sociological nor the psychological dynamics within Black and minority ethnic families are neglected or privileged.

Such an approach could have benefited the study in that ethnic and cultural influences on ethnic minority families' parenting practices would have been understood in their historical context, thus laying a basis for comparison of situated practices. In her review of approaches to narrative research, Squire (2008) describes this as the sort of inclusiveness that is particularly beneficial in enabling researchers to extend analyses to multiple levels.

As Hinchman and Hinchman (1997) note, by focusing on eliciting retrospective narratives of experience, BNIM facilitates the expression and detection of suppressed implicit perspectives that could illuminate the intersection of biography, history, and society. This makes it better suited for longitudinal process studies that seek to capture incident experiences with a clear sequential order that connects the complexity of historic events in a meaningful way. Critics of BNIM argue that it places greater emphasis on the individual rather than the social context in which life is lived (Connelly and Clandinin, 1990; Riessman and Quinney, 2005). I chose not to use it because, like ethnography, data collection is time intensive.

Research participants

The participants for this study represented several cultural and ethnic identities. This mix of participants provided a rich source of data in that despite their differences, their narratives converged towards a common view about the efficacy of evaluations of culturally informed parenting. For example, although ethnic characteristics such as parents' countries of origin, religious persuasions, and belief systems were different, they all expressed the view that parenting competence evaluations had failed to appraise their parenting practices within the context of the cultural goals they sought to achieve when socialising their children. In this regard, parents saw themselves as being a homogenous group whose cultural approaches to parenting were not accepted in the UK.

Equally, the social workers were from several ethnic and cultural backgrounds but viewed themselves as a homogenous group. They articulated this as being evident in the criteria they use to evaluate all parenting, as well as the language that they use, to generalise their clients' behaviour, for example, in using statements such as "*I know in your culture physical punishment is acceptable*", when assessing BAME parents where concerns of physical chastisement have been made.

Data collection

The participants for this study were initially selected using purposive sampling techniques. However, the initial numbers were too small. This led me to employ snow ball sampling to recruit participants who met the research criteria whilst maintaining the purposive sampling approach (Polkinghorne, 2005). Participant selection made it necessary to have inclusion criteria in place so that participant characteristics were clear from the onset. Ritchie and Lewis (2003) explain many different forms of purposive sampling including heterogeneous, homogenous, typical, critical, and extreme (or deviant) samples. I selected participants for this study based on their ethnicity.

My criteria were simple: participants had to be parents from Black and minority ethnic backgrounds, whose parenting had been assessed by social workers. I began the process of identifying potential participants through my connections in the local authorities where I had previously been employed and from friends and colleagues within the social care industry. The recommendations from these connections gave me access to gate keepers and minimised some of the bureaucratic processes that I would have otherwise had to follow to access potential participants.

The pragmatic approach I adopted in selecting the organisations I approached to recruit participants ensured that the sample remained relevant to the aims of the study. In other words, I was still able to recruit participants who met the predefined characteristics; that is, Black and minority ethnic parents as well as social workers who had experience of being involved in parenting competence evaluations. I felt that this would not adversely impact on the findings because the data collection was still guided by the foundational aims of the study (Creswell, 1994).

That said, some of the debate within research literature questions the use of pragmatic approaches. Mertens (2003) for example, asserts that it is not enough to base methodological choices solely on practicality. She argues that studies that take pragmatic approaches to data collection often fail to clarity whose practicality and benefit are being prioritised, and to what end.

Data analysis

My approach to the task of data analysis followed the recommendation of Coffey and Atkinson (1996) who postulate that data analysis is better achieved by exploring data from a variety of perspectives. This was congruent with my methodology in which the data will be collected using a variety of methods. According to

Van Manen (1990), phenomenological research should not be subjected to rigid rules. Instead, researchers should allow the direction of studies to be informed by continual analysis. This process of simultaneous data collection and analysis is the hallmark for research that relies on participants' narratives to understand phenomena (Lofland and Lofland, 1995).

Given that this study was guided by a phenomenological research philosophy, I relied heavily on frame analysis to analyse the data. Bruner (1986) explains that there are two main approaches to analysing literary accounts: paradigmatic or narrative. In the paradigmatic approach, text and structure are analysed for criteria that might enable a researcher to reinforce hypothesis, while the narrative approach focuses on understanding the meaning of stories by studying them within their contexts (Dautenhahn, 2000; Coffey and Atkinson, 1996).

By using the narrative analysis approach, I focused on participants' lived experiences and, through their narratives, identified themes and patterns associated with their experiences. This was achieved by using data collected from observing and interviewing participants to draw conclusions about the meaning of narratives. Because the research was designed to ensure that participants told their own stories and described their experiences, they had control over their narratives. This allowed power sharing (Dominelli, 2002) in that I informed participants of their right to terminate sessions at any point.

The challenge, as Van Manen (1990) puts it, is that researchers often know too much about the phenomenon they are studying. Therefore, they must bridle their assumptions and pre-understandings (e.g. personal beliefs and theories) to allow for potentially surprising findings (Dahlberg, 2006). However, as I explained earlier in this chapter, rather than separate myself from the study, I embraced this challenge by allowing my thoughts and experiences to run parallel to those of the participants (Giorgi, 1994; Halling et al, 2006; Finlay, 2009). By doing this, I was in a better position to concentrate on participants' narratives whilst also reflecting on my thoughts and experience.

The data collection methods also helped minimise bias. By using field notes taken during focus groups and one-to-one interviews, audio recording of participant sessions, journal records (which captured my reflections), and from notes about the where, when, and of the circumstances surrounding participants' narratives, I became more aware of emerging themes. This also offered the advantage of creating a more meaningful picture by capturing participants' narratives within the contexts of the stories they told (Polkinghorne, 2005; Clandinin, 2006; Reissman, 2008).

As Clandinin (2006) points out, it is through synthesising collective descriptions and storied events that we can discover and understand lived experiences. Therefore, I analysed the experiences that participants considered to be significant as well as how they reflected on those experiences. This added to the overall identification of the themes and patterns that were analysed.

According to Clandinin and Connelly (2000), making sense of participants' narratives requires researchers to ask questions that point in four directions: "inward, in order to capture internal conditions such as feelings, hopes, moral dispositions and aesthetic reactions; outward in order to capture existential conditions associated with the environment; and backward and forward, in order to capture the temporality of past, present and future" (p. 50). During data collection process, some participants found this to be challenging as they became emotional about expressing their lived experiences. In some ways, participants' emotional expressions elicited the tensions that helped give a better understanding of how they experienced parenting competence evaluations. The qualitative approach adopted for this study helped in the identification of emerging themes and patterns.

Ethical considerations

Researching participants who have experienced social services involvement raises some ethical issues. These include issues of power dynamics, consent, confidentiality, data protection, social justice, partiality, researcher safety, dependency in relationships, and cultural differences (Bowling, 2002). Moriarty (2011) argues that because questions of ethics are inherent in all studies, no research methodology is ethically privileged.

My approach to addressing ethical issues was to ensure methodological rigour. However, as I had anticipated, the ethical problems I encountered were subtle. They were mainly embedded in the construction of the relationship of power between myself and participants. This is because research processes create tensions between aims to make generalisations for the good of others and participants' rights to maintain privacy (Orb et al, 2001; Moriarty, 2011). I addressed by maintaining clear ethical standards. In addition to addressing research process tensions, clear ethical standards provide a crucial indicator of the quality of a study. It was for this reason that I sought ethical approval from research ethics committees. I was also guided by relevant social work codes of conduct.

For this study, I submitted applications for ethics approval to York University's Health and Social Care Ethics Committee (HSSEC) and to the Social Care Institute of Excellence (via the Integrated Research Application System – IRAS). The Social Care Institute of Excellence (SCIE)'s position was that research proposals that have met the requirements of reputable higher institutions of learning, such as the University of York, did not need separate approval (see appended email). I also applied to the Association of Directors of Children's Services Research Group.

Although the ethics boards scrutinised my research proposal to ensure that participants were protected, I was ultimately responsible for anticipating and taking steps to address potential harm to my research participants. Therefore, I considered the ethical questions associated with qualitative studies, including issues relating to interactions between myself and the participants. These considerations, as discussed later, are reflected in the appropriateness of the research and methodological designs and informed the research project from data collection through to the write up and dissemination.

I approached the issue of ethics from my reflection on how biomedical and communitarian research ethics correspond with the social work codes of ethics put forward by Banks (2006). Biomedical research ethics are based on values of autonomy, non-malfeasance, beneficence, and justice. These values inform principles of informed consent, honesty, avoidance of harm, respect to privacy, research integrity, and confidentiality. Communitarian research ethics, on the other hand, are based on feminist philosophy and posit that a community's moral values should guide any research that is conducted within that community's domain (Denzin, 1989). The implication is that research ethics are always con-textual and therefore oblige the researcher to be sensitive to community concepts such as kindness, neighbourliness, care, shared governance, and moral good.

The relationship between participants and researchers has something to con-tribute to subjectivity or objectivity. Therefore, I conducted the research with sen-sitivity to feminist concepts such as empowerment and the participatory nature of research. This is because doing so helped facilitate non-hierarchical dialogue between myself as the researcher and the research participants.

The communitarian perspective on moral good and shared governance corre-sponds well with social work values on user involvement. According to Banks (2006), social work codes of ethics are categorised as: 1. respect for individuality; 2. promotion of self-determination; 3. promoting the best interest of others; and 4. promoting social justice. I considered these codes of ethics alongside research principles such as informed consent, avoidance of harm, care, and moral good.

Both perspectives are also consistent with the phenomenological philosophy that underlies this study in that they can be applied to engage, interpret, and reflect participants' narratives with respect to how personal, social, and cultural circum-stances influence their experiences. This enabled me to conduct the research and navigate through the tensions between concrete and universal experiences in rela-tion to issues such as gender, politics, and social status. That is, I allowed partici-pants to express their views about these issues and how they related to parenting competence evaluations without seeking to add to their narratives.

That said, I remained within the mainstream approach and only adopted guid-ing assumptions from biomedical and communitarian research ethics that were congruent with social work codes of ethics (Shaw and Gould, 2001). Specifically, I ensured that the study was conducted in a manner that reflected commitment to the wellbeing of the research participants. This meant that my paramount consid-eration was to make sure that the participants understood the purpose of the study, were offered anonymity, and that those who consented to participating did so willingly and without coercion (Wiles et al, 2005). This was achieved by inform-ing participants of the general parameters of the study before obtaining their con-sent. Feminist concerns about ethical issues around consent relate to participants exposing themselves to an undesired extent.

Informed consent was obtained in accordance with the legal frameworks and regulations such as Article 8 of the Human Rights Act 1998 and the Data Protec-tion Act (1998). These had relevance to this research as they specifically relate to issues of respect for private and family life as well as access to the information that organisations hold about their clients (Montgomery, 2003; Masson, 2004).

Consent was also obtained throughout the research as a continual process. This is because of the potential for intrusion and exploitation associated with using participants' narratives as a research method (LaRossa et al, 1981; Alderson, 2004). By obtaining consent at different stages throughout the research process, I was also advancing the case that ethical considerations are not a one-off process and must be negotiated at several stages of the research project.

Initially, the organisations through which participants were recruited approached potential participants and invited them to take part in the study. At that stage, participants were given the project information sheet and asked to attend an information session. During the information session, I explained the research in terms of my role and identity, the purpose of the research, the scope it will take, the questions I am likely to ask during sessions, the use to which the study will be put, the method of anonymity, and the extent to which their narratives will be used in the final report. I also reminded participants about their right to end sessions at any time during the study.

Conversely, questions of confidentiality and anonymity were especially important in ensuring that participants' identities were protected. Anonymity was offered to all participants, and no identifying information is included in the final thesis. I kept all research data locked away and used fictitious names to represent participants' responses.

According to Morris (2006), power differentials and structural inequalities between the researcher and participants need to be addressed to ensure that research participants are not excluded from the analysis process. This study addressed power and structural issues by using a bottom-up approach, which recognises participants as actors and agents whose input into is to be respected.

Additionally, the multilayered in-depth approach that was used for this study made it necessary for me to consider issues of gender, alongside power, and structural inequalities. This also has advantages for scholarship, as well as ethical and political reasons in that it influences the way we thread individual and/or family narratives.

Aspects of the research design, such as the interview dynamics, prioritised participants' interests over the need to collect data that might have added to validating the conclusions made here. For example, using Thompson's (1992) framework for conducting qualitative research, I asked all the parents who took part how they felt about being interviewed by a male researcher and whether any arrangements needed to be made to ensure that they were comfortable. This also included obtaining consent for the anonymous use of interview data and omitted parts of their narratives that they did not wish to be included in the data analysis.

Data protection issues were addressed by transcribing all the data that were collected as part of the study and saving those electronically. This was being done on a password-protected hard drive that was kept locked in a desk drawer in the researcher's home office. All paper documents including participant identifiers were shredded and audio recording deleted after the information had been converted to electronic versions.

Another area of ethical consideration related to the need to conduct a study on Black and minority parenting that bears critical methodological scrutiny. This implied that the data had to be transparent and robust enough to withstand critique and to facilitate nuanced understanding. My research questions addressed this by providing a base from which to draw findings that are resonant with and relevant to participants' lived experiences. The participants were recruited from multiple sites. However, I did not intend to set a control group. Nevertheless, all the parents who took part turned out to be first-generation immigrants.

My background and interests were implicated in the study. This informed rather than skewed the research agenda, questions asked, and the framework within which data were interpreted. However, I was also keen to ensure that the study did not crossover from scholarship to advocating for Black and minority ethnic parents. As Kvale (1996) notes, semi-structured interviews are particularly vulnerable to these pitfalls because they allow the researcher to focus discussions on areas of interest to them. This increases the potential for bias, especially in research encounters where participants are reluctant to express themselves.

Participants' reluctance to express themselves resulted in me focusing on elements of their narratives that resonated with the research agenda. This meant collecting and analysing information that was important for evaluating and informing social work practice.

Validity and credibility

My approach to validity was in the context of establishing the extent to which the findings were a true and certain reflection of participants' experiences. For this, I used methodological triangulation in order to increase internal validity. This involved cross-checking data from the focus groups and one-to-one interviews to ensure that I had captured participant narratives that related to the research questions and that my descriptions and conclusions were credible. Patton (2002) suggests that this can be achieved by analysing research questions from multiple perspectives. However, he cautions against making the goal of such analyses arriving at consistency across data sources or approaches. In Patton's view, inconsistencies should be welcomed as opportunities to uncover deeper meaning from the data.

Thus, the triangulation process only involved interviewing BAME parents and social workers to get their perspectives on the efficacy of evaluations of culturally informed parenting and drawing parallels between both. The aim was to determine areas of agreement and divergence. The validity of the conclusions drawn from the research data was then enhanced by presenting direct quotations from the interviews as a way of demonstrating the relationship between themes and participants' narrative.

Morse et al (2002) implore qualitative researchers to reclaim research credibility by implementing verification strategies that are inherent and self-correcting during the research process. Credibility checks for this study included using my supervisor and social work colleagues to audit the data from each research question with focus on the themes created.

6   BAME parents' perspectives

Profiles

This phase of the study focused on obtaining group perceptions of safe parenting and their experiences of being assessed by social workers. A total of eight BAME parent focus groups were held between April 2012 and June 2013. Each group consisted of eight participants and lasted from 60 to 106 minutes. There were five parents in each focus group.

I did not achieve the initial goal of recruiting participants from the same ethnic groups. Instead, the groups were diverse and the main homogenous characteristics were that all participants were first-generation BAME parents whose parenting had been assessed by children's social services. For example, a group of mainly Polish participants also contained two Chinese parents. Likewise, focus groups of African parents were made up of parents from different countries in Africa.

I facilitated the group discussions using an open-ended interview protocol. All focus group discussions were recorded on an I-phone, with the permission of the participants. The anonymity of participants in the focus groups is protected in this report in that the report only presents the summary of the group discussions. Similarly, the reasons for social care involvement with participants were obtained from self-reports. No attempt was made to clarify the circumstances either through the organisations from which participants were recruited or from the local authorities that had been involved with them.

Focus group

Focus group interview recordings were transcribed and went through several phases of analysis. The initial analysis was conducted to get a general sense of the data and reflect on its meaning. This was followed with a more detailed analysis and data were divided into units that reflected participants' thoughts, attitudes, and experiences. This process culminated in the generation of a list of topics that were then labelled and categorised as the key findings. Data from across all focus groups were analysed and organised into the identified categories to determine the interconnectedness of issues and conditions that may have given rise to the categories. This gave a general picture of participants' perceptions about how parenting competence evaluations incorporate issues of culture and ethnicity.

Each participant group data were also analysed separately to determine whether there were trends unique to each group. There were no significant distinguishable differences. Instead, there were high levels of agreement and significant consistency in how participants talked about issues within the groups. That said, there was discernible difference in how some issue were articulated in different groups. For example, restricting children's socialisation was talked about in all focus groups, but some groups emphasised religion, whilst others emphasised differences in moral values as their main reason for seeking to restrict their children's socialisation.

Twelve themes emerged. Overall, 12 themes relating to participants' perceptions about and experience of parenting competence evaluations, as well as their perceptions of the influence of culture and ethnicity on their parenting practices were identified from the analysis of focus group discussion transcripts. These findings included traditions, religion, acculturation, aspiration, protection, children's development, gender roles, identity, social support, building resilience to discrimination and racism, views about professionals' preconceptions, and view about what constitutes competence.

The insight into BAME parents' attitudes, feelings, and beliefs about the influence of culture and ethnicity was that cultural parenting scripts are partially independent of individual family circumstances or social setting. The consensus expressed in one of the focus groups put it as follows: *"the way we raise our children is how people in our culture have been doing it for centuries. So, it doesn't matter where you go, all Punjab parents anywhere in the world do it the same way"*. But, whilst the pervading view was that culture and ethnicity exert significant influence on the parenting practices of Black and minority ethnic parents, some participants stated that their parenting practices were not at all influenced by culture and ethnicity.

Focus group discussions also highlighted that Black and minority ethnic parents did not feel that social workers sought to understand why parents approach parenting in the way they do. This, they argued, meant that social workers failed to properly appraise parenting competence and instead limited the use of information about parents' culture and ethnicity to identification purposes.

Another key finding was that religion is intricately interwoven with other aspects of culture and ethnicity. Indeed, within the focus group discussions, participants tended to illustrate points with reference to religion and culture used interchangeably to explain their parenting practices.

All the aforementioned themes were also identified from the one-to-one interviews. As such, I chose to focus the presentation and elaboration of findings on illustrations from the one-to-one interviews. This is not to suggest that data from the one-to-one interviews were more important than data from the focus groups. Rather it is, first, to minimise repetition and, second, to focus on gaining nuanced understanding of how Black and minority ethnic parents perceive and experience parenting competence evaluations, as well as whether, and if so how, culture and ethnicity influenced their individual parenting practices.

One-to-one interviews

Parents within the interview sample were originally from four Black and minority ethnic backgrounds as defined by their countries of origin. These comprised Polish, Pakistani, Indian, and African. The participants who described themselves as African were originally from Ghana, Kenya, Uganda, Senegal, Nigeria, and Sierra Leone. This level of diversity within the sample has implications for generalisability. The implications are discussed in Chapter 8 that discusses what the findings mean.

What is important to point out at this stage is that all the participants also had several characteristics in common, namely, they described themselves as being of Black or minority ethnic background; they were first-generation immigrants; their parenting competences had been previously assessed by social workers; and they had at least one child who had been previously made subject to either child protection plans or who had been taken into local authority care.

The reasons for social care involvement with participants' families had been obtained at the initial stages of recruitment. As aforementioned, what I knew of the reasons for social work involvement with participants' families was what the parents told me. The reasons were widely varied, and I was not able to verify the information. However, all participants (focus group and one-to-one interviews) had had social care involvement for more than 3 months. The participants who went on to take part in the focus group interviews had had their cases escalated and their children either made subject to child protection plans or removed from their care.

As stated in the methodology chapter, the 15 participants for the one-to-one interviews were drawn from a total sample of 40. Although the majority of the 15 participants either had long-term partners or were married, it was only the women who attended the one-to-one interviews. The explanations that the mothers attending the interviews gave were that the fathers either had to be at work or were looking after the children to allow the mother to take part in the interview. What was also noteworthy was that most of the participants who took part in the one-to-one interviews were either unemployed or worked part-time (*demographic details of the parents who took part in the interviews are provided in Table 6.1*).

What was immediately evident from the one-to-one interviews was that in all cases, the children involved were younger than 13 years. In fact, there were only two parents who had children who were older than ten years.

What the data from the interviews or focus group do not highlight is the nature of the organisations from which participants were recruited. The organisations stated that they offered a range of support services aimed at helping their clients. This help was not exclusively about issues to do with parenting. The organisations described their support as being tailored to clients' needs but that it included services such as interpreting, advocacy, signposting, and providing social events to connect the organisations' clients with people from similar ethnic backgrounds within the community. What was curious in all cases was that all the organisations had support groups for parents who had been involved with children's social services.

Table 6.1 Participants (parents)

Participant	Age	Ethnicity	Number of children	Level of social worker involvement	Length of social work involvement	Employment status	Parental relationship status
Agnes	27	Polish	3 (two girls and a boy)	CP	6 Months	Unemployed	Partner
Patricia	32	Polish	2 (a boy and a girl)	CP	3 Months	Part-time cleaner	Single
Aria	26	Pakistani	4 (two girls and two boys)	LAC	6 Months	Unemployed	Married
Noreen	28	Indian	4 (four girls)	CP	6 Months	Unemployed	Married
Deborah	35	African	2 (two boys)	CP	6 Months	Part-time	Single
Olivia	33	African	3 (three girls)	CP	8 Months	Unemployed	Partner
Ruth	37	Pakistani	1 child – boy	CP	6 Months	Unemployed	Single
Rachael	29	African	3 (two boys and one girl)	LAC	6 Months	Part-time cleaner	Single
Sarah	32	Indian	4 (four girls)	LAC	8 Months	Part-time in a school	Married
Verona	36	African	2 (one girl and one boy)	CP	9 Months	Unemployed	Partner
Rebecca	38	Pakistani	2 (one girl and one boy)	CP	6 Months	Unemployed	Married
Lillian	30	African	2 (two boys)	CP	7 Months	Unemployed	Married
Susan	28	African	1 child – boy	LAC	8 Months	Unemployed	Partner
Jessica	34	Indian	3 (two girls and one boy)	CP	6 Months	Unemployed	Single
Carolyn	38	Polish	2 (one girl and one boy)	CP	8 Months	Unemployed	Partner

Key: CP – Child Protection; LAC – Looked After Child/ren

In terms of their policies, the organisations were clear that supporting parents who were or had been involved with social care was not the focus of their work. Rather, where support was being provided to clients who were having interventions from children's social care, it was being provided insofar as it helped safeguard the welfare of clients' children. Typically, the support was offered in the form of client-run open drop-in groups that were facilitated by a member of staff.

Findings

When thinking about how I was going to present the findings, I considered whether presenting some of the findings using quantitative data would provide better illustration and lend greater credibility to the research. This was mainly because during the data collection process, I had obtained significant quantitative data such as the number of participants and their demographic make-up (e.g. age ranges, gender split, and ethnic background). I saw the inclusion of quantitative data as offering great benefit not only in drawing meaningful results from large volumes of qualitative data but also in allowing me to focus on the more nuanced aspects of the data by separating out the quantifiable components.

However, I took the view that presenting the findings using quantitative data would not be in keeping with the inductive theoretical perspective underpinning the research. Throughout this study, experiential meaning was an important aspect of this study. Therefore, I did not want to risk suggesting through quantitative data that there is an objective reality that can be measured and statistically analysed to understand the parenting practices of Black and minority ethnic parents.

As such, the findings presented here are exclusively based on qualitative data and presented in the form of themes, which are evidenced using verbatim quotes from participants' interviews. The reason for using verbatim quotes is to illustrate participants' perceptions about the links between parenting practices and issues of culture and ethnicity. The quotes give insight into participants' experiences by presenting the words that participants use to describe how they make sense of their word. This helps us understand why each participant believes or parents as they do. Each quotation is labelled with the research participants' pseudonym and their ethnicity. So, for example, (Sara, Pakistani mother), would represent a research participant of Pakistani origin whom I refer to as Sara.

The themes are presented in subheadings and reflect the key issues that emerged during the analysis. They also represent participants' conceptualisations of culture and ethnicity as constituent dimensions of parenting and their perspectives of how issues of culture and ethnicity are incorporated within parenting capacity assessments. The presentation of themes about how parents say they do parenting is followed by themes about parents' views on whether social workers incorporated ethnicity and culture in their assessments of the participants' parenting capacity.

That said, I recognise that some of the phrases I used in presenting the findings, such as 'most', 'some', and 'a few', also carry with them an element of quantifying data. But, every effort was made to ensure that quotations remained as close to the transcribed text as possible albeit, conversational prompts, silences between responses and non-verbal utterances such as 'hmmm', 'oh', 'ah', are not included. This is because the focus of the study was to understand content rather than discourse. Therefore, I felt that including conversational prompts or describing participants' 'body language' as they responded to questions would detract from the text.

How participants say they do parenting

The findings indicate that participants' parenting practices were influenced by a range of factors mostly from their own experiences of being parented but also modified through necessity and exposure to other forms of parenting from social connections and media. Participant's responses suggested that their parenting practices were a result of how they understood messages about being parents from their families, friends, professionals, and the media. One participant expressed it as follows:

> *Yes, culture comes into it but they don't pull you aside as a child and tell you how to become a parent. You do what you saw your parents doing and what your friends' parents were doing but you also learn as you go . . . you make mistakes, and you see what your friends are doing with their children, what experts on TV say and you pick-up from there. That's how I do it. I am an international mother. I pick from here and there.*

(Jessica, Indian mother)

Theme 1: tradition

Most participants viewed traditions as a key influencing factor in shaping their parenting practices. In other words, they saw their parenting practices as a repertoire of skills that had been passed down through generations. This was expressed in two different ways: first, participants described it in the form of gender expectations and explained that their children had to be socialised to demonstrate certain gender competences because it is this that will prepare them for the different gender roles they will perform as adults.

> *My daughter has to learn how to keep a home from an early age. Who is going to marry her if she can't cook or clean? So, she must learn. Otherwise what good am I as a mother?*

(Sarah, Indian mother)

> *Traditionally, you can't raise boys and girls the same way. A girl cannot be lazy otherwise her family will not eat. But because now we are in England, it is called child abuse when you try to teach your daughter responsibility early.*

(Julia, Pakistani mother)

I remember my mother teaching me these things when I had my first child. She used to say that you have to feed children warm things so that they get some warmth in their body and she would say that it is not good to always carry a child when it cries. Sometimes you have to leave them to cry. The lady from social, she didn't understand this tradition things.

(Susan, Ugandan mother)

Second, tradition was spoken about in terms of it being an innate characteristic of parenting.

I don't really know where my knowledge comes from. You just know it. It is there. It is tradition. That is how everyone does it where I come from. I don't know. May be if you are raised in a certain culture you just find yourself parenting in the traditional way that you know.

(Ruth, Pakistani mother)

Some participants spoke of tradition in terms of seeking to maintain a sense of belonging. For some participants maintaining traditional parenting practices was an important marker of identity.

A lot of these traditions did not mean much to me when I was in Ghana. But somehow they have become important since I came to England and I want to make sure that my children don't lose that part of their Ghanaian identity. So for me the language, the behaviour and the dress are important.

(Lillian, Ghanaian mother)

The need to parent in ways that hold on to tradition was particularly evident in participants who claimed to have traditional rites of passage into adulthood. These participants expressed parenting in practical terms, such as teaching their children the ancestral language as well as cultural norms concerning behaviour and preparing them for adult life. This also extended to areas of disciplining/sanctioning children for what parents felt was as poor behaviour. Participants reiterated an embedded sense of tradition within their parenting by highlighting the importance of teaching children about their culture from an early age.

Where I come from, it is traditional for children to knell when they greet adults. All my children have been raised like that from a young age so for them it is natural. But when the social worker came, she took it the wrong way. Knelling is a traditional sign of respect and children are taught this from very young.

(Susan, Ugandan mother)

Children have to start wearing the traditional wear when they are teenagers. At this time, they are traditionally mature and have to learn important cultural behaviour. This is where the problem started with the girls. They wanted to be like their White friends. But we have to keep our traditions. This is who we are, this is how we dress.

(Rebecca, Pakistani mother)

Theme 2: religion

Participants were not specifically asked questions about religion, but it became evident during the interviews that religion was very important to most participants. Many of the participants spoke of religion as having a significant influence on the way they parent. Some parents spoke of using religion as a way of socialising their children, while others said that their parenting practices were drawn directly from religious teachings. For some participants, religious beliefs and faith were expressed as a guide for parenting that met the cultural traditions that parents were practicing in their countries of origin and the expectations of parenting in England.

I love my children. Therefore, I have to discipline them. There is nothing wrong in that. Even the bible says that the person who loves their child must chastise them. Of course, you don't just do it for the sake of it. You do it to teach them. That is why they say spare the rod and spoil the child.

(Olivia, Nigerian mother)

I use the church to teach my children how to behave. It helps with teaching children modesty and about respecting their elders. At least this is the same as African values and no one can say that it is child abuse if it is from the church.

(Verona, Sierra Leonean mother)

Others suggested that their parenting practices were influenced by religion because they had been brought up to be religious in line with family expectations at the time. They, therefore, saw religion and culture as being intertwined.

In Pakistan, religion and culture are the same. A good Muslim child is a good child. It's all the same. This means we must teach them about religion. Then only will they be grow up to be good citizens. This is not just about praying. Praying is good but also, if they are fearing God then also they are doing good things for their self and for the country.

(Aria, Pakistani mother)

Narratives such as the ones expressed in the quotations earlier suggest that for some participants, at least in part, parenting from a religious perspective was established at an early age, through dominant social discourse at an early age. There is also some suggestion of a sort of relinquishing of parental responsibilities. In other words, some participants used religion to provide guidance and boundaries for their children, without necessarily taking parental responsibility for setting and maintaining appropriate boundaries within the home.

> *When they get to a certain age, it is easier to use church. For example, who wants to talk about sex and contraception to a thirteen-year-old? That is what the church is there for. I say, no sex until you are married. Therefore, no need to learn about contraception. Not my rules, God's rules.*
>
> (Deborah, Kenyan mother)

Theme 3: acculturation

Acculturation refers to the process of cultural and psychological change that develops as a result of individuals and groups from different cultural backgrounds meet. Participants expressed the effects of acculturation in terms of striving to maintain the parenting practices of their countries of origin whilst also adapting to new ways of parenting. This was particularly apparent in interviews with participants who had faced or were facing difficulties with parenting teenage children. The following participants, for example, talked about the challenges of adapting new parenting practices as a way of making sure that their children did not become socially excluded:

> *I always knew that smacking doesn't work. I never liked it as a child. So coming to England was a good way to try a new way of disciplining children. The trouble is that somethings are not easy to change. My husband still thinks that the child is the mother's responsibility and he doesn't help at all. This is difficult in a country where we don't have support.*
>
> (Lillian, Ghanaian mother)

> *It is not easy to adjust but you change your style. What I struggled with was the amount of power that this country gives to children. For me I was shocked when my child threatened to report me to social services. But you learn how to start talking to them differently and accept that what you know is not how things work here.*
>
> (Noreen, Indian mother)

Other participants expressed assimilation with a slightly different emphasis: they spoke about the opportunity to combine the good aspects of their traditional parenting practices with what they saw to be good about parenting practices in England. Parenting for these participants was a deliberate decision to choose the better of two 'worlds'.

> *It is hard to say what influences my parenting. I pick what I think will benefit my children from different places. For example, I like the confidence that Western children have. So, I have no issue with my children having sleepovers unlike many Indian and Pakistani families I know. I think it is a good*

way for children to grow up together. At the same time, I don't agree with children bringing girlfriends or boyfriends home to stay overnight at thirteen.

(Ruth, Pakistani mother)

Why does it have to be one or the other? I allow my children to embrace the culture here but I also make sure that they keep their Asian values. You should see some of the clothes that the girls here wear. I can't allow my daughter to leave the house dressed like that. No wonder they become sexually active when they are still very young. I want my daughters to believe that they are as good as anyone but at the same time I want them to be respectable people in the community.

(Aria, Pakistani mother)

A few participants spoke of their parenting as being influenced by child welfare policies and described their parenting practices as having changed because they now lived in England. For these parents, child welfare policies constitute an onslaught on traditional parenting and undermine parent autonomy.

It is pure nanny state. The government wants to tell you how to raise your child and they say if you don't we take the child away. Since when does a child decide what goes on in the family? But if you teach them the right way, the state says you are too harsh and they taking them and giving them money and saying 'don't worry, it's okay'. This doesn't help them grow.

(Patricia, Polish mother)

The government makes it hard for parents. Of course children are children. They will do things which are not good for them and someone has to make sure they don't go astray. For some children that means being harsh. I know my daughter, the naughty step will never work. But they give children so much power and this changes the relationship in the home.

(Jessica, Indian mother)

As can be seen in the earlier quotes, participants commonly referred to state intervention when discussing parenting practices that they took on reluctantly. A key example was about how children are sanctioned for behaviour that parents found unacceptable. This suggests that participants held a degree of uneasy about child welfare policies that seemed to spell out how children should be parented. By referring to state intervention, participants seemed to be recognising that their parenting was transient and that factors such as social policy can thwart the ways in which they prefer to raise their children.

Theme 4: aspiration

Aspiration refers to the hope or ambition that parents have for their children to achieve something. While some participants spoke of tradition and religion being important aspects of parenting, most participants acknowledged that holding on exclusively to traditional and religious values could limit parent's aspirations for their children. Indeed, many participants felt that the aspirations they had for their children were arguably the single most significant influence on their parenting as all parenting decisions and parenting practices were geared towards ensuring that the children achieved the future that their parents envisioned for them.

> *At the end of the day, all parenting is about making sure that your children have the best future.*
>
> (Noreen, Indian mother)

Another participant spoke at length about how state intervention in parenting undermines parents' aspirations for their children. Her narrative pointed to the view that the aspirations she had for her children were undermined when her children were taken into care.

> *My daughter was a very bright girl. Averaging A-stars. But when she went into care she suddenly had a lot of freedom and independence and it all went to her head. I don't think she will achieve what she could. Her behaviour is atrocious. This is not what I wanted for her.*
>
> (Carolyn, Polish mother)

Responses such as the ones quoted earlier suggest that parents are intentional about developing the skills that their children need for the kinds of lives that the parents would like them to lead. Participants acknowledged that the aspirations they have for their children meant that the parenting practices needed to be fluid rather than being rigidly dictated by tradition or religion. For these participants, parenting must continually be redefined for it to maintain validity. This means that the parenting process is deliberate and overt as opposed to being unplanned and implicit as suggested by other participants.

> *I have to parent with the times because I want my children to achieve far more than I have been able to. So, for me, it is insane to keep doing the same thing that my parents did with me.*
>
> (Verona, Sierra Leonean mother)

Participants were aware that the aspiration they have for their children may change as the children grow (particularly as the children have different ambitions for themselves) and that this may require a re-evaluation of their parenting approaches. In this sense, aspiration highlights that participants understood aspirational parenting as an evolving rather than fixed construct.

Different aspirations were evident: some participants highlighted the need to ensure that their children excelled academically and spoke of their parenting practices as being geared towards making sure that their children had a good education and, ultimately, a good income. Others placed emphasis on socialising their children to be the best behaved and saw this as the gateway to future success.

In both instances, participants seemed to take a range of practical and pragmatic approaches to ensure that their aspirations for their children were realised. One of the approaches commonly mentioned by participants was 'being in it for the long haul'. Many felt that the influence they had as parents was continually being undermined by government policies and they therefore felt that they needed to adjust their parenting to adapt to new expectations:

> *You have to be prepared to accept that the government will decide on things like when your child will learn about sex, sexual relationships, sexuality and contraception. They even want to tell you how to discipline your child.*
>
> (Ruth, Pakistani mother)

Other participants adopted their parenting in different ways. For example, rather than accept that their children might be socialised in ways that they did not approve of, they adapted by exercising the options available to them within policy:

> *I read up about the policies and when it came to the sex classes, I opted for my children not to attend. I didn't want them learning things they were too young to understand because it is me who would be picking-up the pieces. This is what politicians don't understand. Real people have to deal with the consequences of their policies.*
>
> (Noreen, Indian mother)

Theme 5: protection

A significant number of participants saw their parenting practices as being informed by the need to protect their children from what they described as the negative things within the community. One participant explained it as follows:

> *When your child comes back home and says to you that another child was teasing them because of their accent or because of the colour of their skin, you make sure that your child does not continue to play with those children.*
>
> (Olivia, Nigerian mother)

Participants saw the need to protect their children as being a fundamental factor informing their parenting practices. This was verbalised in a variety of different ways as participants highlighted a range of issues from which they sought to protect their children. The issues were not just about race and ethnicity but also included the need to protect children from dangers such as encountering paedophiles, people with severe mental health problems and negative peer influences. For example, a number of participants felt that their children were at high risk of being victims of abuse from paedophiles "*because this is a country where this kind of people are allowed to walk around freely and they can harm another victim*" (Rebecca, Pakistani mother).

Sentiments about the risk from paedophiles or from people with severe mental health problems were quite common with participants expressing real anxiety that their children are not safe.

> *One of the first things that you hear over here is the high number of people who interfere with children. I was shocked. My friend told me to be careful about people who want to play with your child on the bus. They can be targeting your child for abuse.*
>
> (Susan, Ugandan mother)

> *What I fear the most is the number of people with mental health issues on the street. You are always hearing on the news that someone killed innocent people because the voices in their head told them to do it. I can't take the risk for that to be my child.*
>
> (Carolyn, Polish mother)

In some cases, participants felt that they had perhaps been over zealous in seeking to protect their children and that in doing so they did not allow the children to develop age-appropriate socialisation and independence skills. This was expressed in terms of strained parent–child relationships.

> *When I think about it now, I can understand what the social worker was saying. Maybe my daughter felt that the only way to tell me that I was being too much was to rebel. I wish she had not gone after the wrong relationships. It just broke my heart to discover what she was doing with men older than her parents. On top of it, we had social services looking into our parenting.*
>
> (Jessica, Indian mother)

Participants also stated that they needed to protect their children from what they saw as the harmful aspects of British culture. Again, this was expressed in a variety of ways with some participants pointing to attitudes about sex and sexuality as being issues they were concerned about.

> *It's hard not to worry when you think about these things. The clothes that some of the children wear leave nothing to the imagination. And you know, some parents even allow their teenage daughters to have a boyfriend. This happened with my own daughter's friend. The mother allowed the girl's boyfriend to stay over and to share a room. This totally sends the wrong message to the child. It can't happen in a Pakistani home.*
>
> (Ruth, Pakistani mother)

The influence of culture on parenting

Alongside understanding how Black and minority ethnic parents say they do parenting, the study also sought to understand how culture and ethnicity influence parenting practices. Participants were invited to first explain how they defined culture and ethnicity and then to share how they felt their parenting practices had been shaped by culture and/or ethnicity.

Participants' definition of culture

What I had in mind when inviting participants to offer a description or definition of culture and ethnicity was to explore how participants' definitions framed the way in which they understood their parenting roles and thus impacted on their parenting practices. The definitions offered varied significantly, but the most common terms used by participants to describe culture and ethnicity were 'shared values', 'shared way of life', 'shared belief systems', and 'shared ancestry'.

Participants also made a distinction between culture and ethnicity in that they saw them as separate concepts. The majority viewed culture as a belief system of shared values and ways of doing things, while ethnicity was seen in terms of national and racial identity. Among the participants who viewed ethnicity in terms of national identity, some viewed ethnicity and skin colour as being intertwined. Others viewed culture and ethnicity as being inseparable concepts and spoke of them as the same thing.

But, regardless of how participants defined culture and ethnicity, the majority felt that their parenting practices were influenced by culture and ethnicity. Participants expressed this in terms of their deliberate efforts to socialise children to develop the skills they needed for the kind of lives they (the parents) expected them to lead.

> *Everything is about children being able to do certain things by the time they are a certain age. For example, where I come from, by ten-years-old, a girl should be able to cook a meal for the family.*
>
> (Agnes, Polish mother)

For some participants, the emphasis was about equipping their children to be ready for post-18 independence; for others, it was about ensuring that their children were equipped to perform gender roles in their own families as adults, and for others still, socialising was about ensuring that the children achieved or maintained a certain social and/or economic status.

Theme 6: understanding children's development

Participants stated that facets of culture helped shape their understanding of child development. This was expressed in terms of how they understood developmental milestones. Several participants described it as a rite of passage with the majority giving examples that pointed to the transition from childhood to adulthood. In other words, when they talked of child development, they expressed it in terms of the developmental milestones that children were expected to have reached before they are considered to be adults. For example:

> *In my culture, by twelve-years old, a child is independent and mature enough to be left to look after their younger siblings. This is normal.*
>
> (Noreen, Indian mother)

There was some suggestion that the communal approach to parenting that is favoured in most participants' countries of origin plays a key role in shaping parents' thinking about child development. This was evident in participants' views about when children should be given greater responsibility of their own decisions. For example, some participants expressed this in terms of parenting decisions around levels of supervision.

> *For us, when a child reaches seven-years-old we say that he is now fully formed into the person he will be for the rest of his life. He is still a child, but all you can do is give him guidance till he is twelve. After that, he can make his own decisions.*
>
> (Sarah, Indian mother)

There was evidence that participants derived confidence and comfort from knowing that parenting traditions offered clear guidance on parenting. This was expressed by participants who talked about their culture and ethnicity as offering a pragmatic way of understanding what children need at different stages of their development. Participants who expressed this view saw their ethnicity and culture as providing the basis from which to align their parenting practices. They articulated it as a feeling of confidence in the knowledge that the cultural practices they were applying had been proved to work over several generations within their genealogy. For example, several participants discussed how they used traditional parenting practices to inform the diet choices they made for their children at different stages of development, the way they disciplined them and the social skills they sought to promote within their children.

> *It helps to be able to do things the way your parents did them because you don't really know what you are doing as a parent. At least the traditional ways work. They have been tried and tested for generations.*
>
> (Jessica, Indian mother)

Many participants also voiced that they tended to revert to cultural ways of parenting when they were unsure of how to manage their children's behavioural challenges. For some, this was the last resort option to ensure that their children achieved their full potential.

> *I could not just stand by and see my daughter ruin her life. Talking was not working. Grounding her wasn't working. And the way she was talking to me; she was beginning to think that me and her were equal. In my culture they say a child that will not listen is managed by the rod. So, I gave her one.*
>
> (Olivia, Nigerian mother)

Theme 7: gender roles within the family

Participants talked about culture and ethnicity as being fundamental in shaping views about gender roles within a family. This was expressed in two main ways:

first in terms of parental gender roles and second, as aforementioned, in terms of how they socialise their children. Regarding how culture influences parental gender roles, most participants stated that because they are mothers, their cultures expected them to take a more hands-on role in parenting the children. Participants who expressed this view went on to explain that cultural perspectives about which parent is responsible for the day-to-day care of the children mean that even when fathers are present, they have very little or no direct care responsibilities for the children.

> *For us this is not an issue. He is responsible for providing for the family and my job is to cook and look after the children.*
>
> (Jessica, Indian mother)

Most participants expressed the influence of culture and ethnicity on gender roles in parenting as a positive aspect and talked about it in terms of efficiency. For example, one participant expressed as follows:

> *If you think about it, it is actually the best way to survive in England. When you do not have family or the neighbours to help, the best way to get things done is if one of you stays home and looks after the children and the other goes to work.*
>
> (Deborah, Kenyan mother)

Other participants who shared the view that culture and ethnicity offer positive benefits by separating gender roles in parenting expressed it in terms of parents modelling behaviour for children.

> *It is definitely a good thing. My sons now know what it means to be a man because they see their dad and my daughters know what it is to be a woman because they see me. I think this is how it should be. Not about what they see on tele.*
>
> (Jessica, Indian mother)

> *It is simple. Culture and ethnicity help us to teach children what we expect from them. You know, in our culture this means dressing modest. Also you don't allow the girls to play with boys after they have had their first period. You know, she is a woman now.*
>
> (Aria, Pakistani mother)

For some participants, culture and ethnicity were seen as exerting a negative influence on parenting. This was expressed in terms of the manner in which culture and ethnicity reinforced notions of patriarchy that excluded women from making key parenting decisions.

> *My husband he just likes to dictate. He doesn't do anything in the house because he is the man. I see it as a backward way of doing things. Why should*

it be the man that decides everything? I worry that my son is going to become like that. He is the youngest but he still likes to order his sisters around.

(Verona, Sierra Leonean mother)

Participants who expressed similar views explained that it is by defining gender roles that culture and ethnicity has the greatest influence on parenting. However, they felt that it was not necessarily a good or bad thing. Rather, it was about how each family interprets and applies aspects of their culture to their parenting role and how others view the way that people from a particular culture parent their children.

Of course there are good and there are bad aspects of culture and ethnicity. The problem is that some parents overdo it and spoil it for the rest of us. Then when you have a social worker, they think that everyone from that culture is the same.

(Susan, Ugandan mother)

It is what you make of it really. I like to think of it as a guide. There are no chores for boys or girls in my house. Just chores.

(Deborah, Kenyan mother)

Theme 8: identity

Participants saw the transmission of cultural and ethnic values as an integral to providing children with a sense of identity. Most participants recognised the influence of culture and ethnicity in shaping how they guided their children on issues of identity. This was articulated in terms of discouraging behavioural choices that participants disapproved of. In other words, participants parented in ways that sought to prevent the likelihood of their children behaving in ways that did not necessarily fit with their cultural and ethnic values.

It is difficult for any parent. You have to teach your children to take pride in their identity. But there is also pressure from their friends and from the media. But if you don't teach them to have pride in their African identity, then they will go with anything and in the end it is you who loses.

(Olivia, Nigerian mother)

When my daughter is being lazy, I tell her Polish women are never lazy. We work hard. That is who we are. This helps her.

(Agnes, Polish mother)

More generally, participants considered that it was important for children to be taught about cultural and ethnic identity from early childhood. Doing so was seen as a way of ensuring that children developed the confidence to resist external pressures on their traditional ways of life and choices.

*If the child loses sight of their African-ness, they lose their essence and it is
only a matter of time before they become a burden to society.*

(Verona, Sierra Leonean mother)

Many participants tended to hold positive views about the role of culture and
ethnicity in influencing their parenting practices regarding shaping their children's sense of identity. However, some participants expressed mixed views about
whether a sense of identity that was rooted in cultural and ethnic difference was
appropriate in the modern world.

*My problem with all of this is that a lot of things about our culture and eth-
nicity no longer apply in today's society. Cultural and ethnic traditions that
are intolerant to difference no longer have a place in society today. I think it
would be wrong to say to children that this is what defines you. Let them be
who they want to be.*

(Olivia, Nigerian mother)

Theme 9: social support

In the main, despite some of the differing views about how much influence culture and ethnicity should have on parenting practices, participants felt that it
was important to get support from people who fundamentally prioritised similar
values. This was a pragmatic way for parents to ensure that their social support
conformed to similar parenting approaches. Many participants expressed strong
conviction that it was important for children to see similarities in the way that
their peers were being parented.

*This whole culture of sleepovers worries me. So, sleepovers are either at my
house or at my sister's house. That way I know that we see and do things the
same way.*

(Lillian, Ghanaian mother)

A few participants described geographical location as being equally important
in ensuring access to social support that reinforced their cultural and ethnic convictions. Participants who expressed this view explained that living in the same
geographical location as people from one's ethnic background helped minimise
the challenges of determining the right balance between retaining the cultural and
ethnic values of their countries of origin and the culture values of Britain.

*It is less headache if you stay with your own people. The children have fewer
things to complain about because everyone is doing it the same way. Even
simple things like wearing the traditional clothes is easy when you live in an
Asian area.*

(Aria, Pakistani mother)

> *When you live in the same area as other Asians it is easy to make changes possible because you all share the same concerns. My sister lives in an area where there are lots of Asians. Because a lot of parents had children in the same school and some sat on the board of governors, they asked for changes in the school's sex education curriculum.*

> (Noreen, Indian mother)

A significant number of participants frequently spoke of how culture and ethnicity reinforced oppressive parenting practices. They continually referred to ways in which either their parents or their partners' parents exerted their influence on them in adult life and felt that this was made possible because they lived in areas where the demographic makeup was predominantly of people from the same background.

> *It is a sword with two edges. On one hand you have access to support from family and friends who share similar values as yourself but with that you also get some of the things about your culture that you don't want your children to experience.*

> (Jessica, Indian mother)

> *I think it is okay to live in areas where there are many Polish. But only because it is easy to find the food. I don't like to live in these areas because Polish people like too much drinking and fighting. So, I make sure that my children don't see this side of Polish culture.*

> (Agnes, Polish mother)

Theme 10: building resilience

Participants saw culture and ethnicity as being important in building resilience in children. This was voiced as a way of offering children a belief system that enabled them to retain aspects of their background that reinforced a sense of pride in their identity. Some participants described it as giving children confidence in their identity so that they develop the ineffable ability to retain resolve in times of challenges.

> *I tell my children that Nigerians might have a bad name in England but at least no one can say we lack confidence. So, I say, if people make fun of you being Nigerian, hold your head up high because what they are really saying is that you are confident.*

> (Olivia, Nigerian mother)

When talking about resilience, participants spoke about the stressors they encounter as they settle in the UK. According to most participants, holding on to aspects of their cultural and ethnic identity that promote a sense of pride helped children to navigate through the challenges of settling into a new environment.

Most participants talked about resilience as a necessary skill for their children to have reflected on it within the context of settling into a new culture. These participants saw parenting as being context driven and felt that was only by holding onto their cultural and ethnic values that they would promote resilience in their children. One participant articulated it as follows:

> *People underestimate the challenges that children go through when they move to a new country and a new way of doing things. In Africa, everything is about communal cohesion. So, when you uproot a child from a place where parenting was all about making sure that they get along with everyone around them, it can be difficult for the child to adjust in a country where is individualistic. You have to help them overcome this by going back to the basics of your culture. This is how they become resilient.*
>
> (Verona, Sierra Leonean mother)

There were also a few participants who talked about the need to build their children's resilience but were not sure whether it was best achieved by reinforcing messages of cultural and ethnic identity or by promoting assimilation. These participants mainly reflected on their thoughts without giving a definitive view. However, they tended to share the view that there was a danger that using culture and ethnicity to promote resilience would raise unrealistic expectations about what culture and ethnicity can achieve in a foreign environment. For these participants, the role that culture and ethnicity play in influencing parenting practices is only evident within the cultural setting that promotes such practices.

> *A lot of the things are very different from how people do things in this country. That is why most of us had social services. May be the best is to forget what you know from your own country and do everything the way it is done here. To be honest, I don't know what works.*
>
> (Noreen, Indian mother)

Participants who shared a similar view to had strong convictions that what culture and ethnicity can achieve in the context of parenting in the UK is strongly conditioned by what Western society defines as normal. There was also a tendency for such participants to describe resilience as an unplanned and implicit quality that children develop on their own as part of their growth as opposed to a quality that a child can be trained to develop. In general, these participants also expressed a degree of uncertainty about whether socialisation processes within the family and wider community embody or function in ways that reinforce core cultural beliefs and values.

> *I don't think that culture and ethnicity have anything to do with whether a child is strong or not. They either are or they are not. Who can say whether they are strong because of their cultural beliefs and values? Maybe it is possible; who knows*
>
> (Susan, Ugandan mother)

Some participants expressed resilience in terms of making children aware of issues such as racial discrimination and teaching them how to deal with it. For these participants, resilience was only seen as a relevant only insofar as it helped children to cope with the effects of racial discrimination.

Participants' perspectives about parenting competence evaluations

This study also sought to gain an understanding of participants' views about the effectiveness with which social workers incorporated issues of culture and ethnicity when assessing their parenting competence. This had relevance because the research starts from the premise that culture and ethnicity play an important role in parenting.

Theme 11: preconceptions

Participants stated that most social workers approached the assessment process with preconceptions about parents. Participants felt that while this was not necessarily a bad thing, it was the failure to adjust their thinking that was a problem. Participants who expressed this view tended to feel that social workers saw culture as being conservative and inflexible in nature. According to these participants, although social workers had considered issues of culture and ethnicity, this was largely superficial. One participant explained it as follows:

> *Yes, they asked about culture. But it was clear that it was really about ticking boxes. They asked about surface things like whether we are religious, what food we feed the children and if there are cultural activities we like doing.*
>
> (Olivia, Nigerian mother)

Most participants felt that social workers did not show any motivation to understand the extent to which culture and ethnicity influence parenting practices. Participants who expressed this view also saw social workers as only being interested in issues of culture and ethnicity that reinforced their preconceptions. These participants typically felt that social workers were blinded to their own partiality. This was voiced in the form of complaints that social workers were not willing to entertain the possibility that they might hold subjective views, which could be implicated in their assessments. The participants stated that, in their view, social workers made no overt attempts to recognise and address their own biases.

> *I don't think there is any genuine attempt to understand why we parent the way we do. As far as they are concerned the only right way to parent children is the way that it is done in this country. It did not matter what I said to her, I was always going to be wrong.*
>
> (Verona, Sierra Leonean mother)

Theme 12: competence and confidence

Most participants perceived social workers as professionals who held and used their power as a form of control as opposed to using it to support families. Participants felt that social workers genuinely sought to support families but that they did not have the competence to understand the complexity of family arrangements that were different from their own.

> *I thinks she genuinely wanted to help but she made things worse. All she was focused on was that my husband was controlling because he did all the talking. When I tried to explain that this is how it is where we come from, she said I was minimising and that if I cannot see this, I cannot protect my children.*
>
> (Noreen, Indian mother)

In most cases, participants described social worker interventions as being well meaning but often unhelpful. Participants who expressed this view said that social work interventions had done more to alienate some family members and, in the process, exacerbated conflicts within the family. These participants felt that social workers needed to have specific skills to assess the parenting competence of parents whose parenting practices may be heavily influenced by cultural and ethnic beliefs and values

Some participants perceived social workers to have shown confidence in recognising and addressing signs of operation. These participants stated that social workers had demonstrated competence and made it easy for participants to work with them in collaborative partnerships.

Overall, participants stated that they responded to social workers according to what they felt was the overarching stance that the social worker had taken. For example, several participants said that once they had realised that social workers were not prepared to unlearn their preconceptions, they responded by either being overtly uncooperative or pretended to go along with what social workers were saying. Participants who felt that social workers were competent tended to be more collaborative.

> *Like I keep saying in our meetings, some of them are never going to change their views no matter what you say to them. It is better if you just go along with them. After all, this is their country, their rules.*
>
> (Olivia, Nigerian mother)

Theme 13: feminism

Although participants were not specifically asked questions about feminism, it emerged as a pervasive theme throughout the interviews. Participants felt that feminist ideology permeated most social worker's approach and that this interfered with social workers' ability to fully assess family dynamics within the contexts of patriarchal family structures.

> *I learnt very quickly that there was no point in trying to explain anything to her. She decided that he was oppressive and I was a victim and that was it.*

But in our family we had to play good cop bad cop. That's how we got the children to behave. In the end he thought I had given her the impression that he was aggressive. The relationship was difficult after that.

(Verona, Sierra Leonean mother)

A significant number of participants described social workers' approaches as appearing to be led by ideology. Many of the participants who expressed this view felt that social workers had assumed that the family arrangements they found were designed by the husbands and partners to deliberately oppress. According to these participants, social workers failed to effectively assess the importance of culture and ethnicity in influencing the parenting practices that were being used within the family.

Like I say, it is not a good or a bad thing. They are probably right that it is not fair. But just because that is not how you would do it doesn't mean it is wrong. If they were being fair, they would ask themselves if our way of doing things makes the children to be damaged. Not who is in the kitchen.

(Noreen, Indian mother)

Participants stated that social workers whose perspectives on parenting are that there should not be gender role difference within the family imposed their own values rather than sought to understand the value that BAME parents attach to their parenting.

7 Social workers' perspectives

Focus group discussions

Much of the group discussions focused on highlighting the complexities of incorporating culture in evaluations of safe parenting. Indeed, there were impassioned and extensive debates about the value that should be attached to issues of culture when evaluating safe parenting. The consensus was that culture matters. Nevertheless, some social workers felt that the focus of assessment should remain 'squarely' about whether children are suffering harm because of the parenting they receive, rather than seeking to understand why parents take a certain approach to parenting. Some social workers were suspicious of parents who point to their culture to explain their parenting practices. One of the groups strongly felt that some BAME parents use culture as "*a smoke screen to hide abuse*".

Another issue that drew extensive debate within the focus groups was that social workers felt that the questions of this research should have been directed towards policy makers rather than at practitioners. They pointed to the practical challenges of seeking to understand cultural parenting scripts within the context of resource constraints and suggested that it is only through explicit policies that the focus of assessment can change.

Analysis of group discussions identified 11 themes explaining how social workers said they evaluate culturally informed parenting. These themes included the use of assessment tools; professionals' experience; the role of social workers; time constraints; supervision; the use of colleagues' expertise and knowledge; research; sensitivity to culture and ethnicity in practice situations; the boundaries of culture and ethnicity; oppressive practice and constraints in accessing resources.

The way the themes were discussed within the groups raised questions about the extent to which social workers' individual cultures are implicated in assessment. For example, some social workers pointed out that determining safe parenting can be highly subjective. The social workers who expressed this view argued that there is a need for a culturally sensitive assessment tool that minimises and tests subjectivity. This view was counted by social workers who felt that the professional already has a range of assessment tools, which helps structure assessments and reduces the likelihood of subjectivity. The majority view was that focusing on culture would make assessment difficult because, for example, expectations around developmental stages vary across cultures.

Social worker profiles

There were several characteristics that were common with all social workers who took part in this study (demographic details are given in Table 7.1):

1 They all had at least 5 years post-qualification experience.
2 The minimum level of academic qualification was an undergraduate degree.
3 They had all previously assessed the parenting competence of at least three BAME parents no more than 12 months prior to the interview.
4 They all worked within statutory children's social care departments.
5 They had all qualified from a British University.

However, the social workers were from different local authorities and different ethnicities. This has implications for generalisability.

The themes identified from the focus group discussions were the same as those from the one-to-one interviews. As such, I chose to focus the presentation in this chapter on the findings from the one-to-one interviews. Throughout this chapter, I use verbatim quotations to illustrate how participants conceptualised culturally informed parenting. All participants' names have been changed to keep their anonymity.

In keeping with the phenomenological approach of this research, I present participant's narratives with a focus on describing rather than explaining their

Table 7.1 Participants (social workers)

Name	Gender	Age	Ethnic background	Post-qualification experience	Academic qualification
Rochelle	Female	34	White-British	6 years	Masters
Karen	Female	36	White-British	8 years	Masters
Ben	Male	43	Black-African	10 years	Masters
Kirsty	Female	35	White-British	5 years	Bachelors
Grace	Female	38	Caribbean	7 years	Bachelors
Yvonne	Female	36	Black-African	5 years	Bachelors
Janet	Female	29	Black-African	5 years	Bachelors
Anne	Female	45	Caribbean	11 years	Bachelors
Harriet	Female	33	Black-African	6 years	Bachelors
Gregory	Male	47	White-British	15 years	Masters
Jesse	Male	38	Black-African	7 years	Masters
Jaz	Female	36	British-Asian	9 years	Bachelors
Pretti	Female	35	Indian	8 years	Masters
Monica	Female	28	White-British	5 years	Bachelors
Thomas	Male	37	Black-African	9 years	Bachelors

experiences. While I acknowledge that there is some form of interpretation involved in deciding what to select and how to express it, my aim in this chapter is to, insofar as is possible, limit my own biases and remain faithful to participants' narratives.

Theme 1: assessment tools

All participants stated that they evaluate the parenting competence of Black and minority ethnic parents using standardised assessment tools. Most participants expressed this in terms of drawing on a vast body of scientific knowledge to make sense of how families function but that objectivity in assessment was achieved by using the same assessment tool for everyone. Participants who expressed this view also stated that they used the framework for the assessment of children in need and their families as the main tool for evaluating parenting.

> *You don't approach assessments differently just because the parent is from a black and minority ethnic group. Everyone is treated equally using the assessment triangle. I think it is the fairest way to assess parenting. Otherwise how can you be sure that the same standard is applied to everyone?*
>
> (Karen, White-British Social worker)

> *I personally don't think it should make a difference what the parents' background is. Don't get me wrong. I know that culture and ethnicity is important. I just don't think it should influence the outcome of assessment.*
>
> (Monica, White-British Social worker)

The framework for the assessment of children in need and their families was seen by most participants as an effective tool for evaluating the parenting competence of Black and minority ethnic parents. This was expressed by participants who also held the view that cultural diversity in the UK meant that need, risk, and rights are interpreted differently by the different groups of people whose parenting is likely to be assessed.

> *There is no right or wrong way of doing things in our profession. It all boils down to how you balance needs, risks and rights; regardless of the client's culture or ethnicity. The assessment triangle gives you an objective way of assessing and I think it works just as effectively for black and ethnic minorities.*
>
> (Gregory, White-British Social Worker)

Not all participants who used the framework for the assessment of children in need and their families thought that it was effective in evaluating the parenting competence of Black and minority parent. Some participants felt that issues of culture and ethnicity within Black and minority ethnic families were quite significant, and a different assessment tool was needed if their parenting competence is to be assessed effectively.

> *The problem is that what we know about parenting is based on Eurocentric views and Western research. It does not necessary apply to people from different backgrounds.*
>
> (Ben, Black-African Social Worker)

> *I think the assessment triangle is a blunt tool at best when it comes to assessing parenting with black and minority parents. Think about it; all parenting takes place within the context of culture. The triangle is suited for assessing parenting in Western cultures but can only loosely assess parents for whom dimensions such as stimulation, independence, community participation or emotional warmth are interpreted differently.*
>
> (Thomas, Black-African Social Worker)

There was a commonly held view among participants that assessment tools were important in helping them to focus their work but that they were not always helpful in enabling them to draw conclusive views about parents' competence.

Some participants felt that this was because organisational policies too often influenced how information was interpreted and presented. Participants who held this view expressed it in the form of criticism that organisational focus on audits and performance indicators meant that they were not able to focus on parenting issues of specific groups of clients.

> *In an ideal world, you would like to explore what it is about their culture or ethnicity that makes them parent the way they do. But, when you have eighteen other families to assess within set timescales, you have to have an approach that can treat everyone the same.*
>
> (Kirsty, White-British Social worker)

> *Assessment tools help highlight what the parent is doing or not doing in certain specified aspects of parenting but you ultimately have to make a judgement about whether you think they are a good parent or not. Imagine the challenges if they are from a black or minority ethnic background.*
>
> (Pretti, Indian Social Worker)

The framework for the assessment of children in need and their families was not the only tool that participants used to evaluate parenting competence. The three most used tools for assessing parenting were framework for the assessment of children in need and their families, signs of safety, and the continuum of need. Participants talked about using a variety of different models to inform their views about parenting competence. However, parenting competence was assessed using tools specified by the organisation in which they worked. Many participants stated that this left them feeling uncomfortable about assessing the parenting competence of Black and minority parents.

You only have a small window in any family's life to make a judgement about their parenting. It is more difficult when it is a family from a black or minority ethnic group because you know that a lot of what they do may be perfectly acceptable where they come from but obviously it is not in this country. Assessment tools do not capture that.

(Gregor, White-British Social Worker)

Participants felt that it was important to have a way of effectively assessing issues of culture and ethnicity within parenting but that this did not have to mean adopting a different assessment tool to evaluate the parenting competence of Black and minority ethnic parents.

Issues of culture and ethnicity are becoming increasingly common place in assessment of parenting but what is needed is a knowledge base in this area rather than a separate assessment tool for black and minority ethnic families. Perhaps the approach should be similar to the way we assess substance misuse or mental health issues within parenting.

(Grace, Caribbean Social Work)

The issue of black and minority ethnic families being over represented in care statistics is not new. I suspect it is to do with us not understanding the influence of culture and ethnicity on the way they parent. This is what needs to change. Not the way we assess but how we assess these aspects within all parenting.

(Rochelle, White-British Social Worker)

Participants who felt that there needed to be a way of evaluating the impact of culture and ethnicity on parenting also stated that effectiveness in incorporating this within assessment was dependent on individual practitioners' experience rather than organisational focus.

Theme 2: professional experience

Most participants stated that it was their experience that gave them the confidence in assessing the parenting competence of Black and minority ethnic parents. This was expressed in terms of being able to recognise that a parents' culture or ethnicity played a significant part in shaping the way they parent.

The thing is that not every black or Asian parent is doing parenting because they are black or Asian. Understanding this makes a difference when you are assessing parenting. Otherwise you make unhelpful assumptions that could risk leaving a child in a dangerous environment.

(Anne, Caribbean Social Worker)

You build more confidence from working with parents from black and minority ethnic background. This is what helps you to understand how culture and

ethnicity influences the way they parent. If you don't have the experience, I
don't think you can do a good job no matter which assessment tool you use.

(Monica, White-British Social Worker)

Most participants talked about the need to understand issues of culture and ethnicity as they specifically relate to the parents being assessed. However, participants who expressed this view also stated that it was not practical for any social worker to be expected to know about every client's culture. Participants saw experience as the main means through which their gaps in knowledge about assessing the parenting competence of Black and minority ethnic parents were bridged.

Look, we are not just talking about two or three different cultures or ethnicities. The spectrum is too wide. It is the practitioners' experience, specifically with working with people from black and minority ethnic backgrounds that equips them to effectively incorporate issues of culture and ethnicity when assessing parenting competence.

(Thomas, Black-African social Worker)

Experience is massively important in this area. We just need to cast our minds to the issue of female genital mutilation. Until it became a national focus, it was only social workers with experience of working with families for whom that was a common practice that were able to incorporate it in assessment. Most social workers will have stereotyped and dismissed it.

(Jesse, Black-African Social Worker)

Participants who viewed experience of working with Black and minority ethnic people as an important aspect of assessment talked about in terms of enabling balanced evaluation of parenting. This was expressed in terms of what participants saw as the benefits of separating risk of harm to children from the need to re-educate parents about their parenting approach.

We have all panicked about some of the parenting practices we have seen from black and minority ethnic families at some point in our carer. But, with experience, you begin to learn that in the majority of cases, it really is a matter of re-educating parents about their approach.

(Karen, White-British Social Worker)

Participants also associated experience as being necessary to alleviate 'fears' and enable social workers to build relationships with Black and minority ethnic parents and improve assessments. This was expressed in terms of enabling social workers to feel less anxious about assessing Black and minority ethnic parents.

I can remember feeling really anxious when I was first asked to assess this Caribbean parents. The husband was so intimidating. I don't think I did that assessment justice. It was rushed and I only captured how he made me feel. I would certainly do it different now.

(Monica, White-British Social Worker)

You do need a certain level of experience to interpret and break some of the barriers that stand in the way of assessing black and minority ethnic parent. These are more than language. It can be things like the subtle cultural norms around social interactions between adults and children that can, for example be misinterpreted for a lack of emotional warmth.

(Ben, Black-African Social worker)

Theme 3: the role of social workers

A significant number of participants saw their social work role as being integral to the way that they assessed the parenting competence of Black and minority ethnic parents. This was expressed in terms of ensuring that the focus remained on the child. Participants who held this view stated that all parenting competence was assessed within the context of social justice from the child's point of view. For these participants, it did not matter what the family's cultural or ethnic background was. One participant expressed it as follows:

At the end of the day, my responsibility is to the child and the child's welfare.

(Jaz, British-Asian Social Worker)

Participants also stated that the purpose for which the assessment was required also played a significant part as it decided the stance. Some examples given were that assessments required by courts were more thorough in comparison to those completed as part of 'normal' local authority assessments. Participants stated that the purpose for which the report was required meant that more time was allocated to completing and that this allowed for more complex issues of culture and ethnicity to be considered fully.

In the normal run of the mill social work, you don't really have the time to focus on issues of culture and ethnicity. They are far too subtle to draw the attention of managers. But, when you are in the Court arena, you have to be thorough otherwise some wise barrister might ask you whether you considered their client's culture and ethnicity when you made certain conclusions about their parenting.

(Ben, Black-African Social Worker)

I think our roles as children's social workers has a big influence. I don't think it is easy to look at issues of culture and ethnicity if your focus is on whether the child has suffered harm. In the vast majority of cases, it is not easy to separate the child's welfare from the way the parents approach their parenting tasks. Yet, parents' approach is often determined by their culture and ethnicity.

(Pretti, Indian Social Worker)

A significant number of participants stated that there is a need for issues of culture and ethnicity in parenting to be assed but strongly that this should not be done by the same worker assessing parenting competence. This was mainly expressed in terms of the overwhelming demands on social workers.

> *Assessing the impact of culture and ethnicity on the parenting of black and minority ethnic parents should be done by a separate professional from the one doing the parenting capacity assessment. All too often social workers are asked to take more tasks and blamed for weak assessments. You need experts in this area in the same way that we have experts in substance misuse or child sexual abuse.*
>
> (Kirsty, White-British Social Worker)

Theme 4: time

Almost all participants stated that the time they were allocated to complete assessments was a crucial factor in determining the extent to which issues of culture and ethnicity were incorporated in parenting competence assessments. Many participants talked about not delving beyond aspects that would be relevant for matching children with prospective carers. Participants who expressed this view felt that understanding the impact of culture and ethnicity on parenting required them to invest more time in building relationships with Black and minority ethnic parents.

> *Everything is so rushed these days that you can't help but wonder whether you assessment of a family was a fair reflection of what is really going on.*
>
> (Monica, White-British Social Worker)

> *Open and honest engagement with parents, of whatever background, takes time to develop. Sometimes, a little more time with a family can reveal a different picture about their parenting practices.*
>
> (Yvonne, Black-African Social Worker)

For most participants, the need to fit assessments within tightly specified time frames meant that they risked losing sight of the influence that culture and ethnicity have on parenting practices. Participants saw this as disadvantaging parents from Black and minority ethnic groups.

> *The problem with the tight deadlines is that you have to fit all parenting into the same mould so to speak in order to meet the assessment timescales. Parents who do not conform to that mould can find themselves being assessed as not being good enough. Sadly, that is most black and minority ethnic parents.*
>
> (Thomas, Black-African Social Worker)

Participants who talked about time as being an issue in the assessment of parenting competence, also often referred to time being associated with the role of social work. This was expressed in terms of social work roles and responsibilities being too wide to be effective within tight assessment deadlines. One participant put it as follows:

> *You are expected to do it all: arrange meetings, chair them, write the minutes, arrange contact, supervise it; and not just for one family. Naturally, there is not enough time to be thorough about issues of culture and ethnicity.*
>
> (Janet, Black-African Social Worker)

A few participants stated that some managers recognised the need to allow more time for issues of ethnicity and culture to be explored in assessments. In most participants' experience, this was only done if cases were in court proceedings.

> *You tend to be given more time if your case is in Court proceedings. But if you have a manager who understands issues of culture and ethnicity, they will allow more time to explore the impact that these issues might have on parenting practices.*
>
> (Harriet, Caribbean Social Worker)

Most participants did not see culture and ethnicity as the only important factor to consider when assessing the parenting competence of Black and minority ethnic parents. Nevertheless, they felt that sufficient time was required in order to assess some root problems affecting parenting competence in Black and minority families. Examples given included issues such as poverty, poor housing, and racism.

> *You need time to produce thorough assessments. Even more so with black and minority ethnic parents. This is mainly because the issues they face are complex and unique to them but it is wrong to assume that it is only about the impact of culture and ethnicity. Other aspects such as poverty, poor housing and access to resources play a far more important role.*
>
> (Anne, Caribbean Social Worker)

Theme 5: supervision

Participants stated that supervision made a fundamental contribution to how they assess the parenting competence of Black and minority ethnic parents. This view was expressed by participants who also saw assessment of Black and minority ethnic parents as being fraught with dangers associated with misinterpreting parents' behaviour, reinforcing practitioners' subconscious stereotypes, or causing offence in the process of assessment.

> *I have been doing social work for a long-time now, but I still get anxious about assessing black and minority ethnic parent. Not on the clear cut things, like domestic abuse or substance misuse; It is on the more subtle practices associated with their culture and ethnicity. Things like how they enforce the*

whole idea of respect. It can seem oppressive and you need good supervision
if you are to get the balance right.

(Rochelle, White-British Social Worker)

Supervision is absolutely key. It is easy to be misunderstood especially when
dealing with issues of culture and ethnicity. Supervision comes into its own
when you can debate these issues and make sure you are not being biased or
stereotyping.

(Kirsty, White-British Social Worker)

Most participants who viewed supervision as being integral to the effectiveness with which they assessed Black and minority ethnic parents' parenting competence explained the benefits in terms of enabling critical analysis of the meaning of parenting practices. This view was typically expressed by participants who saw supervision as a forum for reflecting on their assessments as well as sharing decision making.

It is easy for a parent to lead you down the garden path because they are
aware that you can't possibly know about their culture. Supervision allows
you to critically evaluate parenting practices that cause concern. For me
marriage ranks high among some of the most controversial cultural practices
that parents promote as part of how they raise their children.

(Monica, White-British Social Worker)

Participants who saw supervision as a forum for reflecting on issues of culture and ethnicity talked of supervision as a way of minimising cultural relativism in their approach to assessment. This was expressed in terms of allowing social workers to evaluate whether the cultural and ethnic value bases of Black and minority ethnic parents enhance or detract from safe parenting. Participants stated that it was during supervision that they sounded out their reflective awareness of working with client groups from different backgrounds.

The thing to remember is that the different value bases that are reflected in
the parenting practices of many black and minority families do not necessar-
ily translate into child welfare concerns. But you need good supervision to
help you minimise the likelihood of oppressive practice that looks at Western
parenting as the gold standard.

(Pretti, Indian Social Worker)

A few participants talked of supervision in terms of shaping how much focus was given to issues of culture and ethnicity in assessment. Participants who expressed this view stated that they used supervision to gauge whether issues of culture and ethnicity needed to be considered beyond factual demographic information. Most participants explained the reasoning for this practice in terms of the pressures to meet assessment timescales.

Obviously issues of culture and ethnicity are important when assessing parenting. But let's be honest; untangling the meaning of cultural parenting practices is a complex matter. You need supervision to guide you on how much time and focus to give it in your assessment.

(Anne, Caribbean Social Worker)

I don't think culture and ethnicity should necessarily be the focus of all assessments of the parenting capacity of black and minority ethnic parents. Identifying when it is necessary to explore culture and ethnicity in great detail is crucial and it saves time. Most times the presenting issues are to do with child abuse concerns that are a result of environmental factors. If you think about the impact of things like poor mental health, substance misuse or domestic abuse; the effects on parenting are the same regardless of the family's ethnicity and culture.

(Gregory, White-British Social Worker)

Theme 6: colleagues

A small but significant number of participants talked about using their colleagues to guide their assessment of Black and minority ethnic parents. This was expressed in terms of attempts to understand culturally specific parenting practices. There were two main ways in which participants said they used colleagues: the first was as informal supervisory support and the second was as 'insider' informants of the meaning of cultural and ethnic parenting practices associated with the parents being assessed. Participants who talked about using colleagues as informal supervisory support talked about drawing on colleagues' professional experience of assessing families from similar backgrounds.

The diversity of the clients we now have to work with is just mind gobbling. Luckily, there is always someone within the team who has dealt with families from the same background; they become the team expert on families from that background.

(Kirsty, White-British Social Worker)

There is definitely a need for a separate assessment tool. Without it, one has to rely on the expertise of colleagues who have assessed parents from a similar or the same background for guidance.

(Jesse, Black-African Social Worker)

The reality is that all cultures and ethnicities approaches parenting differently. We risk misinterpreting some parenting practices because we don't understand them or don't have the time to try to understand them. The danger is that you err on the side of caution and in doing so become oppressive in your practice. Having a colleague who has walked the same path before, so to speak, helps make sure that you are, if nothing else, being fair in your assessment and are capturing the right things.

(Harriet, Black-African Social Worker)

Participants also talked about drawing on the research knowledge that colleagues might have accumulated over the course of their practice.

> *The diversity is just so wide it is impossible to know the inner workings of every culture. Even within the same ethnicity and culture there are important differences. In my team we have two colleagues that we have dubbed the encyclopaedias on all issues cultural in assessment. Their research knowledge is astounding.*
>
> (Karen, White-British Social worker)

Participants who talked about using colleagues as insider' informants stated that they used colleagues from the same cultural and ethnic backgrounds as the parents they were assessing to understand and/or verify the meaning associated with specific parenting practices. Participants gave several examples highlighting how their colleagues help give insight into the belief and value bases that had informed the parenting practices of the clients they were assessing. The examples given were typically about trying to understand parents' beliefs and value bases about issues such as respect, tradition, sex, relationships, sexuality, gender, and gender roles.

> *It can get quite complicated when you consider that black and minority ethnic parents approach the task of parenting from distinctively different belief and value systems. Having a colleague from the family's cultural and ethnic background can help explain even practices as simple as why it is important for the children to dress a certain way or why the girl in the family seems to do a lot more chores than the boys.*
>
> (Jaz, British-Asian Social Worker)

> *From time to time one comes across parental practices within black and minority ethnic families that appear rigid, oppressive and do not make sense from a Western perspective. In such situations, it helps to have a colleague who understands the culture of the parents you are assessing and can explain how to intervene to address the welfare issues without appearing to disrespect the family's beliefs and value systems.*
>
> (Janet, Black-African Social Worker)

Within the responses that participants gave, there was an overall recognition that even colleagues from the same cultural and ethnic backgrounds as the families being assessed didn't always know or understand the parenting approaches that families had adopted. This, according to some participants, heightened anxieties in completing assessment.

> *I know that some colleagues do not like being used to assess people from their own cultural and ethnic background because they do not want to be seen as the expert in that culture. But, I think it is easy to become more defensive in*

your practice when a colleague from the same ethnic background says they too do not understand the family you are assessing.

(Grace, Caribbean Social Worker)

Theme 7: research

A significant proportion of participants said that they relied on research to inform their judgements about the parenting competence of Black and minority ethnic parents. Most participants who express this view talked about it in terms of standardising assessments and avoiding practice that might be perceived as being oppressive. One participant expressed it as follows:

The complexity involved in trying to understand the value bases and functioning of black and minority ethnic families means that if you are not careful as a practitioner, you risk making arbitrary decisions which bias the outcome of assessment. What research does is remove the tendency to guess or experiment with families by suggesting helpful ways of assessing parents from black and minority ethnic backgrounds.

(Thomas, Black-African Social Worker)

Participants felt that research evidence was helpful in enabling them to understand the contexts within which Black and minority parents socialise their children. This was seen by many participants as a way of providing objectivity in assessment and as evidence of good practice in social work.

Obviously you are going to be less likely to be biased if you base your assessment on research. Basically what you are doing is using best evidence to inform your assessment of the parenting capacity.

(Monica, White-British Social Worker)

Drawing on research is a crucial way of making sure that assessments are as effective as they can be. It is basic good practice.

(Ben, Black-African Social Worker)

All participants stated that they generally use research to inform their assessments of the parenting competence of Black and minority ethnic parents. But almost all participants also talked about the barriers to using research, with the majority mentioning time as being a key barrier.

We cannot deny that quite often research offers insightful understanding of the clients we work with and that is no different for black and minority ethnic parents. The real issue is whether, as a practitioner you always have the time to dig up research on every client group.

(Gregory, White-British Social Worker)

Apart from the lack of time, participants stated that research in the area of assessing parenting within Black and minority ethnic families was scarce. Some participants also felt that where research was available, it was not always accessible. The main reasons given for this were that research papers tend to be long and use language that is not always easy to understand. A small number of participants also stated that their use of research was inconsistent because they felt that they did not have the skills to critically evaluate the evidence base of the research they read.

> *There is actually not a lot of evidence base that is specific to parenting in black and ethnic minority families.*
>
> (Thomas, Black-African Social Worker)

> *The benefits are clear and undeniable but the reality is that a lot of the research that is available is obviously written by academics for fellow academics. It doesn't always have practical application in the field.*
>
> (Pretti, Indian Social Worker)

> *A lot of research papers, in my view, live in an ideal world. Besides, trolling through research papers to write an assessment always feels like you are reducing clients' experiences into academic pursuits. People's lives are far more complex and it doesn't help to make them more complicated by requiring them to fit into some academic's philosophical ideal.*
>
> (Anne, Caribbean Social Worker)

A significant number of participants saw research as being helpful in informing assessment, but their narratives focused on the limitations of using research to evaluate parenting competence within the context of culture and ethnicity. Participants such as Anne, quoted earlier, felt that most research did not have practical application in the lives of the Black and minority ethnic parents they saw. Some of the reasons given for this were that research tended to ignore resource issues or did not address culture issues within the context of UK's child welfare policy.

> *The biggest limitation of most research on parenting within black and minority ethnic families is that it is great at explaining cultural influences on parenting but it doesn't tell us anything about what that means within the context of UK legislation and child welfare policy.*
>
> (Rochelle, White-British Social Worker)

7.4 Unanticipated themes

As stated in the introduction to this chapter, I identified five unanticipated themes that are included here because of their relevance to the main research focus. That is, to explore whether, and if so how, social workers incorporate issues of culture and ethnicity in their evaluations of the parenting competence of Black and ethnic minority parents. The first seven themes presented earlier reflect participants' direct responses to the research questions they were asked. The five themes that follow are drawn from the questions that participants asked about the relevance of the research and their explanations for asking the questions. To remain consistent with the aims of this chapter, that is, to present the findings, I focus on describing rather than explaining participants' narratives.

Theme 8: cultural sensitivity in practice situations

During the group discussions and in the interviews, participants asked whether the research questions would have yielded better insight if they had been directed at policy makers. Most of the participants who posed this question stated that they asked it because they felt that policy exerts significant influence on the importance that social works attach to issues such as culture and ethnicity in assessments. Participants generally explained their stance by pointing out that the assessment guidance on which social workers base their evaluations of parenting competence are informed by policy developments. Most participants suggested that unless policy places more value on the importance of issues of culture and ethnicity, they can only remain relevant as markers of identity that assessing professionals use to inform sensitivity in social care interventions.

> *National and local policies are notoriously ambiguous on the issue of culture and ethnicity. Take for example the policy developments that followed the death of Victoria Climbie. The changes required social workers to demonstrate greater cultural sensitivity in assessment. But the reality of practice is that culture and ethnicity is often used by parents as a smoke screen to hide abuse. If black and minority ethnic parents are to be assessed differently, it is absolutely crucial for child welfare legislation and policy to be clear about the weight that should be given to culture and ethnicity when assessing parenting capacity.*
>
> (Gregory, White-British Social Worker)

All participants who queried whether the research questions would have been better directed at policy makers stated that it is important for social workers to demonstrate ethnic and cultural sensitivity in their interactions with Black and minority ethnic families. A significant proportion of participants felt that ethnic and cultural sensitivity should be limited to understanding the contexts within which parenting occurs rather than inform evaluations of parenting competence. The illustrations that most participants used to emphasise this view focused on explaining that while it was important to understand why cultural parenting practices are important to some Black and minority ethnic parents, their culture and ethnicity should not be used to evaluate their parenting competence.

> *The thing is, all parenting is culturally defined. What might appear perfectly acceptable in one culture may be seen as abuse in another. It would be chaotic to try and assess parenting capacity based on parents' culture and ethnicity. A good example is the issue of the physical chastisement of children.*

*For some cultures, perhaps due to the influence of religion, physical chas-
tisement is seen as perfectly acceptable way of disciplining children. It is not
acceptable in the UK. I think cultural sensitivity should stop at understanding
and respecting why the parent might think their form of parenting is okay, but
their parenting capacity has to be assessed based on the parenting standards
of the UK.*

(Kirsty, White-British Social Worker)

A few participants who shared the view that the research questions might have been
best directed at policy makers expressed the view that culture and ethnicity needed
to be central in all evaluations of the parenting competence of Black and minority
ethnic parents. Participants who expressed this view explained that assessors who
mainly use culture and ethnicity to inform how they interact with their clients inevitably oppress Black and minority ethnic parents and contribute to the disproportionate overrepresentation of Black and minority ethnic children in care statistics.

*The context of parenting has to be given central focus when assessing parent-
ing capacity. A parent who falls short of British standards of parenting is not
necessarily a bad parent. Therefore, assessments that do not consider ethnicity and culture at a deeper level than for political correctness or identity
cannot have been thorough.*

(Thomas, Black African Social Worker)

Theme 9: the boundaries of culture

A significant number of participants queried whether it was necessary for issues
of culture to be considered beyond defining identity. Participants expressed this
by asking, rather rhetorically, what culture and ethnicity offered Black and minority ethnic families besides a sense of identity. The majority of participants who
expressed this view stated that culture and ethnicity matters and should be incorporated in assessment but should be limited to informing support decisions rather
than evaluating parenting competence.

*Yes, it (culture and ethnicity) matters because it gives people a sense of sta-
bility, especially for families who are new to this country. Assessments should
therefore consider why parents parent the way they do. But they should not be
assessed according to what is acceptable in their culture, which is what the
questions seem to be suggesting.*

(Jaz, British-Asian Social Worker)

Participants who shared the view that issues of culture and ethnicity should be
limited to informing support decisions tended to give examples relating to children being placed in local authority care. They saw culture and ethnicity as being
an important consideration when making decisions about matching children from
Black and minority families with foster carers.

It is important to be aware of the aspects of culture and ethnicity that are important to families because when you place a child, you want to maintain a degree of normality for them. Things like diet, dress, how they treat their hair and the importance of religion, can seem trivial but are surprisingly important.

(Rochelle, White Social Worker)

The most common reason that participants gave to explain why the parenting competence of Black and minority ethnic parents should be limited to defining identity is that the expectations are different. Participants expressed this by explaining that parenting within Black and minority ethnic families is often based on different conceptualisations of childhood and child development than the ones that inform social workers' evaluations of parenting competence. This explanation was often illustrated with examples about the different interpretations that Black and minority ethnic parents tend to have about aspects such as emotional warmth and stimulation, as well as guidance and boundaries.

I can't tell you how many times I have worked with parents from Africa who show no sign of emotional warmth or where the children barely have any toys in the home. To them, these things are not as important as education, respect and children learning to take responsibility from an early age. The intensity that some black and minority ethnic parents enforce these things is often alien to us in this country so we have to hold them accountable to the standards of this country.

(Monica White Social worker)

When you think about it, parenting assessments are not about pointing a finger of blame. We are not really saying that the parent is bad. All we are saying is that the way they are parenting is not how we would parent and we think it is harmful to the child.

(Anne, Caribbean Social worker)

Some participants stated that it was important for the parenting competence of Black and minority ethnic parents to be evaluated within the context of the parents' culture and ethnicity. Participants who expressed this view also stated that restricting issues of culture and ethnicity to defining identity was evidence of the lack of creative thinking within the profession.

I have worked with several colleagues who returned to the office and said there was no emotional warmth with that family. Often what they mean is that the family did not show emotional warmth in the way the social worker expected to see it i.e., there was no hugging and kissing. It is probably true that most African cultures are not tactile. That is not the only way to show emotional warmth.

(Benjamin, Black African Social Worker)

Participants also stated that they did not feel that assessment tools or processes needed to change for the parenting competence of Black and minority ethnic parents to be evaluated on:

> *All parenting is culturally defined. Therefore, assessing black and minority ethnic parents with a Western lens immediately disadvantages them. We don't have to reinvent the wheel to take a different approach. The dimensions of the assessment triangle can be considered within the context of culture and ethnicity without compromising children's safety and welfare.*
>
> (Pretti, Indian Social Worker)

Theme 10: oppressive practice

A significant number of participants asked whether the research was motivated by suggestions that the current assessment processes are oppressive to Black and minority ethnic parents. In questioning whether the research was borne out of suggestions that assessment processes were oppressive, participants advanced two main responses: the first was that Black and ethnic minority parents either fail or are reluctant to engage with parenting competence evaluations and this negatively affects the outcome of assessment. The second was that effective practice requires social workers to be reflectively aware of their client groups. This was helpful in aiding investigative social work. However, participants also felt that reflective awareness also carries with it the risk of reinforcing professionals' stereotypes about the parenting practices of Black and minority ethnic parents, thus perpetuating oppressive practice.

> *Unfortunately, from a Western view point, a lot of culturally defined parenting within black and minority ethnic families can be oppressive and harmful to children. That can be reflected in the views they hold about the importance of women and girls in society or the use of physical chastisement to discipline children. When these issues are being explored and the parents refuse to engage in assessment, you have little choice but to conclude that what your hypothesis is likely to be the children's lived experience within the family.*
>
> (Monica, White Social Worker)

A few participants stated that evaluations of parenting competence can be oppressive. They explained that this has more to do with the adversarial nature of child protection social work and agency structures, which place emphasis on identifying evidence of maltreatment rather than on working to support clients. Participants who expressed this view also pointed out that the system is oppressive to social work clients in general but that Black and minority ethnic parents are perhaps at greater disadvantage because they do not always know how or where to access support. Participants who gave this view stated that some of the disadvantages are that evaluations of parenting competence must necessarily be based on British definitions of what constitutes good parenting.

> *By the time you are assessing parenting capacity, quite often there is already a view that the parenting is short of the minimum expectations. Focus can then easily shift to identifying who is right and what is the best evidence upon which to make a point. Sadly, parents can get lost in this process as we pursue evidence that their parenting has fallen short of the British standards of parenting.*

(Grace, Caribbean Social Worker)

> *The child protection system is itself oppressive. Thresholds keep shifting. For example, we no longer talk of children experiencing actual harm. It is enough for a social worker to argue that there is a likelihood of harm. It is little wonder therefore that when parents actually have problems, they will minimise them to avoid a negative assessment.*

(Jessica, African Social Worker)

Participants generally held the view that Black and minority ethnic children were over represented in welfare statistics because many social workers tend to take what they described as 'defensible' decisions. They stated that many 'defensible' decisions were a result of social workers not having a full understanding of the parenting practices of Black and minority ethnic parents and thus erring on the side of caution to avoid future blame.

Theme 11: the issue of resources

A small number of participants queried whether the research would result in funding resources for Black and minority ethnic parents. Participants who expressed this view discussed it in terms of positive discrimination. They explained that while having resources such as interpreting services was helpful in reducing disadvantage, more needed to be done for Black and minority ethnic parents. They described Black and minority ethnic families as often being vulnerable to structural forms of disadvantage.

> *They (black and minority ethnic families) face a number of challenges which are not always obvious e.g., racism, poverty, overcrowding, exploitation and social isolation. These issues compromise parenting yet they can be lost in the focus on safeguarding. The extra resources allow for more humane consideration when assessing parenting capacity.*

(Yvonne, Black-African Social Worker)

Participants stated that there was a need for funded support resources with expertise around issues of culture and ethnicity. Several suggestions were mentioned to explain how such a service might work. Typical examples included group-specific charitable organisations within the community. Participant stated that the advocacy support that the charitable organisations provided helped social workers understand the inner working of families and thus reach balanced assessments of parenting competence.

> *Those groups (charitable organisations) help the parent and the social worker. I once worked with an Afghan charity helping a family who were just not willing to engage. It helped me understand the hierarchy within the family which, interestingly was the paternal grandmother. That information changed the focus of assessment and resulted in better outcomes for that family. We need more of such resources if we are to work effectively with people from different backgrounds.*
>
> (Pretti, Indian Social Worker)

When espousing the need for extra funding to support evaluations of the parenting competence of Black and minority ethnic parents, participants suggested that it needed to be a specialist resource-like substance misuse or domestic abuse support. Distinctions were made between specialist and charitable resources in that participants felt that charitable resource run the risk of being biased and limited to the group they support while professional resources would take a more even handed and inclusive approach.

> *I suspect that many black and minority ethnic parents are sent to parenting classes because that is what is available rather than because it necessarily addresses any issues raised. A service with ethnicity and culture expertise could work with such families to teach them about aligning their practice to British parenting values. It is a totally different focus.*
>
> (Thomas, Black-African Social Worker)

> *A funded resource would remove the challenge of trying to know and understand the parenting practices of different cultures. You would simply refer the family and get a report about how they do things in that culture. That way, you avoid making unhelpful assumptions.*
>
> (Yvonne, Black-African Social Worker)

Theme 12: the culture of social workers

Although participants did not talk about their own culture and ethnicity having any bearing on the assessments they conducted, their narratives suggested that their personal and professional culture were implicated in assessments. This was evident in statements that contained connotations of value judgements about the parenting practices of Black and minority ethnic parents as well as in narratives that inferred the Black and minority ethnic parents use their culture and ethnicity to perpetuate harmful parenting approaches.

[S]ome cultures openly prefer sons and will channel all their resources to ensure that the sons are treated better than the daughters.

(Kirsty, White-British Social worker)

[O]bviously where they come from things might be done differently, and it may be okay there. But you have to explain to them that in this country, that is not how we do things. It is not okay to smack your child or threaten them with a stick in the corner.

(Monica, White Social Worker)

I initially saw social workers as primarily from the 'culture' of social work but realised that the range of backgrounds was a distinctive, unusual, and valuable feature of my study.

8   What it all means

For many BAME families, culture provides a sense of identity and belonging. As such, some parents go to great lengths to preserve their cultural beliefs and values. This can influence how they respond to parenting situations. Because of their shared experiences, families from the same cultural backgrounds tend to socialise their children in broadly similar ways. The challenge for social workers assessing culturally informed parenting is that the value bases of many BAME parents are often at odds with Western values. For example, in areas such as morality (Corby, 2000; Simpson and Littlechild, 2009), the differences often mean that BAME parents can respond to parenting situations in ways that are distinctly different from the majority population. This creates contentions in relation to defining actions that constitute child abuse.

The social workers who took part in this study described the contentions that arise during assessments of parenting as differences in opinion between BAME parents and assessing social workers. However, other studies (e.g. Phoenix and Husain, 2007; Lonne et al, 2009; Simpson and Littlechild, 2009; Chase, 2010; Littlechild, 2012) note that cultural misunderstandings contribute to some of the negative outcomes of assessments. Whilst empirical evidence has not unveiled a single and objective method of assessing culturally informed parenting, it highlights the need to find robust ways of evaluating safe parenting within BAME families. This includes enhancing social workers' abilities to interpret the cultural issues specific to the family being assessed.

As others have noted (e.g. Sawrikar, 2017; Keller et al, 2019), our understanding of the influence of culture on parenting is limited by dependence on studies that have mainly focused on Western, Educated, Industrialised, Rich and Democratic (WEIRD) populations. Professor Keller, a renowned German psychology academic, and her colleagues point out that WEIRD populations represent only about 5% of the world's population, yet more than 90% of scholarship on culturally informed parenting draws conclusions from studying WEIRD populations. Even then, the different dimensions of culturally informed parenting complicate assessments.

Parenting literature indicates that there is still much speculation about what constitutes 'good' parenting in different cultures. This calls for emphasis on understanding not only how culturally informed parenting is framed, but also how social workers evaluate safe parenting within BAME families. In the study from which this book draws its insights, many BAME parents talked about feeling threatened and inadequate when interacting with social workers. They explained that the sense of powerlessness led them to accept what they felt were unfair judgements about their parenting and signup for services that they felt did not understand the challenges affecting BAME families. This echoes Page et al's (2007) qualitative case study which found that safeguarding professionals tend to make assumptions about BAME parents based on ethnicity and that the assumption were often unfairly judgmental.

There is, therefore, need for an intersectional way of working that considers the power dynamics between social workers assessing parenting and BAME parents. This also entails seeking to understand the stigmatising experiences of BAME families. Only then can the profession begin to tackle the negative perceptions associated with how practitioners assess BAME families, as well as address the barriers that limit BAME parents' engagement with safeguarding services. For example, most parents who participated in the study referred to in this book said that social workers repeatedly used perceived safeguarding concerns to explicitly and tacitly block or limit their involvement in decision making processes. They felt that this had stymied opportunities for their children to remain in their care or with birth family members.

The view that social workers hinder some BAME children's chances of remaining in the care of their own families highlights aspects of systemic disadvantage. It also brings the issue of unequal distribution of social power to the fore. Addressing disadvantage is important, especially in the context that while children in local authority care remain predominantly White, the population of BAME children has increased over the last 5 years, particularly, children of mixed and Black ethnicity (ONS, 2012). Some have associated this increase with the growing number of unaccompanied asylum-seeking children (see Humphris and Sigona, 2019), but studies such as the one from which this book draws its insights suggest that such a view is too simplistic.

Dr Sawrikar, a social work academic in Australia, points out that adopting one ethnocentric approach to evaluating safe parenting risks leaving children from some groups vulnerable to either abuse or neglect from family perpetrators or from the safeguarding system itself (Sawrikar, 2017). Improving the efficacy of assessing culturally informed parenting, therefore, requires practitioners to recognise that culture interlocks the different influencing factors, by framing how BAME parents engage with their environment. This interlocking effect is associated with why BAME parents challenge hitherto taken-for-granted assumptions about how to socialise children.

How culture frames parenting

The influence that culture exerts on parenting is not always explicit. Rather, it is exhibited in deliberate and overt processes, as well as in implicit and unplanned parenting so that some decisions are, seemingly, made subconsciously. Goffman's

(1974) explanation of 'framing' helps us understand how this plays out. He defined frames as an ongoing process of forming social context. In general, individuals use frames to organise information and construct a point of view that encourages how they interpret the facts of any given phenomenon. What this means, in terms of understanding culturally informed parenting, is that BAME parents draw on surface and deep frames, which contain within them additional information, to make decisions about how to socialise their children. These frames also influence the strategies that parents select to promote cultural competence.

The surface frames are the mental structures associated with how BAME parents describe culture (e.g. practices, beliefs, and values). The deep frames define parents' moral world view and influence their responses to the environment around them. According to Goffman conceptualisation, parents simultaneously activate several frames as they interact with and interpret their environment. The challenge for assessing social workers is to detect which frames BAME parents are drawing on to form a view. Indeed, therein lies the limitation of using frame analysis to understand behaviour or make sense of parents' narrative. But, what Goffman (1974) espouses eloquently is that frames are the 'scaffolds' for any credible stories and therefore indispensable in communication. They are, as Goffman (1974) explains, adopted consciously but most often used unconsciously.

What we can infer from Goffman's ideas about frames is that culture influences parenting in ways that are distinct even in the smallest detail. This means that during assessment, BAME parents and social workers are likely to express implicit but strongly held ideas about what they believed to be the 'right' way to parent. So, for example, parents who give more house chores to their daughters compared to their sons may have drawn on cultural frames about gender roles, family hierarchy, and family member responsibilities. Conversely, a social worker may draw on feminist frames to interpret that scenario as evidence of boys being preferred over girls within a family they are assessing.

Culture and socialising children

The subtlety of culturally informed constructions of parenting influence how BAME parents construe issues such as gender and the role of women in families. For example, a parent might state that they understand why social workers are concerned about their parenting practices, but justified how they parent in terms of what they believed to be appropriate and beneficial to their children within the context of their culture. One participant expressed it as follows:

> *I know it looks as if we do not value the girls because they do more house-work than the boys; but in our culture it is the women who will have responsibility for running the home and they have to start learning early.*

In this regard, responses from most BAME parents suggested that they had not considered how their parenting practices perpetuated what they described as the gender stereotypes and biases they sought to redress. For example, participants whose cultural belief was that modesty in women is reflected in how they dress, attached great importance to the way their daughters presented in public. One participant who expressed this view reflected on how with hindsight, she could see that the way she sought to reinforce modesty was more forceful than it needed to be.

Equally, participant social workers generally acknowledged that they approached parenting competence assessments with culturally constructed preconceptions about gender equity. This was evident in responses which expressed the view that most BAME cultures subjugate women. Social workers who expressed this view went on to state that they felt that parents had to adjust their parenting to fit within the constructs of socially acceptable gender equity in England. Most social workers explained this as being a pragmatic approach that would ultimately benefit BAME parents, rather than a cultural construct. They reasoned that because parenting competence is evaluated based on Western ideas about socialising children, it was prudent for BAME parents to align their parenting to Western ideals.

From a frame analysis point of view, the descriptors that participants used represented the surface frames from which parenting practices were understood. BAME parents saw their parenting practices as being influenced by tradition, beliefs, morals, and values. This was perceived to be true for themselves, as well as for the 'other' and can be described as the surface frame. Participants' perceptions about the culture of the 'other', in comparison to their own, provide the deep frame from which safe parenting is understood. What is intrinsic within this frame is that BAME parents perceived their parenting to be safe but expressed uncertainty about how social workers view their approaches to socialising children.

Socialising children includes aspects of stimulating, as well as providing guidance and boundaries. This includes shaping ideas about what constitutes stability within families' environmental settings. For example, a significant number of BAME parents reported experiencing high levels of conflict with their children over issues such as 'curfew' times, use of make-up, dress styles, and lifestyle choices. Parents who expressed this view also stated that conflict with their children often resulted in the use of high levels of overt discipline regimes to guide and manage behaviour and to provide safety and stability.

Attention to stimulation, guidance, and boundaries suggests that culturally informed parenting seeks to achieve parenting outcomes that are consistent with what empirical evidence lists as the four fundamental components of parenting that transcend cultural contexts: basic care; safety and protection; emotional care and stimulation; and providing behavioural boundaries and stability (see Woodcock, 2003; Roopnarine and Gielen, 2005; Johnson et al, 2006; Jones, 2010). The cultural beliefs that BAME parents hold about stimulating and guiding their children serve the purpose of creating parenting pathways that ensure that children are prepared for the economic, psychosocial, and physical environments in which they will grow and develop.

However, most social workers expressed concern when expressing views about how BAME parents stimulate and guide their children. This was mainly articulated in terms of social workers feeling that culturally informed parenting often lacks basic understanding of children's development. A recurring theme was that social workers were often concerned that BAME parents tended to provide inappropriate levels of supervision in relation to their children's ages or levels of development. One social worker expressed that:

> *I was surprised that this mother could not see the risk associated with leaving a seven-year-old to cook the family meal on a gas hob. Another mother left a nine-year-old to look after her three and five-year-old siblings overnight, so that she could go to work on a night shift.*

(Karen, White-British Social worker)

The question about how children should be socialised highlighted a conflict between how BAME parents and social workers construe safe parenting. This conflict is not directly apparent in the surface frames but is reflected in the way that both sets of participants responded to questions about safe parenting.

It is from deep frames that participants organise culture into a context from which to parent. What this means, in the context of culturally informed parenting, is that tensions between BAME parents and social workers are a result of their expectations and understanding of children's developmental stages. For example, respondent social workers expressed approaching parenting assessments with concerns about protecting children from unsafe levels of supervision. They gave many examples about BAME parents giving children responsibilities that social workers did not deem to be age appropriate or using harsh strategies to discipline their children. Consequently, social workers saw culture as a complicating factor that had the potential to perpetuate abuse.

Conversely, BAME parents construed safe parenting in the context of preserving cultural identity. This was expressed in terms of promoting their children's social competence and sense of belonging. As such, they saw social workers' approaches to evaluating safe parenting as having a monoculture focus that undermines the value of BAME parents' parenting practices. The different perspectives directly challenge social workers' theories of parenting in that they raise the possibility that issues of risk can be presented as differences in perspective.

The way that participants perceived culturally informed parenting suggests to us that the deep frames they held defined the general relationship that BAME parents and social workers have with parenting evaluations. The surface frames reinforce that relationship. For example, social workers who approach assessments from the deep frame that culturally informed parenting is unsafe will reinforce that frame with a surface frame that defines the BAME parents as falling short of the minimum standards of safe parenting. Consequently, they are more likely to prefer parenting that aligns to Western values over culturally informed parenting. But, as Butler and Williamson (1994), Owen and Farmer (1996), and Littlechild (2012) observe, social workers' perceptions of parenting are themselves shaped by personal as well as professional cultural ideals.

Modelling parental behaviour

Another way that culture frames parenting practices is by modelling parental behaviour. This was evident in the narratives of BAME parents which suggested that their childhood experiences of being parented had influenced their attitudes and long-term parenting behaviour, including how they went on to parent their own children. A significant number explained that their current parenting practices had been borne out of their own experiences of being parented. Participants articulated this in terms of the practices they either wanted to retain or discard from their parenting. This is consistent with parenting literature that asserts that experience of parenting models future parenting (see Madge, 2001; Woodcock, 2003; Madge and Willmont, 2007).

The study in this book highlighted interesting differences in the way that BAME parents and social workers articulated the impact of parenting experience during childhood. Social workers tended to suggest that parenting practices that were seen to be punitive or neglectful were a result of the absence of positive parental modelling. They explained that practices such as regimes used to discipline children (e.g. physical chastisement) were a remodelling of their own childhood experiences. Social workers' interpretations appeared to draw from Bandura's (1962, 1977) social learning theory, which asserts that people learn from one another through observation, imitation, and modelling. Social workers' who expressed this view explained that the parenting practices of many BAME parents ended to cause concern.

Overall, BAME parents shared similar views as those illustrated by social workers. This was expressed both in terms of parenting being modelled during their own childhoods and in terms of their endeavours to parent in distinctively different ways from the parenting they received as children. Parents who expressed this view were keen to point out that the cultural values and beliefs did not have a strong influence on their parenting. They explained that they were constantly evaluating messages about parenting from their friends, families, and professionals to adjust their parenting.

The views expressed by BAME parents indicated that cultural parenting scripts function as flexible systems. This means that while the way that many BAME parents socialise their children may be rooted in the cultural ideals modelled by previous generations parents adjust their parenting to fit their environment. The implication, for social workers, is that they need to strike a balance between evaluating safe parenting in the contexts of existing knowledge, as well as consider families' cultures and environments. Child welfare legislation appears to take this into consideration by requiring assessments to make provision for families' cultural backgrounds as well as their expressed views and preferences (Department of Health, 1991).

Contentions in assessment arise because of the difference in how social workers and BAME parents frame culture. For example, some social workers appeared to hold a traditional frame of culture – i.e., one that BAME parents have brought into a new country. Social workers who held this view suggested that culture was static. They explained that many BAME parents were unable to engage with intervention because they could not break away from their traditions to confront and resolve the damaging effects of their own experiences of being parented. On the other hand, many BAME parents framed culture as an evolving characteristic. They talked about their parenting in terms of adjustments they had made because they were now in a new country.

Variance in how respondents framed culture suggests that it holds a complex meaning and is defined from several deep and surface frames. These frames influence how social workers and parents interpret safe parenting. Furthermore, because individual assessors draw on personal and professional frames, there is always the risk of social workers making unhelpful generalisations about the parenting practices of BAME parents. This difference in how BAME parents and social workers frame culture highlights tensions that mirror wider research on assessing culturally informed parenting.

The absence of universally accepted minimum standards of parenting (Budd and Holdsworth, 1996; Budd, 2001; Page and Whitting, 2007; Phoenix and Husain, 2007) adds to the challenges that exist between how BAME parents and social workers perceive safe parenting. This emphasises the need for nuanced understanding of culturally informed parenting. Otherwise, social work interventions with BAME families could be guided by unexamined assumptions that the parenting practices of BAME parents in Western countries will culminate in assimilation.

Identity, meaning, and context

Culture provides the context within which parenting is shaped and becomes meaningful. BAME parents talked about culture as the context within which their parenting derives meaning. However, they were keen to emphasise that it provides more than a context for meaning. Many parents also felt that culturally informed parenting identified them as belonging to a specific group. This perspective is consistent with findings from previous studies (e.g. Modood et al, 1997; Super and Harkness, 2002; Weisner, 2002; White, 2005; Phoenix and Husain, 2007) that argue for the need for parenting to be analysed in the context of culture.

That said, a significant number of the BAME parents interviewed explained that the contention they had with social workers arose because social workers insisted on limiting the parents' cultures to identity whilst evaluating their parenting according to Western ideals and standards. Parents who expressed this view illustrated it with examples that social workers did not appear to consider the dynamics and interactive nature of cultural identity. This was associated with views that the parenting practices exhibited by some BAME parents did not always align with social workers' conceived ideas of what was deemed to be normative.

Researchers and academics (e.g. Gelfand and Fandetti, 1986; Dominelli et al, 2001) share similar observations about social work interventions when working with BAME families. Dominelli et al (2001), for example, advance the view that social work has not engaged appropriately with issues of diversity and thus perpetuates oppressive practice. They argue that the effectiveness of social work interventions is limited by failure to acknowledge the nature of social relations and the importance of culture among BAME families. This results in assessments that focus on observable outward appearances, rather than explore how culture influences perceptions about what is acceptable within a given culture – for example, minimum standards of parenting, gender socialisation, supervision, and hierarchy within families.

Without nuanced understanding of why BAME parents approach parenting the way they do, evaluations of safe parenting create a dichotomy of expectations. For example, about how parents should address gender issues. This was evident in the responses from BAME parents who felt that when social workers were evaluating their parenting, they tended to focus almost exclusively on their own preconceptions about gender equity, as expressed in the participant quotation:

> *[S]he started to look at why the girls were doing more housework than the boys but didn't try to understand. Instead, she said that I was doing this because I was raised in an environment where women are not valued and that is what I know but it is not right.*

(Noreen, Indian mother)

Narratives such as the one illustrated earlier indicate that culture frames parenting contexts within families and their wider community by not only embodying core beliefs and values but also functioning to communicate and reinforce those beliefs and values. This is congruent with findings from previous studies (e.g. McDaniel and Tepperman, 2000; Quah, 2003) that show that cultural and ethnic affiliations serve to provide group identity and parenting contexts that significantly influence parenting practices.

In her study of parenting styles among Singapore families, Quah (2003) found that over time, culture is modified but not eliminated by other variables. The implication is that parents, as well as social workers, filter their perception of parenting in ways that highlight cultural aspects more noticeably than other factors that influence parenting, for example, education, social class, poverty, and geographical location (Utting, 2007; Waylen and Stewart-Brown, 2010; Bornstein, 2012). Studies of parenting within the countries of origin of some of the parents who took part in the study that this book is based on (e.g. Keller et al, 2005; Tuli, 2012) highlight similar findings to Quah (2003). For example, Keller et al's (2005) study of Nso and German mothers found that socialisation practices reflected the conscious nature of parenting as a shared cultural activity. This suggests that it is inadequate to use culture only as a descriptor of identity.

The findings of this study show that evaluations of safe parenting among BAME families fail to fully appraise the dynamic nature of culture and how cultural beliefs and values affect parenting over time. This finding is consistent with debate within parenting literature that associates the over representation of BAME children in welfare statistics, with social workers' failure to fully evaluate the meaning and context of cultural parenting scripts (Lonne et al, 2009; Littlechild, 2012). Only by fully engaging with issues of culture and ethnicity can evaluations move beyond the socially constructed dichotomy of White majority and ethnic minority approaches to parenting.

Conceptualisation of parenting competence

Social workers and BAME parents generally agree that parenting is culturally defined. But what is accepted as safe parenting in any one culture cannot be 'normative'. Tensions were evident when participants described and shared their perspectives about the efficacy of parenting competence evaluations, specifically, in appraising the value of cultural parenting scripts to children's welfare and development. What seemed to emerge from the frames that participants used to define parenting and the efficacy of evaluations of safe parenting highlighted a degree of mistrust between BAME parents and social workers. The section that follows explores how both sets of participants construed safe parenting.

Constructions of child development

Child development was one of the dominant frames in the narratives of almost all respondent social workers and some BAME parents. Respondent social workers articulated it more in the context of empirical research rather than from a frame of culture. In other words, their perceptions about how children develop were framed by research. As such, they emphasised the importance of parents having knowledge of empirical evidence on child development and felt that parents whose knowledge of child development was not consistent with empirical research were more likely to parent in ways that compromised children's safety and welfare.

Conversely, respondent parents articulated child development in the context of culture. They used this frame to make sense of their own understanding of how children develop. This was expressed in terms of how children acquire the social skills and competences that they are expected to have within their cultural group. For the respondent parents, the way that children acquire culture was integral to their development. Both sets of participants argued that there was a knowledge gap on the part of the 'other'. For example, respondent social workers felt that BAME parents generally lacked the requisite child development knowledge to provide safe parenting for their children. Equally, respondent parents felt that social workers lacked the skills or desire to effectively appraise child development within the context of culture.

The perspectives that both sets of participants espouse reflect the frames from which they appear to define child development. Despite the variance, both positions are reflected in empirical research. For example, a large body of research on ecological systems suggests that children's development is influenced by a range of contextual and immediate environmental factors (including culture) that are different for every family and ethnic group (see, e.g. McDaniel and Tepperman,

2000; Barn, 2002; Woodcock, 2003; Quah, 2003; Utting and Pugh, 2004; Belsky and Jaffe, 2006; Barn, 2006b). Parenting and, by association, children's development, is a series of connected events across which families participate over time.

When participants' descriptions and conceptualisation of safe parenting are brought together under the lens of frame analysis, it becomes clear that for most BAME parents, culture embeds assumptions about parenting. Through recurrent interactions with their environments, BAME parents get drawn into parenting assumptions central to their cultural constructions. Conversely, social workers draw heavily on scientific knowledge about what is known to work. The issue is that both sets of participants use different frames to inform their knowledge of child development.

Parenting literature suggests that effective evaluation of safe parenting can be achieved when social workers involve parents in their evaluations (Buckley et al, 2006; McGhee and Hunter, 2011). This is also recognised within child welfare legislation that emphasises the importance of taking account of families' cultural backgrounds. The findings from the study in this book are congruent with this literature. BAME parents engage more openly with assessing social workers who show respect for their culture. When social workers are critical of culturally informed parenting scripts, it can cause conflict and decrease the likelihood of meaningful engagement.

Given that ideas about child development are framed by different psychosocial, cultural, and legislative processes, gaining a better understanding of how frames influence parenting practices helps improve the efficacy of evaluations of safe parenting. Indeed, one of the ways in which this study contributes to the literature is by illuminating the frames from which BAME parents and social workers derive their perspectives about how children develop.

Preventing harm – tradition vs. assessment tools

The overriding concern expressed by social workers was that BAME parents often lacked the willingness or capacity to protect children from harm. A few social workers suggested that culturally informed parenting carried the risk of harm to children. Social workers who expressed this view referred to legal guidance as the frame through which they appraised safe parenting. However, their narratives suggested a focus on appraising the presence or absence of abuse rather than safe parenting. This is congruent with Woodcock's (2003) work on social work assessment of parenting. In her study, Woodcock found that rather than evaluate the quality or adequacy of parenting practices, as recommended within parenting literature, social workers construed parenting competence based on whether parents were abusive.

In general, there were many similarities within social workers' narratives about what constitutes safe parenting. Social workers' narratives suggested that their ideas about harmful parenting were framed from training, professionals' experience and knowledge, as well as their personal experiences of parenting (both from being parented and from being parents). But, while most social workers stated that they were confident about identifying harmful parenting from BAME parents, they expressed feeling less confident about evaluating competence within the context of parents' cultures. One social worker expressed it as follows:

> *[I]t is not as straight forward as that. Harm is harm; you have the law and you have guidance to help you decide when parenting is harmful. The problem with determining whether parenting practices are good enough is that it is all subjective and very difficult to pin down.*
>
> (Gregory, White-British Social Worker)

Parents felt that in most cases, social workers attributed problems to them that they did not recognise in themselves. The narratives from parents tended to view social workers' approaches to the issue of safe parenting as negative and rigid. Many parents explained that socialisation processes within their cultures meant that their children had attained significant levels of independence at earlier ages than their Western counterparts. Typical explanations related to the ages at which BAME parents felt that children were ready to be left in charge of their younger siblings or given responsibilities such as cooking family meals and other house chores.

While some parents reported that social workers had shown understanding of the cultural contexts of their parenting, a significant number of parents felt that during assessment, social workers were often accusatory and unwilling to understand. Parents who expressed this view argued that social workers employ a rigid approach to evaluating safe parenting, which exacerbates conflict between BAME parents and social workers. One parent illustrated it as follows:

> *I was never going to win that argument. As far as the social worker was concerned, if I could not see things her way, I was minimising issues and therefore could not protect my children. What then do you do? You have to accept what they are saying.*
>
> (Noreen, Indian mother)

The finding illustrated by the earlier narrative indicates that BAME parents view evaluations of safe parenting as negative. This then causes mistrust and hinders attempts for BAME parents and social workers to work more closely together. This finding is consistent with the literature (e.g. Corby et al, 2002; Millar and Corby, 2006; Dumbrill, 2006; Kellett and Apps, 2009), which highlights the presence of enforced compliance in response to assessment. As Kellett and Apps' (2009) study found, the focus on identifying abuse meant that relationships between social workers and parents were strained during assessment. Often to the extent that parents' engagement during and after assessment was either superficial or blatantly aggressive towards assessing social workers.

Bias, racism, and discrimination

The narratives of both BAME parents and social work participants who took part in this study suggest that some decisions about safe parenting were based on the stereotypes that social workers held about certain BAME groups. This racialisation, if left unchallenged, fuels biases that can become tools for justifying discriminatory practice. For example, a social manager who denies or makes it difficult for BAME families to access financial support because they believe that certain BAME groups are prone to being untruthful or fraudulent.

Studies on diversity show that there are disparities in the experiences of BAME groups in all areas of life affected by public organisations with some ethnicities experiencing more pronounced disadvantage than others. Some have argued that disparities exist because of historic enduring racism and biases. In their article on the sociology of racism, Clair and Denis (2015) define racism as individual- and group-level processes and structures that are implicated in the reproduction of racial inequality. They argue that systemic racism happens when structures or processes are implemented by groups with power, for example, schools and government departments, including social services. Inquiries into the experiences of BAME groups repeatedly highlight, that systemic issues of racism and bias are not openly discussed within organisations.

In practice, social workers may not consciously be aware that some of their decisions carry connotations of discrimination for BAME families. However, their learned biases and detachment can translate into being unable to effectively advocate for BAME parents. The difficulties seem to be in how safeguarding structures evaluate culturally informed parenting scripts. Often, professionals' biases become actions that they justify as a need to err on the side of caution. For example, a social worker might consciously or unconsciously believe that BAME fathers are more likely to be abusive or repressive towards women and children. This could cause them to become anxious if they perceive a BAME father to be angry. The social worker's actions can range in severity from labelling the parent as aggressive, to seeking to 'protect' the rest of the family by asking the parents to separate, for their children's safety despite having scant evidence of domestic abuse.

Gender – identity, power, and feminism

A key theme to emerge in defining what constituted positive parenting related to how both sets of participants framed the issue of gender – both in terms of gender roles and hierarchies of authorities within families. For most BAME parents, the goal of parenting was to ensure that their children succeed in what they saw as a new and often hostile environment. Participants' narratives highlighted tensions in the way they interpreted cultural aspects in areas such as respect, hierarchy of authority, sexuality, and parental roles. This was evident in participants' expressed views about how culture frames issues of gender.

The parents who took part in the one-to-one interviews were all mothers. During the interviews, they stated that they had actively passed on gender role attitudes to their children by communicating culturally informed gender expectations. This included role modelling as well as encouraging gender-specific behaviours and activities. Most BAME parents explained that gender identity was a key feature of culturally informed parenting scripts. This was articulated in terms of the separation of gender roles within the family, as well as differential treatment of daughters and sons. Most BAME parents felt that their perspectives of cultural definitions of gender were undergoing shifts but that social workers' assessments had continued to stereotype them.

The literature on the socialisation of gender asserts that gender relations are culturally unique. For example, individualist and collectivist cultures will have different views regarding earlier maturity around sex or other aspects around gender. That said, there is little detailed research focusing on why BAME parents perpetuate gender socialisation practices that they are not always in agreement with. Studies (e.g. Bornstein, 2012; Chimba et al, 2012) tend to focus on the general variations of cultural approaches to parenting, such as whether cultures prioritise independence or collectivist ideals. This limits our understanding to cultural meanings and practices that explain parenting in general terms rather than on the contrasting interconnections between culture and socialisation aspects such as gender roles.

Nevertheless, parenting literature recognises that parental attitudes towards issues of gender are adapting to changing socioeconomic realities. In the study that this book is based on, parents reported they were actively embracing ideas of gender equality in terms of economic aspirations but held on to traditional expectations when it came to parental roles, household chores, and family security. Given increase mobility and globalisation, nuanced understanding of gender socialisation is important. As culture boundaries widen, traditional ways of viewing gender issues will become either troublesome or inadequate.

During the interviews in this study, narratives from social workers suggested that they held feminist perspectives about the gendered nature of culture. This was evident in perspectives that disapproved of parenting practices that they saw as perpetuating disadvantage in the way that girls are socialised. Participants typically illustrated this point by asserting that BAME parents tended to socialise their daughters in ways that encouraged dependence, conformity, and domestication, whereas boys were socialised to be self-reliant, competitive, and dominant. According to one social worker:

> *[S]ome cultures openly prefer sons and will channel all their resources to ensure that the sons are treated better than the daughters.*
>
> (Kirsty, White-British Social worker)

Gender socialisation was seen by both sets of participants as an important marker of identity. This was expressed in terms of securing support from within the extended family as well as community networks. For most BAME parents, cultural artefacts such as physical presentation (traditional dress) as well as behavioural traits (e.g. perceptions of promiscuity or being able to prepare traditional meals) were also deemed to be important identity markers. These perceptions contrasted with those expressed by social workers who generally saw such gender socialisations as environments in which relations of oppression are constituted.

Emotional availability and sensitivity – acculturation vs. assimilation

Most participant social workers stated that BAME parents tended to lack insight into their children's emotional needs. Social workers who expressed this view articulated their perspective as being derived from observations of lack of empathy from parents. This led social workers to conclude that parents were putting their needs (often for financial improvement) over their children's emotional development needs. One social worker expressed it as follows:

> *[T]heir perception was that they love their children and were working hard to make sure that the children had everything they needed. But they could not see that the children's behavioural challenges were a result of not spending quality time with their parents.*
>
> (Thomas, Black-African Social Worker)

On the other hand, most BAME parents expressed feeling that social workers expected them to express emotions of affection in a manner that was alien to them:

> *We do not express emotions in the same way. Western cultures are heavy on sharing information with others from the onset. Our approach is that people must qualify for what you share.*
>
> (Olivia, Nigerian mother)

In the main, the way that social workers' perceptions about how parents should express emotional availability was framed by Western constructions. That is, social workers who suggested that BAME parents did not show emotional warmth expected to observe parents exhibiting overt expressions of receiving and reciprocating affection towards children. They saw BAME parents' failure to align their parenting to Western ideals as a failure to fully assimilate in their new community.

BAME parents expressed feeling that social workers lacked an understanding of the challenges that parents face in trying to maintain the parenting practices of their countries of origin whilst also adapting to new ways of parenting. Parents associated this with social workers having poor grasp of issues of culture. They argued that social workers lacked the motivation to improve their understanding of cultural parenting scripts beyond a focus on defining identity through aspects such as parents' religious persuasions, type of food families ate, and grooming regimes. Most BAME parents described these attributes as important but peripheral issues when faced with the prospect of having their children placed in local authority care.

The contrasting conceptualisations of safe parenting are complicated by the frames that both sets of participants draw on to inform their perspectives. For examples, while social workers talk about drawing on research knowledge, legislation, and their agencies' policies, BAME parents draw on their experiences in the community and on their cultural scripts. The issue is that there is a perceived dichotomy in parenting approaches across the world. This dichotomy is associated with the different socialisation priorities within individualist and collectivist cultures. The different expectations inform perspectives about parenting aspects such as maturity around sex, appropriate levels of supervision, and how individuals express emotional warmth.

The findings suggest that further complexity arises because social workers' perspectives about how culturally informed parenting should be interpreted to address issues such as identity, meaning, and context. Many social workers seemed to draw on their individual as well as their professional backgrounds. Drawing on these different frames when assessing safe parenting in BAME families contributes to variations in assessment outcomes.

Culture and social work values and codes of practice

Social work values and professionals' codes of conduct make it incumbent on social workers to understand the cultural issues of the clients they work with. This is a crucial starting point to avoiding unfair discrimination against culturally different groups. However, this study suggests that the value bases of BAME parents and social workers vary widely and are often at odds. This can limit the effectiveness of the strength-based interventions when dealing with issues around morality and ethics.

Most BAME parents want social workers to understand how the parent in the context of their cultural beliefs, values, and social circumstances rather than from Western value bases. The limitation is that much of what we know about parenting in BAME families tends to stop at recognising that constructions of parenting and children's developments vary across and within different cultures. Additionally, the literature suggests that when parents are under scrutiny by safeguarding agencies, they may choose to respond with resistance (Simpson and Littlechild, 2009; Chase, 2010).

In his article on values and cultural issues in social work, Professor Brian Littlechild provides a helpful summary of social work professional values and codes of conduct and moves on to advocate for greater awareness of the role that cultural factors play in the structures and outcomes of child safeguarding practice (Littlechild, 2012). The findings of this study reflect his point that social work practice can be affected by personal and structural issues surrounding cultural differences. This carries the risk of reinforcing perceptions of 'otherness'. There is, therefore, a need for social workers to reflect on how they work with BAME parents to address parenting that is perceived to be harmful to children.

Previous studies and policy reviews (e.g. Chand, 2001; Chimba et al, 2012) have suggested that the over representation of BAME children in child welfare and youth justice statistics in England is associated with systemic approaches that impact on social workers' abilities and creativity to appropriately address issues of culture. Without greater appreciation of the influence of culture on parenting, social workers risk unintentionally reinforcing discrimination and oppression towards BAME groups.

Rather than advance a case for cultural relativism, this study suggests that social workers can achieve greater insight into the parenting of BAME parents and work more effectively with them, by understanding the cultural frames from which parents draw their perspectives about family, children's development, and socialisation. This requires social workers recognise and acknowledge with parents that when families move from their countries of origin, they bring with them their own traditions, customs, and beliefs about how to bring up their children. As BAME parents adjust to Western traditions and child rearing norms, they may encounter difficulties such as discrimination, hostility, poverty, and social isolation that re-frame their approaches to parenting.

Greater understanding of how culture frames parenting helps minimise the likelihood of practice that perpetuates negative stereotypes and oppressive practice. It also enables social workers to focus on re-framing parents' perspectives about how they can achieve the socialisation goals they seek to promote with their children. Chand's (2001) review of social workers' assessments of BAME families, for example, found that social workers were prone to accepting stereotypes about culturally informed parenting and tended to view cultural parenting scripts as having 'weaknesses' rather than 'strengths.

References

Adams, R, Dominelli, L and Payne, M (2009) *Critical Practice in Social Work*. Second Edition. England: Palgrave Macmillan.

Adcock, M and White, R (1985) *Good Enough Parenting: A Framework for Assessment*. London: British Association for Adoption and Fostering (BAAF).

Adler, L and Gielen, U (Eds.) (2003) *Immigration, Emigration and Migration in International Perspective*. Westport, CT: Greenwood.

Adoption Act (1976) https://www.legislation.gov.uk/ukpga/1975/72/contents

Ainsworth, M D S (1967) *Infancy in Uganda: Infant Care and the Growth of Love*. Baltimore: The Johns Hopkins Press.

Ainsworth, M D S and Bell, S M (1969) *Some Contemporary Patterns in the Feeding Situation*. In: Ambrose, A (Ed.) *Stimulation in Early Infancy* (pp. 133–170). London: Academic Press.

Ainsworth, M, Blehar, M, Waters, E and Wall, S (1978) *Patterns of Attachment*. Hillsdale, NJ: Lawrence Erlbaum Associates.

Akilapa, R and Simkiss, D (2012) *Cultural Influences and Safeguarding Children*. Paediatrics and Child Health, Vol. 22 (11): pp. 490–495.

Alderson, P (2004) *Ethics*. In: Fraser, S, Lewis, V, Ding, S, Kellett, M and Robinson, C (Eds.) *Doing Research with Children and Young People*. London: Sage.

Aldgate, J, David, J, Wendy, R and Carole, J (Eds.) (2006) *The Developing World of the Child*. London, UK: Jessica Kingsley.

Allen, M, Svetaz, M V, Hardeman, R and Resnik, M D (2008) *What Research Tells Us about Latino Parenting Practices and Their Relationship to Youth Sexual Behaviour*. Washington, DC: Latino Initiative Advisory Group.

Amato, P R and Fowler, F (2002) *Parenting Practices, Child Adjustment and Family Diversity*. Journal of Marriage and Family, Vol. 64 (33): pp. 703–716.

Anastas, J W (2010) *Teaching in Social Work: An Educator's Guide to Theory and Practice*. New York: Columbia University Press.

Aquilino, W S and Supple, A J (2001) *Long-Term Effects of Parenting Practices during Adolescence on Well-Being: Outcomes in Young Adulthood*. Journal of Family Issues, Vol. 22 (3): pp. 289–308.

Arnett, J J (2002) *The Psychology of Globalisation*. American Psychologist, Vol. 57: pp. 774–783.

Asmussen, K and Weizel, K (2010) *Evaluating the Evidence Fathers, Families and Children*. London: National Academy for Parenting Practitioners (NAPP).

Azzopardi, C and McNeil, T (2016) *From Cultural Competence to Cultural Consciousness: Transitioning to a Critical Approach to Working Across Differences in Social Work*. Journal of Ethnic and Cultural Diversity in Social Work, Vol. 25 (4): pp. 282–299.

Bandura, A (1962) *Social Learning through Imitation.* In: Jones, M R (Ed.) *Nebraska Symposium on Motivation.* Lincoln: University of Nebraska Press.

Bandura, A (1977) *Social Learning Theory.* Upper Saddle River, NJ: Prentice-Hall.

Banks, S (2006) *Ethics and Values in Social Work.* Third Edition. Basingstoke, UK: Palgrave Macmillan.

Barlow, J, Fisher, J and Jones, D (2012) *Systematic Review of Models of Analysing Significant Harm.* Department for Education. Manchester, United Kingdom.

Barlow, J, Shaw, R and Stewart-Brown, S (2004) *The Effectiveness of Parenting Programmes for Ethnic Minority Parents.* York, UK: Joseph Rowntree Foundation.

Barn, R (2002) *Parenting in a "Foreign" Climate: The Experiences of Bangladeshi Mothers in Multi-racial Britain.* Social Work in Europe, Vol. 9 (3): pp. 28–38.

Barn, R (2002) *Exploring the Unsaid: Risk and Creativity in Working Cross-culturally.* In Mason, B and Sawyerr, A (Eds) Ethnicity and Child Welfare. London, UK: Karnac.

Barn, R (2006a) *Improving Services to Meet the Needs of Minority Ethnic Children and Families.* Briefing Paper 13, Research in Practice. Making Research Count. London: Department for Education and Skills.

Barn, R (2006b) *Parenting in Multi-racial Britain.* York, UK: Joseph Rowntree Foundation.

Barn, R, Ladino, C and Rogers, B (2006) *Parenting in Multi-Racial Britain.* York, UK: Joseph Rowntree Foundation.

Barnardo's (2011) *Reaching Families in Need: Learning from Practice in Barnardo's Children's Centres.* Essex, UK: Barnardo's.

Barth, F (1969) *Ethnic Groups and Boundaries.* Oslo, Norway: Scandinavian University Books.

Bartholomew, K and Shaver, P R (1998) *Methods of Assessing Adult Attachment: Do They Converge?* In: Simpson, J A and Rholes, W S (Eds.) *Attachment Theory and Close Relationships* (pp. 25–45). New York: The Guilford Press.

Bates, R (1983) *Modernisation Ethnic Competition and the Rationality of Politics in Contemporary Africa.* In: Rothchild, D and Olorunsola, V (Eds.) *State Versus Ethnic Claims: African Policy Dilemmas.* Boulder, CO: Westview Press.

Bateson, G (1972) *Steps to an Ecology of Mind: Collected Essays in Anthropology, Psychiatry, Evolution, and Epistemology.* Chicago, IL: University of Chicago Press.

Batool, S and Mumtaz, A N (2015) *Development and Validation of Parenting Style Scales.* Pakistan Journal of Psychological Research, Vol. 30 (2).

Baumrind, D (1967) *Child Care Practices Anteceding Three Patterns of Preschool Behaviour.* Genetic Psychology Monographs, Vol. 75: pp. 43–88.

Baumrind, D (1968) *Authoritarian v. Authoritative Parental Control.* Adolescence, Vol. 3: pp. 255–271.

Baumrind, D (1991) *The Influence of Parenting Style on Adolescent Competence and Substance Use.* Journal of Adolescence, Vol. 11: pp. 56–95.

Bayer, M (2009) *Reconsidering Primordialism: An Alternative Approach to the Study of Ethnicity.* Ethnic and Racial Studies, Vol. 32 (9): pp. 1639–1657.

Bebbington, A C and Beecham, J (2003) *Children in Need 2001: Ethnicity and Service Use.* PSSRU University of Kent. Canterbury, England.

Becher, H and Husain, F (2003) *Supporting Minority Ethnic Families: South Asian Hindus and Muslims in Britain: Developments in Family Support.* London: National Family and Parenting Institute.

Beishon, S, Modood, T and Virdee, S (1998) *Ethnic Minority Families.* London: Policy Studies Institute.

Bell, M (2007) *Safeguarding Children and Case Conferences.* In: Wilson, K and James, A (Eds.) *The Child Protection Handbook.* Third Edition (pp. 283–300). London: Balliere Tindall.

Bell, M, Shaw, I, Sinclair, I, Sloper, P and Rafferty, J (2007) *An Evaluation of the Practice, Process and Consequences of the ICS in Councils with Social Services Responsibilities.* York, UK: University of York.

Belsky, J (1984) *Determinants of Parenting: A Process Model.* Child Development, Vol. 55: pp. 83–96.

Belsky, J, Fish, M and Isabella, R A (1991) *Continuity and Discontinuity in Infant Negative and Positive Emotionality: Family Antecedents and Attachment Consequences.* Developmental Psychology, Vol. 27 (3): pp. 421–431.

Belsky, J and Jaffe, S R (2006) *The Multiple Determinants of Parenting.* In: Cicchetti, D and Cohen, D (Eds.) *Developmental Psychopathology: Risk, Disorder and Adaptation.* Second Edition. New York: Wiley.

Benson, J B and Marshall, M H (Eds.) (2009) *Social and Emotional Development in Infancy and Early Childhood.* Cambridge, MA: Academic Press.

Bernard, C and Gupta, A (2006) *Black African Children and the Child Protection System.* The British Journal of Social Work, Vol. 38 (3): pp. 476–492.

Bernard, C and Harris, P (2016) *Safeguarding Black Children: Good Practice in Child Protection.* London: Jessica Kingsley Publishers.

Berreman, G D (1981) *Social Inequality: A Cross-Cultural Approach.* In: Berreman, G D (Ed.) *Social Inequality: Comparative and Developmental Approaches.* New York: Academic Press.

Berrie, L and Mendes, P (2011) *The Experiences of Unaccompanied Asylum-Seeking Children in and Leaving the Out-of-Home Care System in the UK and Australia: A Critical Review of the Literature.* International Social Work, Vol. 54 (4): pp. 485–503.

Berry, J W (2005) *Acculturation: Living Successfully in Two Cultures.* International Journal of Intercultural Relations, Vol. 29 (6): pp. 697–712.

Berry, J W, Phinney, J S, Sam, D L and Vedder, P (2006) *Immigrant Youth in Cultural Transition.* Mahwah, NJ: Erlbaum.

Berscheid, E and Regan, P (2005) *The Psychology of Interpersonal Relationships.* New York: Psychology Press.

Bhatti-Sinclair, K (2011) *Anti-Racist Practice in Social Work.* Basingstoke: Palgrave MacMillan.

Biehal, N (2005) *Working with Adolescents: Supporting Families, Preventing Breakdown.* London: BAAF.

Bogdan, R and Taylor, S J (1975) *Introduction to Qualitative Research Methods: A Phenomenological Approach to the Social Sciences.* New York: Wiley.

Booth, M (2002) *Arab Adolescents Facing the Future: Enduring Ideals and Pressures for Change.* In: Brown, B B, Larson, R and Sarsawthi, T S (Eds.) *The World's Youth: Adolescence in Eight Regions of the Globe.* New York: Cambridge University Press.

Bornstein, M H (2012) *Cultural Approaches to Parenting.* Parenting, Science and Practice, Vol. 12: pp. 212–221.

Bornstein, M H (2013a) *Approaches to Parenting in Culture.* Parenting: Science and Practice, Vol. 12: pp. 212–221.

Bornstein, M H (Ed.) (2013b) *Cultural Approaches to Parenting.* Hillsdale, NJ: Lawrence Erlbaum Associates.

Bornstein, M H (2013c) *Parenting and Child Mental Health: A Cross Cultural Perspective.* World Psychiatry, Vol. 12 (3): pp. 258–265.

Bornstein, M H (2019) *A Developmentalist's Viewpoint: "It's About Time!" Ecological Systems, Transaction, and Specificity as Key Developmental Principles in Children's Changing Worlds.* In: Parke, R and Elder Jr., G (Eds.) *Children in Changing Worlds:*

Sociocultural and Temporal Perspectives (pp. 277–286). New York: Cambridge University Press.

Bornstein, M H and Lansford, J E (2010) *Parenting*. In: Bornstein, M H (Ed.) *Handbook of Cultural Developmental Science* (pp. 259–277). New York: Psychology Press.

Bornstein, M H, Putnick, D and Suwalsky, J T D (2018) *Parenting Cognition to Parenting Practices to Child Adjustment? The Standard Model*. Development and Psychopathology, Vol. 30 (2): pp. 399–416.

Bowlby, J (1951) *Maternal Care and Mental Health*. Geneva, Switzerland: World Health Organisation.

Bowling, A (2002) *Research Methods in Health*. Buckingham, UK: Open University Press.

Bradshaw, J (Ed.) (2016) *The Wellbeing of Children in the UK*. Fourth Edition. Bristol, UK: Policy Press.

Bradshaw, J, Stimson, C, Skinner, C and Williams, J (1999) *Absent Fathers*. London: Routledge.

Brandon, M, Bailey, S, Belderson, P, Gardner, R, Sidebotham, P, Dodsworth, J, Warren, C and Black, J (2009) *Understanding Serious Case Reviews and Their Impact: A Biennial Analysis of Serious Case Reviews 2005–07*. Research Report DCSF-RR129. University of East Anglia.

Brandon, M, Belderson, P, Warren, C, Howe, D, Gardner, R, Dodsworth, J and Black, J (2008) *Analysing Child Deaths and Serious Injury through Abuse and Neglect: What Can We Learn? A Biennial Analysis of Serious Case Reviews 2003–2005*. Nottingham: Department for Children, Schools and Families.

Brechwald, W A and Prinstein, M J (2011) *Beyond Homophily: A Decade of Advances in Understanding Peer Influence Processes*. Journal of Research on Adolescence, Vol. 21 (1): pp. 166–179.

Broadhurst, K, Grover, C and Jamieson, J (Eds.) (2009) *Critical Perspectives on Safeguarding Children*. Chichester, UK: Wiley-Blackwell.

Broadhurst, K, Hall, C, Wastell, D, White, S and Pithouse, A (2010) *Risk, Instrumentalism and the Humane Project in Social Work: Identifying the Informal Logics of Risk Management in Children's Statutory Services*. The British Journal of Social Work, Vol. 40 (4): pp. 1046–1064.

Broadhurst, K, Wastell, D, White, S, Hall, C, Peckover, S, Thompson, K, Pithouse, A and Davey, D (2009) *Performing Initial Assessment: Identifying the Latent Conditions for Error at the Front-Door in Local Authority Children's Services*. British Journal of Social Work, Vol. 40 (2): pp. 352–370.

Brody, G, Dorsey, S, Forehand, R and Armindstead, L (2002) *Unique and Protective Contributions of Parenting and Classroom Processes to the Adjustment of African American Children Living in Single-Parent Families*. Child Development, Vol. 73: pp. 274–284.

Brody, G H and Flor, D L (1998) *Maternal Resources, Parenting Practices, and Child Competence in Rural, Single-Parent, African American Families*. Child Development, Vol. 69: 803–816.

Bronfenbrenner, U (1979) *The Ecology of Human Development*. Cambridge, MA: Harvard University Press.

Brooks, J (1987) *The Process of Parenting*. Second Edition. Mountain View, CA: Mayfield Publishing Company.

Brown, K W, West, A M, Loverich, T M and Biegel, G M (2011) *Assessing Adolescent Mindfulness: Validation of an Adapted Mindful Attention Awareness Scale in Adolescent Normative and Psychiatric Populations*. Psychological Assessment, Vol. 23 (4): pp. 1023–1033.

Brubaker, R (1996) *Nationalism Reframed: Nationhood and the National Question in the New Europe* (pp. 13–22). Cambridge: Cambridge University Press.

Bruner, J (1986) *Actual Minds, Possible Worlds*. Cambridge, MA: Harvard University Press.

Bryman, A and Burgess, R G (Eds.) (1994) *Analyzing Qualitative Data*. First Edition. London: Routledge.

Bryne, M K, Eve, M P and Gagliardi, C R (2014) *What Is Good Parenting? The Perspectives of Professionals*. Family Court Review, Vol. 52 (1): pp. 114–127.

Buckley, S, Bird, G, Sacks, B and Archer, T (2006) *A Comparison of Mainstream and Special Education for Teenagers with Down Syndrome: Implications for Parents and Teachers*. Down Syndrome Research and Practice, Vol. 9 (3): pp. 54–67.

Budd, K S (2001) *Assessing Parenting Competence in Child Protection Cases: A Clinical Practice Model*. Clinical Child and Family Psychology Review, Vol. 4 (1): pp. 4–18.

Budd, K S (2005) *Assessing Parenting Capacity in a Child Welfare Context*. Children and Youth Services Review, Vol. 27: pp. 429–444.

Budd, K S and Holdsworth, M I (1996) *Issues in Clinical Assessment of Minimal Parenting Competence*. Journal of Clinical Child Psychology, Vol. 25: pp. 1–14.

Budd, K S, Poindexter L M, Felix, E D and Naik-Polan, A T (2001) *Clinical Assessment of Parents in Child Protection Cases: An Empirical Analysis*. Law and Human Behavior, Vol. 25: pp. 93–108.

Burr, V (1995) *An Introduction to Social Constructionism*. London: Taylor & Frances/ Routledge.

Burt, S A, Barnes, A R, McGue, M and Iacono, W G (2008) *Parental Divorce and Adolescent Delinquency: Ruling Out the Impact of Common Genes*. Developmental Psychology, Vol. 44 (6): pp. 1668–1677.

Butler, I and Williamson, H (1994) *Children Speak: Children, Trauma and Social Work*. London: Penguin Longman Publishing.

Butt, J and Mirza, K (1996) *Social Care and Black Communities*. London: HMSO.

Bywaters, P, Brady, G, Bunting, L, Daniel, Featherstone, B, Jones, C, Morris, K, Scourfield, J, Sparks, T and Webb, C (2017) *Inequalities in English Child Protection Practice Under Austerity: A Universal Challenge?* Hoboken, NJ: John Wiley and Sons.

Bywaters, P, Brady, G, Sparks, T and Bos, E (2016) *Child Welfare Inequalities: New Evidence, Further Questions*. Child and Family Social Work, Vol. 21 (3): pp. 369–380.

Caldwell, B M and Bradley, R H (1984) *Home Observations for Measurement of the Environment*. Fayetteville, AR: University of Arkansas.

Caliendo, S M and McIlwain, C D (2011) *The Routledge Companion to Race and Ethnicity*. London: Routledge.

Cameron, G, Coady, N and Adams, G (2007) *Moving towards Positive Systems of Child and Family Welfare: Current Issues and Future Directions*. Ontario, Canada: Wilfred Laurier University Press.

Carra, C, Lavelli, M, Keller, H and Kartner, J (2013) *Parenting Infants: Socialisation Goals and Behaviour of Italian Mothers from West Africa*. Journal of Cross-Cultural Psychology, Vol. 44 (8): pp. 1304–1320.

Cashmore, E (2004) *Encyclopedia of Race and Ethnic Studies*. London: Routledge.

Chahal, K and Ullah, I (2004) *Experiencing Ethnicity: Discrimination and Service Provision*. York: Joseph Rowntree Foundation.

Chamberlayne, P, Rustin, M and Wengraf, T (Eds.) (2002) *Biography and Social Policy in Europe: Experiences and Life Journeys*. Bristol, England: The Policy Press.

Chan, H T V (2012) *Understanding the Practice of Frontline Child Protection Social Workers with Black, Asian and Minority Ethnic (BAME) Families*. Queensgate, Huddersfield: The University of Huddersfield.

Chand, A (2000) *The Over Representation of Black Children in the Child Protection System: Possible Causes, Consequences and Solutions*. Child and Family Social Work, Vol. 5: pp. 67–77.

Chand, A (2001) *The Over Representation of Black Children in the Child Protection System: Possible Causes, Consequences and Solutions*. Child and Family Social Work, Vol. 5 (1): pp. 67–77.

Chandra, K (2004) *Why Ethnic Parties Succeed*. New York: Cambridge University Press.

Chandra, K and Wilkinson S (2008) *Measuring the Effect of "Ethnicity"*. Comparative Political Studies, Vol. 41 (4–5): pp. 515–563.

Chao, R (1994) *Beyond Parental Control and Authoritarian Parenting Style: Understanding Chinese Parenting through the Cultural Notion of Training*. Child Development, Vol. 65: pp. 1111–1119.

Chao, R (2000) *The Parenting of Immigrant Chinese and European American Mothers: Relations between Parenting Styles, Socialisation Goals and Parental Practices*. Journal of Applied Developmental Psychology, Vol. 21 (2): pp. 233–248.

Chase, E (2010) *Agency and Silence: Young People Seeking Asylum Alone in the UK*. British Journal of Social Work, Vol. 40 (7): pp. 23–37.

Cheetham, J, Fuller, R, Mcivor, G and Petch, A (1992) *Evaluating Social Work Effectiveness*. Buckingham, England: Open University Press.

Chen, X, Bian, Y, Xin, T, Wang, L and Silbereisen, R K (2010) *Perceived Social Change and Childrearing Attitudes in China*. European Psychologist, Vol. 15 (4): pp. 260–270.

Chess, S and Thomas, A (1999) *Goodness of Fit: Clinical Applications for Infancy through Adult Life*. Philadelphia, PA: Bruner/Mazel.

Children Act (1908) https://www.legislation.gov.uk/ukpga/Edw7/8/67/contents/enacted

Children Act (1975) https://www.legislation.gov.uk/ukpga/1976/36/contents

Children Act (1989) https://www.legislation.gov.uk/ukpga/1989/41/contents, accessed 3rd March 2020.

Children Act (2004) https://www.legislation.gov.uk/ukpga/2004/31/contents

Childcare Act (2006) https://www.legislation.gov.uk/ukpga/2006/21

Children and Adoption Act (2008) https://www.legislation.gov.uk/ukpga/2008/23/pdfs/ukpga_20080023_en.pdf

Children and Young People Act (1932) https://www.legislation.gov.uk/ukpga/Geo5/23-24/12, accessed 4th March 2020.

Children and Young Persons Act (1963) https://www.legislation.gov.uk/ukpga/1963/37

Children and Young Persons Act (1969) https://www.legislation.gov.uk/ukpga/1969/54/contents

Children and Young Persons Act (2008) https://www.legislation.gov.uk/ukpga/2008/23/contents

Chimba, M, Davey, D, Villiers, T and Khan, A (2012) *Protecting Black and Minority Ethnic Children: An Investigation of Child Protection Interventions of Child Protection Interventions*. Cardiff, Wales: Bawso.

Choate, P W (2009) *Parenting Capacity Assessment in Child Protection Cases*. The Forensic Examiner, Vol. 18 (1): pp. 52–59.

Chodorow, N (1978) *The Reproduction of Mothering: Psychoanalysis and the Sociology of Gender*. Berkeley, CA: University of California Press.

Chuang, S S and Tamis-LeMonda, C (2009) *Gender Roles in Immigrant Families: Parenting Views, Practices and Child Development*. Sex Roles, Vol. 60 (7–8): pp. 451–455.

Clair, M and Denis, J S (2015) *Sociology of Racism*. In: Wright, J D (Eds.) *The International Encyclopaedia of the Social and Behavioural Sciences* (Vol. 19, pp. 857–863). Burlington: Elsevier Science.

Clandinin, D J (2006) *Narrative Inquiry: A Methodology for Studying Lived Experience*. Research Studies in Music Education, Vol. 27: pp. 44–54.

Clandinin, D J and Connelly, F M (2000) *Narrative Inquiry: Experience and Story in Qualitative Research*. San Francisco, CA: Jossey-Bass.

Cleaver, H and Freeman, P (1995) *Parental Perspectives in Cases of Suspected Child Abuse*. London: HMSO.

Cleaver, H, Nicholson, D, Tarr, S and Cleaver, D (2007) *Child Protection, Domestic Violence and Parental Substance Misuse: Family Experiences and Effective Practice*. London: Jessica Kingsley Publishers.

Cleaver, H and Unell, I (2011) *Children's Needs-Parenting Capacity: Child Abuse, Parental Mental Illness, Learning Disability, Substance Misuse and Domestic Violence*. Bristol, UK: The Stationary Office.

Cleaver, H, Unell, I and Aldgate, J (2011) *Children's Needs – Parenting Capacity*. London: Her Majesty's Stationary Office.

Cleaver, H and Walker, S (2004) *From Policy to Practice: The Implementation of New Framework for Social Work Assessment of Children and Families*. Child and Family Social Work, Vol. 9 (1): pp. 81–90.

Cleveland (1988) *The Report of the Butler-Sloss Inquiry into Child Abuse in Cleveland*. HMSO, Cm 412.

Coakley, J (2012) *Primordialims and the Study of Nationalism. The Multicultural Dilemma: Migration, Ethnic Politics and State Intermediation*. London, UK: Taylor and Francis Group.

Coffey, A and Atkinson, P (1996) *Making Sense of Qualitative Data, Complementary Research Strategies*. London, Thousand Oaks, CA and New Delhi: Sage Publications.

Cohen, A (1969) *Custom and Politics in Urban Africa: A Study of Hansa Migrants in a Yoruba Town*. London: Routledge and Kegan.

Cohen, A (1974) *Two-Dimensional Man: An Essay on Power and Symbolism in Complex Society*. London: Routledge.

Cohen, L, Manion, L and Morrison, K (2000) *Research Methods in Education*. Fifth Edition. London: Routledge.

Cohn, H W (2002) *Heidegger and the Roots of Existential Therapy*. London: Continuum.

Collier, P and Hoeffler, A (2004) *Green and Grievance in Civil War*. Oxford Economic Papers, Issue 56: pp. 563–595.

Collins, W A, Maccoby, E E, Steinberg, L, Hetherington, E M and Bornstein, M H (2000) *Contemporary Research on Parenting: The Case for Nature and Nurture*. American Psychologist, Vol. 55, pp. 218–232.

Comunian, A and Gielen, U (Eds.) (2001) *International Perspectives on Human Development*. Lengerich, Germany: Pabst.

Connelly, F M and Clandinin, D J (1990) *Stories of Experience and Narrative Inquiry*. Educational Researcher, Vol. 19 (5): pp. 2–14.

Conley, C (2003) *A Review of Parenting Capacity Assessment Reports*. Ontario Association of Children's Aid Societies, Vol. 43 (3): pp. 16–22.

Corby, B (2000) *Towards a Knowledge Base*. Buckingham, UK: Open University Press.

Corby, B, Millar, M and Pope, A (2002) *Assessing Children in Need Assessments: A Parental Perspective*. Practice, Vol. 14: pp. 5–15.

Cornell, S and Hartmann, D (1998) *Ethnicity and Race: Make Identities in a Changing World*. Thousand Oaks, CA: Pine Forge Press.

Cottle, T J (1972) *The Garden of Children: Education in the Suburbs*. Urban Education, Vol. 6 (4): pp. 373–392.

Cox, D H and Cox, M J (2000) *Families with Young Children: A Review of Research in the 1990s*. Journal of Family, Marriage, Vol. 62 (4): pp. 876–895.

Crabtree, B and Miller, W (Eds.) (1999) *Doing Qualitative Research*. Second Edition. London, UK: Sage.

Craig, C, Glendinning, C and Clarke, K (1996) *Policy on the Hoof: The British Child Support Act in Practice*. In: May, M, Brunsdon, E and Craig, G (Eds.) *Social Policy Review*. London: SPA.

Crawford, J (2011) *Bringing It Together: Assessing Parenting Capacity in the Child Protection Context*. Social Work Now: pp. 18–26.

Creasy, R and Trikha, S (2004) *Meeting Parents' Needs for Information: Evidence from the 2001 Home Office Citizenship Survey (Home Office Online Report 48/04)*. London: Home Office.

Creswell, J W (1994) *Research Design: Qualitative and Quantitative Approaches*. Thousand Oaks, CA: Sage.

Creswell, J W (2009) *Research Design: Qualitative, Quantitative, and Mixed Methods Approaches*. Third Edition. Los Angeles, CA: Sage Publications.

Dahlberg, K (2006) *The Essence of Essences: The Search for Meaning Structures in Phenomenological Analysis of Lifeworld Phenomena*. International Journal of Qualitative Studies on Health and Wellbeing, Vol. 1 (1): pp. 11–19.

Dalzell, R and Sawyer, E (2007) *Putting Analysis into Assessment: Undertaking Assessment of Need – A Toolkit for Practitioners*. London: National Children's Bureau.

Dalzell, R and Sawyer, E (Eds.) (2011) *Putting Analysis into Assessment: Understanding Assessment of Need*. Second Edition. London: National Children's Bureau Enterprises.

Daniel, B, Taylor, J and Scott, J (2009) *Recognition of Neglect and Early Response: Summary of a Systematic Literature Review*. International Journal of Child and Family Welfare, Vol. 12 (4): pp. 120–133.

Daniel, B, Taylor, J and Scott, J (2011) *Recognizing and Helping the Neglected Child: Evidence-Based Practice for Assessment and Intervention*. London: Jessica Kingsley.

Darling, N (1999) *Parenting Style and Its Correlates*. Champaign, IL: ERIC Clearinghouse on Elementary and Early Childhood Education.

Darling, N, Cumsille, P, Cadwell, L and Dowdy, B (2006) *Predictors of Adolescent Disclosure to Parents and Perceived Parental Knowledge: Between and Within Person Differences*. Journal of Youth and Adolescence, Vol. 35: pp. 659–670.

Darling, N and Steinberg, L (1993) *Parenting Styles as a Context: An Integrative Model*. Psychology Bulletin, Vol. 113: pp. 487–496.

Data Protection Act (1998) London, UK: Office of Public Sector Information (OPSI).

Dautenhahn, K (2000) *Socially Intelligent Agents and the Primate Social Brain: Towards a Science of Social Minds*. Proc. AAAI Fall Symposium Socially Intelligent Agents — The Human in the Loop. AAAI Technical Report FS-00-04, AAAI Press, pp. 35–51.

Davies, G (1998) *Child Support in Action*. Oxford: Hart Publishing.

DeMause, L (1974) *The Evolution of Childhood*. In: DeMause, L (Ed.) *The History of Childhood: The Untold Story of Child Abuse* (pp. 1–73). New York: Peter Bedrick Books.

Demo, D H and Cox, M J (2000) *Families with Young Children: A Review of Research in the 1990s*. Journal of Family, Marriage, Vol. 62 (4): pp. 876–895.

Denzin, N K (1989) *Interpretive Biography*. Thousand Oaks, CA: Sage.

Department of Health (1991) *Welfare of Children and Young People in Hospital*. London, UK: HMSO.

Department of Health (1999a) *Working Together under the Children Act 1989: A Guide to Arrangements for Inter-Agency Co-Operation for the Protection of Children from Abuse*. London: HMSO.

Department of Health (1999b) *Working Together to Safeguard Children*. London: The Stationary Office.

Department of Health (2000) *Framework for the Assessment of Children in Need and Their Families*. London: HMSO.

Department of Health (2000) Studies Which Inform the Development of the Framework for the Assessment of Children in Need and their Families. London, UK: The Stationary Office.

Department of Health, Home Office, and Department for Education and Employment (2000) *Framework for the Assessment of Children in Need and Their Families*. London: The Stationary Office.

Ditch, J, Barnes, H, Bradshaw, J, Commaille, J and Eardley, T (1995) *A Synthesis of National Family Policies 1994*. European Observatory on National Family Policies, York, United Kingdom: University of York.

Dixon, S D, Tronick, E Z, Keefer, C and Brazelton, T B (1981) *Mother-Infant Interaction among the Gusii of Kenya*. In: Field, T M, Sostek, A M, Wielzer, P and Leiderman, P H (Eds.) *Culture and Early Interactions*. Hillsdale, NJ: Lawrence Erlbaum Associates.

Doherty, P, Stott, A and Kinder, K (2004) *Delivering Services to Hard to Reach Families in On Track Areas: Definitions, Consultations and Needs Assessment. Home Office Development and Practice Report No. 15*. London: Home Office.

Dominelli, L (2002) *Feminist Theory*. In: Davies, M (Ed.) *The Blackwell Companion of Social Work*. London: Blackwell Publishing.

Dominelli, L (2002a) *Anti Oppressive Practice*. Second Edition. London, UK: Palgrave.

Dominelli, L (2017) *Anti-Racist Social Work*. London: MacMillan International.

Dominelli, L, Lorenz, W and Soydan, H (Eds.) (2001) *Beyond Racial Divides: Ethnicities in Social Work Practice*. Hampshire, UK: Ashgate.

Dornbusch, S, Ritter, P, Leiderman, P, Roberts, D and Fraleigh, M (1987) *The Relation of Parenting Style to Adolescent School Performance*. Child Development, Vol. 58 (5): pp. 1244–1257.

Drinkwater, S and Robinson, C (2011) *Welfare Participation by Immigrants in the UK*. IZA – Institute of the Study of Labour. Bonn, Germany.

Dumbrill, G (2006) *Ontario's Child Welfare Transformation: Another Swing of the Pendulum*. Canadian Social Work Review, Vol. 23 (1–2).

Dutt, R and Phillips, M (2000) *Assessing Black Children in Need and Their Families*. In: *Department of Health (Ed.), Assessing Children in Need and Their Families, Practice Guidance*. London: The Stationery Office.

Dutt, R and Phillips, M (2010) *Assessing the Needs of BME Children and Families*. In: Howarth, J (Ed.) *The Child's World: A Comprehensive Guide to Assessing Children in Need*. London: Jessica Kingsleigh.

Dwairy, M and Achoui, M (2010) *Parental Control: A Second Cross-Cultural Research on Parenting and Psychological Adjustment of Children*. Journal of Child and Family Studies, Vol. 19 (1): pp. 16–22.

Eller, J D and Coughlan, R (1993) *The Poverty of Primordialism: The Demystification of Ethnic Attachments*. Ethnic and Racial Studies, Vol. 16: pp. 183–202.

Ellison, G (2005) *Population, Profiting and Public Health Risk: When and How Should We Use Race/Ethnicity?* Critical Public Health, Vol. 5 (1): pp. 65–74.

Entman, R M (1993) *Framing: Towards Clarification of a Fractured Paradigm.* Journal of Communication, Vol. 43 (4): pp. 51–58.

Erikson, E H (1963) *Youth: Change and Challenge.* New York: Basic Books.

Ezzy, D (2002) *Qualitative Analysis: Practice and Innovation.* St Leonards, New South Wales: Allen and Unwin.

Farmer, E and Lutman, E (2012) *Effective Working with Neglected Children and Their Families.* London: Jessica Kingsley.

Farmer, E and Owen, M (1995) *Child Protection Practice: Private Risks and Public Remedies – Decision Making, Intervention and Outcome in Child Protection Work.* London: HMSO.

Farmer, E, Sturgess, W and O'Neill, T (2008) *The Reunification of Looked after Children with Their Parents: Patterns Interventions and Outcomes.* Report to the Department for Children, Schools and Families, School for Policy Studies, University of Bristol.

Farrington, D P (2002) *Key Results from the First Forty Years of the Cambridge Study in Delinquent Development.* In: Thornberry, T P and Krohan, M D (Eds.) *Longitudinal Research in the Social and Behavioural Science.* New York: Kluwer and Plenum.

Fearon, J and Laitin, D (1996) *Explaining Inter Ethnic Cooperation.* American Political Review, Vol. 90 (4): pp. 713–735.

Featherstone, B, Morris, K, White, S and White, S (2014) *Re-imagining Social Work with Families.* Bristol, UK: Policy Press.

Fenton, S (1999) *Ethnicity: Social Structure, Culture and Identity in the Modern World.* London: MacMillan.

Fenton, S (2003) *Ethnicity.* Cambridge: Polity Press.

Fergus, S and Zimmerman, M A (2005) *Adolescent Resilience: A Framework for Understanding Healthy Development in the Face of Risk.* Annual Reviews of Public Health, Vol. 26: pp. 399–419.

Ferguson, H (2011) *Child Protection Practice.* First Edition. London: Palgrave McMillan.

Finlay, L (2009) *Ambiguous Encounters: A Relational Approach to Phenomenological Research.* Indo-Pacific Journal of Phenomenology, Vol. 3: pp. 6–25.

Flegel, M (2007) *"Facts and Their Meaning": Child Protection, Intervention, and the National Society for the Prevention of Cruelty to Children in Late Nineteenth-Century England.* Victorian Review, Vol. 33 (1): pp. 87–101.

Fletcher, A, Bonell, C and Hargreaves, J (2008) *School Effects on Young People's Drug Use: A Systematic Review of Interventions and Observational Studies.* Journal of Adolescent Health, Vol. 42 (3): pp. 209–220.

Fontes, L A (2002) *Child Discipline and Physical Abuse in Immigrant Latino Families: Reducing Violence and Misunderstanding.* Journal of Counselling and Development, Vol. 80: pp. 31–40.

Foulk, S M (2007) *Parenting Children of Affluence.* Proquest, accessed 23rd November 2011.

Fraser, H (2004) *Doing Narrative Research: Analysing Personal Stories Line by Line.* Qualitative Social Work, Vol. 3 (2): pp. 179–201.

Freedman, J and Combs, G (1996) *Narrative Therapy: The Social Construction of Preferred Realities.* W W Norton and Co. London, United Kingdom.

Garcia-Coll, C T, Meyer, E C and Brillion, L (1995) *Ethnic and Minority Parents.* In: Bornstein, M H (Ed.) *Handbook of Parenting*, Vol. II. Hillsdale, NJ: Lawrence Erlbaum Associates.

Gardner, M and Steinberg, L (2005) *Peer Influence on Risk Taking, Risk Preference, and Risky Decision Making in Adolescence and Adulthood: An Experimental Study*. Developmental Psychology, Vol. 41 (4): pp. 625–635.

Geertz, C (1973) *The Interpretation of Culture*. New York: Basic Books.

Geertz, C (1996) *Primordial Ties*. In: Hutchinson, J and Smith, A D (Eds.) *Ethnicity*. Oxford: Oxford University Press.

Gelfand, D E and Fandetti, D V (1986) *The Emergent Nature of Ethnicity: Dilemmas in Assessment*. Social Casework, Vol. 67 (9): pp. 542–550.

Gibbons, J, Conroy, S and Bell, C (1995) *Operating the Child Protection System*. London: HMSO.

Gibbs, A (1997) *Focus Groups*. Social Research Update, Vol. 19 (8): pp. 1–8.

Giddens, A (Ed.) (1993) *Sociology: Introductory Reading*. Cambridge: Polity.

Gillborn, D and Mirza, H S (2000) *Educational Inequality: Mapping Race, Class and Gender*. London: Ofsted.

Gilmore, D D (1990) *Manhood in the Making: Cultural Concepts of Masculinity*. New Haven, CT: Yale University Press.

Giorgi, A (1994) *A Phenomenological Perspective on Certain Qualitative Research Methods*. Journal of Phenomenological Psychology, Vol. 25: pp. 190–220.

Goffman, E (1974) *Frame Analysis: An Essay on the Organization of Experience*. Cambridge, MA: Harvard University Press.

Golombok, S (2014) *Parenting: What Really Counts*. London: Routledge.

Gonzales, N A, Cauce, A M, Friedman, R J and Mason, C A (1996) *Family, Peer and Neighbourhood Influences on Academic Achievement Among African American Adolescents: One Year Prospective Effects*. American Journal of Community Psychology, Vol. 24: pp. 365–387.

Gottlieb, G (1998) *Normally Occurring Environmental and Behavioral Influences on Gene Activity: From Central Dogma to Probabilistic Epigenesis*. Psychological Review, Vol. 105 (4): pp. 792–802.

Green, G B, Rose, S, Bernard, M and Kitzinger, J (1993) *Who Wears the Trousers? Sexual Harassment in Research Settings*. Women's Studies International Forum, Vol. 16: pp. 627–637.

Greenberg, L S, Rice, L N and Elliot, R (1993) *Facilitating Emotional Change: The Moment-by-Moment Process*. New York: The Guilford Press.

Greenfield, P M and Cocking, R R (Eds.) (2014) *Cross Cultural Roots of Minority Child Development*. Columbia, MD: Psychology Press Limited.

Greenfield, P, Keller, H, Fuligni, A J and Maynard, A (2003) *Cultural Pathways Through Universal Development*. Annual Review of Psychology, Vol. 54: pp. 461–490.

Gupta, A and Blewett, J (2008) *Involving Services Users in Social Work Training On the Reality of Family Poverty*. Social Work Education. London, UK: Routledge.

Gupta, A, Featherstone, B and White, S (2016) *Reclaiming Humanity: From Capacities and Capabilities in Understanding Parenting in Adversity*. British Journal of Social Work, Vol, 46 (2): pp. 339–354.

Halling, S, Leifer, M and Rowe, J O (2006) *Emergence of the Dialogal Approach: Forgiving Another*. In: Fischer, C T (Ed.) *Qualitative Research Methods for Psychology: Introduction through Empirical Studies* (pp. 247–278). New York: Academic Press.

Handelman, H (1996) *The Challenge of Third World Development*. Upper Saddle River, NJ: Prentice-Hall Inc.

Harris, J R (1998) *The Nature Assumption: Why Children Turn Out the Way They Do*. Free Press. New York, USA.

Harwood, R L, Leyendecker, B, Carlson, V J, Asencio, M and Miller, A (2002) *Parenting among Latino Families in the United States*. In: Bornstein, M H (Ed.) *Handbook of Parenting: Social Conditions and Applied Parenting*. Second Edition, Vol. 2. Hillsdale, NJ: Lawrence Erlbaum Associates.

Hawes, J M (1985) *American Childhood: A Research Guide and Historical Handbook*. Nineth Edition. Westport, CT: Greenwood Press.

Hayes, M and Williams, C (1999) *Family Law: Principles, Policy and Practice*. London: Butterworths.

Hays, S (1996) *The Cultural Contradictions of Motherhood*. New Haven, CT: Yale University Press.

Heidegger, M (2000) *Introduction to Metaphysics* (Fried, P and Polt, R, Translation). New Haven, CT: Yale University Press.

Heilmann, A, Kelly, Y and Watt, R G (2015) *Equally Protected? A Review of the Evidence on the Physical Punishment of Children*. Scotland: NSPCC.

Held, D, McgGrew, A, Goldblatt, D and Perraton, J (1999) *Global Transformations Revisions: Politics, Economics and Culture*. Cambridge: Policy Press.

Helm, D (2010) *Making Sense of Child and Family Assessment: How to Interpret Children's Needs*. London: Jessica Kingsley Publishers.

Henry, B and Cabot, A M (Eds.) (1996) *Theories of Ethnicity: A Classical Reader*. New York: Werner Sollors.

Herman, H J and Kempen, H J (1998) *Moving Cultures: The Perilous Problem of Cultural Dichotomies in a Globalising Society*. American Psychologist, Vol. 53 (10): pp. 1111.

Herrnstein, R J and Murray, C (1994) *The Bell Curve: Intelligence and Class Structures in American Life*. New York: Free Press.

Hetherington, E M (2006) *The Influence of Conflict, Marital Problem Solving and Parenting on Children's Adjustment in Nondivorced, Divorced and Remarried Families*. In: Clarke-Stewart, A and Dunn, J (Eds.) *The Jacobs Foundation Series on Adolescence. Families Count: Effects on Child and Adolescent Development* (pp. 203–237). Cambridge: Cambridge University Press.

Hewlett, B S, Lamb, M E, Shannon, D, Leyendecker, B and Scholmerich, A (1998) *Culture and Early Infancy among Central African Foragers and Farmers*. Developmental Psychology, Vol. 34 (4): p. 653.

Heywood, C (2001) *A History of Childhood: Children in the West from Medieval to Modern Times*. Cambridge: Polity Press.

Hill, A and Shaw, I (2011) *Social Work and ICT*. London: Sage.

Hill, A K (2012) *Help for Children after Child Sexual Abuse: Using a Qualitative Approach to Design and Test Therapeutic Interventions that May Include Non-Offending Parents*. Qualitative Social Work, Vol. 11 (4): pp. 362–378.

Hill, N E (2006) *Disentangling Ethnicity, Socioeconomic Status and Parenting: Interactions, Influences and Meaning*. Vulnerable Children and Youth Studies, Vol. 1 (1): pp. 114–124.

Hinchman, L P and Hinchman, S K (Eds.) (1997) *SUNY Series in the Philosophy of the Social Sciences. Memory, Identity, Community: The Idea of Narrative in the Human Sciences*. New York: State University of New York Press.

Hinginbotham, A L (1996) *Shades of Freedom*. New York: Oxford University Press.

HM Government (1989) *Children Act, 1989 (c41)*. London: The Stationery Office.

HM Government (2004) https://www.legislation.gov.uk/ukpga/2004/31/contents, accessed 3rd March 2020.

HM Government (2006) *Working Together to Safeguard Children: A Guide to Inter-Agency Working to Safeguard and Promote the Welfare of Children*. London: The Stationary Office.

HM Government (2010) *Working Together to Safeguard Children: A Guide to Inter-Agency Working to Safeguard and Promote the Welfare of Children*. Nottingham. Department of Children, Schools and Family.

HM Government (2013) *Working Together to Safeguard Children: A Guide to Inter-Agency to Safeguard and Promote the Welfare of Children*. London: Department for Education.

HM Government (2015) *Working Together to Safeguard Children: A Guide to Inter-Agency Working to Safeguard and Promote the Welfare of Children*. London: DCSF.

HM Government (2017) *Working Together to Safeguard Children: Changes to Statutory Guidance*. London: Department for Education.

HM Treasury (2003) *Every Child Matters*. London: The Stationary Office.

Hoghughi, M and Long, N (Eds.) (2004) *Handbook of Parenting: Theory and Research for Practice*. London: Sage Publications Limited.

Holden, C, Kilkey, M and Ramia, G (Eds.) (2011) *Social Policy Review 23: Analysis and Debate in Social Policy, 2011*. Bristol, UK: The Policy Press.

Holland, S (2010) *Child and Family Assessment in Social Work Practice*. London: Sage Publications.

Horwath, J (2002) *Maintaining a Focus on the Child? First Impressions of the Framework for the Assessment of Children in Need and Their Families in Cases of Child Neglect*. Child Abuse Review, Vol. 11 (4): pp. 195–213.

Howard, M O, McMillen, C J and Polio, D E (2003) *Teaching Evidence-Based Practice: Toward a New Paradigm for Social Work Education*. Research on Social Work Practice, Vol. 13: pp. 234–259.

Howe, D (1992) *Child Abuse and the Bureaucratisation of Social Work*. The Sociological Review, Vol. 40 (3): pp. 491–508.

Howe, D, Brandon, M, Hinings, D and Schofield, G (1999) *Attachment Theory, Child Maltreatment and Family Support: A Practice and Assessment Model*. Basingstoke, London: MacMillan Press Limited.

Huff, L and Kelley, L (2003) *Level of Organisational Trust in Individualist Versus Collectivist Societies: A Seven-Nation Study*. Organisation Science, Vol. 14 (1): pp. 81–90.

Human Rights Act (1998) https://www.legislation.gov.uk/ukpga/1998/42/contents

Humphris, R and Sigona, N (2019) *The Bureaucratic Capture of Child Migrants: Effects of Invisibility on Children on the Move*. Antipode, Vol. 51 (5): pp. 1495–1514.

Huntington, S (1993) *The Clash of Civilisations*? Foreign Affairs, Vol. 72: pp. 22–49.

Hutchinson, J and Smith, A D (Eds.) (1996) *Ethnicity*. Oxford: Oxford University Press.

Ignatieff, M (1998) *The Warrior's Honour Ethnic War and the Modern Conscience*. London: Chatto and Windus.

Jack, G and Gill, O (2003) *The Missing Side of the Triangle: Assessing the Importance of Family and Environmental Factors in the Lives of Children*. Essex: Barnardo's.

Jack, G and Jordan, B (1999) *Social Capital and Social Welfare*. Children and Society, Vol. 13 (4): pp. 242–256.

Jambunathan, S, Burts, D C and Pierce, S (2000) *Comparisons of Parenting Attitudes among Five Ethnic Groups in the United States*. Journal of Comparative Family Studies, Vol. 31 (4): pp. 395–406.

Jambunathan, S and Counselman, K (2002) *Parenting Attitudes of Asian Indian Mothers Living in the United States and India*. Early Child Development and Care, Vol. 172 (6): pp. 657–662.

Jenkins, R (2008) *Rethinking Ethnicity: Arguments and Explorations*. London: Sage Publications.

Jenkinson, S G (2001) *Child Support: A Comparison of the Old and New Approaches*. Child Support Analysis. http://www.childsupportanalysis.co.uk/guest_contributions/sue_paper/part_1_title.htm, accessed 3rd March 2020.

Jenson, J M (2005) *Connecting Science to Intervention: Advances, Challenges, and the Promise of Evidence-Based Practice*. Social Work Research, Vol. 29 (3): pp. 131–135.

Johnson, J G, Cohen, P, Chen, H, Kasen, S and Brook, J S (2006) *Parenting Behaviours Associated with Risk for Offspring Personality Disorder During Adulthood*. Archives of General Psychiatry, Vol. 63 (5): pp. 579–587.

Jones, D (2010) *Assessment of Parenting*. In: Horwath, J (Ed.) *The Child's World: The Comprehensive Guide to Assessing Children in Need*. London: Jessica Kingsley.

Jones, S (1997) *The Archeology of Ethnicity: Constructing Identities in the Past and Present*. London: Routledge.

Katz, I, La Placa, V and Hunter, C (2007) *Barriers to Inclusion and Successful Engagement of Parents in Mainstream Services*. York, UK: Joseph Rowntree Foundation.

Keller, H, Lavelli, M, Carra, C and Rossi. G (2019) *Culture-Specific Development of Early Mother–Infant Emotional Co-Regulation: Italian, Cameroonian, and West African Immigrant Dyads*. Developmental Psychology, Vol. 55 (9): pp. 1850–1867.

Keller, H, Voelker, S and Yorsi, R D (2005) *Conceptions of Parenting in Different Cultural Communities: The Case of West African Nso and Northern German Women*. Oxford: Blackwell Publishing.

Kellett, J and Apps, J (2009) *Assessments of Parenting and Parenting Support Need: A Study of Four Professional Groups*. York, UK: Joseph Rowntree Foundation.

Kemp, C H, Silverman, F N, Steele, B F, Droegemueller, W and Silver, H K (1962) *The Battered Child Syndrome*. Journal of American Medical Association (JAMA), Vol. 181 (1): pp. 17–24.

Kendall, F E (2012) *Understanding White Privilege*. Second Edition. London: Routledge.

Keniston, K (1977) *All Our Children: The American Family under Pressure*. San Diego, CA: Harcourt Brace Jovanovich.

Kiima, D (2017) *Evaluating the Parenting Competence of Black and Minority Ethnic Parents*. PhD thesis, University of York.

Kmita, G (2015) *Parenting Beliefs and Practices in Poland*. In: Nicolas, G, Bejarano, A and Lee, D L (Eds.) *Contemporary Parenting: A Global Perspective*. New York: Routledge.

Koprowska, J (2014) *Communication and Interpersonal Skills in Social Work*. Fourth Edition. London, United Kingdom: Sage Publications.

Kotchick, B and Forehand, R (2002) *Putting Parenting in Perspective: A Discussion of the Contextual Factors That Shape Parenting Practices*. Journal of Child and Family Studies, Vol. 11 (3): pp. 255–269.

Krauss, S E (2005) *Research Paradigms and Meaning Making: A Primer*. The Qualitative Report, Vol. 10 (4): pp. 758–770.

Kriz, K and Skivenes, M (2010) *Lost in Translation: How Child Welfare Workers in Norway and England Experience Language Difficulties When Working with Minority Ethnic Families*. British Journal of Social Work, Vol. 40 (5): pp. 1353–1367.

Kroeber, A L and Kluckhohn, C (1952) *Culture: A Critical Review of Concepts and Definitions*. Papers. Peabody Museum of Archaeology & Ethnology, Harvard University, Vol. 47 (1): pp. viii, 223.

Krugman, R D and Korbin, J E (Eds.) (2013) *Child Maltreatment: Contemporary Issues in Research and Policy. C. Henry Kempe: A 50 Year Legacy to the Field of Child Abuse and Neglect*. Springer Science. Amsterdam, Netherlands.

Kurtz, S N (1992) *All Mothers Are One: Hindu, India and the Cultural Reshaping of Psychoanalysis*. New York: Columbia University Press.

Kvale, S (1996) *Interview Views: An Introduction to Qualitative Research Interviewing*. Thousand Oaks, CA: Sage Publications.

Lamborn, S D, Mounts, N S, Steinburg, L and Dornbush, S M (1991) *Patterns of Competence and Adjustment among Adolescents from Authoritative, Authoritarian, Indulgent and Neglectful Families*. Child Development, Vol. 62: pp. 1049–1065.

Laming (2003) *The Victoria Climbié Inquiry Report*. London: HMSO.

Laming (2009) *The Protection of Children in England: A Progress Report*. London: HMSO.

Lammy, D (2017) *The Lammy Review: An Independent Review into the Treatment of, and Outcomes for Black, Asian and Minority Ethnic Individuals in the Criminal Justice System*. London: HMSO.

LaRossa, R, Bennett, L A and Gelles, R J (1981) *Ethical Dilemmas in Qualitative Family Research*. Journal of Marriage and the Family, Vol. 43: pp. 303–313.

Lee, E, Bristow, J, Faircloth, C and Macvarish, J (2014) *Parenting Culture Studies*. Kent: Palgrave MacMillan.

Lennings, C (2002) *Decision Making in Care and Protection: The Expert Assessment*. Australian e-Journal for the Advancement of Mental Health, Vol. 1 (2): pp. 128–140.

Lerner, R M (1998) *Theories of Human Development: Contemporary Perspectives*. In: Lerner, R M and Damon, W (Eds.) *Handbook of Child Psychology: Vol. 1. Theoretical Models of Human Development*. Fifth Edition (pp. 1–24). New York: John Wiley and Sons.

Leug, K, Lau, S and Lam, W (1998) *Parenting Styles and Academic Achievement: A Cross Cultural Study*. Merrill-Palmer Quarterly, Vol. 44 (2): pp. 157–172.

LeVine, R A (1994) *Childcare and Culture: Lessons from Africa*. Cambridge: Cambridge University Press.

Levitt, H, Butler, M and Hill, T (2006) *What Clients Find Helpful in Psychotherapy: Developing Principles for Facilitating Moment-to-Moment Change*. Journal of Counselling Psychology, Vol. 53: pp. 314–324.

Leyendecker, B, Harwood, R L, Comparini, L and Yalcinkaya, A (2005) *Socio Economic Status: Ethnicity and Parenting*. In: Luster, T and Okagaki, L (Eds.) *An Ecological Perspective* (Vol. 2, pp. 319–341). Mahwah, NJ: Lawrence Erlbaum Associates Publishers.

Liabo, K (2005) *What Works for Children and What Works in Research Implementation? Experiences from a Research and Development Project in the United Kingdom*. Social Policy Journal of New Zealand, Vol. 24: p. 198.

Lindahl, K M and Malik, N M (1999) *Marital Conflict, Family Processes, and Boys' Externalizing Behavior in Hispanic American and European American Families*. Journal of Clinical Child Psychology, Vol. 28 (1): pp. 12–24.

Littlechild, B (2012) *Values and Cultural Issues in Social Work*. Eris Web Journal, Vol. 5 (1): pp. 62–76.

Lloyd, N and Rafferty, A (2006) *Black and Minority Ethnic Families and Sure Start: Findings from Local Evaluation Reports*. London: NESS.

Local Authority Social Services Act (1970) https://www.legislation.gov.uk/ukpga/1970/42

Locke, J (1693) *Some Thoughts Concerning Education*. Revised Edition by. Quick, R. H (Ed.) (2007). Massachusetts, USA: Harvard University Press.

Lofland, J (1974) *Styles of Reporting Qualitative Field Research*. The American Sociologist, Vol. 9 (3): pp. 101–111.

Lofland, J and Lofland, L H (1995) *Analyzing Social Settings: A Guide to Qualitative Observation and Analysis*. Belmont, CA: Wadsworth.

Lonne, B, Parton, N, Thomson, J, Harries, M (2009) *Reforming Child Protection*. Abingdon: Routledge.

Luthar, S S (2006) *Resilience in Development: A Synthesis of Research Across Five Decades*. In: Cicchetti, D and Cohen, D J (Eds.) *Developmental Psychology: Risk, Disorder and Adaptation*. Second Edition. New York: Wiley.

Maalouf, A (2000) *On Identity*. London: Harvill Press.

Maccoby, E E and Martin, J A (1983) *Socialising in the Context of the Family: Parent-Child Interaction*. In: Mussen, P H and Hetherington, E M (Eds.) *Handbook of Child Psychology*. Fourth Edition: Socialisation, Personality and Social Development. New York: Wiley Publishers.

Madge, N (2001) *Understanding Difference: The Meaning of Ethnicity for Young Lives*. London: National Children's Bureau.

Madge, N and Willmont, N (2007) *Children's Views and Experiences of Parenting*. York, UK: Joseph Rowntree Foundation.

Main, M and Solomon, J (1986) *Discovery of an Insecure-Disorganized/Disoriented Attachment Pattern*. In: Brazelton, T B and Yogman, M W (Eds.) *Affective Development in Infancy* (pp. 95–124). Westport, CT: Ablex Publishing.

Main, M and Solomon, J (1990) *Procedures for Identifying Infants as Disorganized/Disoriented during the Ainsworth Strange Situation*. In: Greenberg, M T, Cicchetti, D and Cummings, E M (Eds.) *The John D. and Catherine T. MacArthur Foundation Series on Mental Health and Development. Attachment in the Preschool Years: Theory, Research, and Intervention* (pp. 121–160). Chicago: University of Chicago Press.

Marshall, M N (1996) *Sampling for Qualitative Research*. Family Practice, Vol. 13 (6): pp. 522–526.

Maslow, A H (1943) *Motivation and Personality*. Third Edition (1987). New York: Addison-Wesley Publishers.

Masson, J (2004) *The Legal Context*. In: Fraser, S, Lewis, V, Ding, S, Kellett, M and Robinson, C (Eds.) *Doing Research with Children and Young People*. London: Sage.

Masten, A S, Burt, K B and Coatsworth, J D (2006) *Competence and Psychopathology in Development*. In: Cicchetti, D and Cohen, D J (Eds.) *Developmental Psychopathology*. Second Edition. New York: Wiley.

Masten, A S and Shaffer, A (2006) *How Families Matter in Child Development: Reflections from Research on Risk and Resilience*. In: Clarke-Stewart, A and Dunn, J (Eds.) *The Jacobs Foundation Series on Adolescence. Families Count: Effects on Child and Adolescent Development* (pp. 5–25). Cambridge: Cambridge University Press.

McDaniel, S and Tepperman, L (2000) *Close Relations: An Introduction to the Sociology of Families*. Toronto, ON: Prentice Hall & Allyn and Bacon Canada.

McGhee, J and Hunter, S (2011) *Involving Parents in Assessment and Decision-Making. Scottish Childcare and Protection Network Briefing*. Scotland: University of Stirling.

McGregor-Smith (2017) *Race in the Workplace: The McGregor-Smith Review*. Cabinet Office. London, United Kingdom.

McIntosh, P (1988) *White Privilege and Male Privilege: A Personal Account of Coming to See Correspondences through Work in Women's Studies*. Massachusetts, USA: Wellesley College Centre for Research on Women.

McLoyd, V, Cauce, A, Takeuchl, D and Wilson, L (2000) *Marital Processes and Parental Socialisation in Families of Colour: A Decade Review of Research*. Journal of Marriage and the Family, Vol. 62 (4): pp. 40–53.

McPhee, D, Fritz, J and Miller, H J (1996) *Ethnic Variations in Personal Social Networks and Parenting*. Child Development, Vol. 67 (6): pp. 3278–3295.

Mertens, D M (2003) *Mixed Methods and the Politics of Human Research: The Transformative Emancipating Perspective*. In: Tashakkori and Teddie (Eds.) *Handbook of Mixed Methods in Social and Behavioural Research*. Thousand Oaks, CA: Sage Publishers.

Middleton, A and DeSoysa, R (2016) *Physical Chastisement: Does It Happen*. Archives of Disease in Childhood, Vol. 101: pp. 359–360.

Miller, M and Corby, B (2006) *The Framework for the Assessment of Children in Need and Their Families: A Basis for a 'Therapeutic' Encounter?* British Journal of Social Work, Vol. 36: pp. 887–899.

Modood, T, Berthoud, R, Lakey, J, Nazroo, J, Smith, P, Virdee, S and Beishon, S (1997) *Ethnic Minorities in Britain: Diversity and Disadvantage*. London: Policy Studies Institute.

Modood, T and May, S (2001) *Multiculturalism and Education in Britain: An Internally Contested Debate*. International Journal of Educational Research, Vol. 35 (3): pp. 305–317.

Monk, G, Winslade, J, Crocket, K and Epston, D (Eds.) (1997) *The Jossey-Bass Psychology Series. Narrative Therapy in Practice: The Archaeology of Hope*. San Francisco, CA: Jossey-Bass.

Montgomery, H (2003) *Children and Violence*. In: Montgomery, H, Burr, R and Woodhead, M (Eds.) *Changing Childhoods: Local and Global*. England: Wiley.

Moon, N and Ivins, C (2004) *Parental Involvement in Children's Education*. London: DfES, RR589.

Moran, D (2000) *Introduction to Phenomenology*. England: Routledge.

Moran, D and Mooney, T (2002) *The Phenomenology Reader*. London: Routledge.

Moran, P, Ghate, D and van der Merwe, A (2004) *What Works in Parenting Support? A Review of International Evidence*. Policy Research Bureau. London, United Kingdom.

Morgan, D L and Kreuger, R A (1998) *When to Use Focus Groups and Why*. In: Morgan, D L (Ed.) *Successful Focus Group*. London: Sage.

Moriarty, J (2011) *Qualitative Methods Overview. Methods Review (1)*. London: NIHR School for Social Care Research.

Morris, T (2006) *Social Work Research Methods: Four Alternative Paradigms*. Thousand Oaks, CA: Sage.

Morrison, G S (1978) *Parent Involvement in the Home, School and Community*. Columbus, OH: Charles E. Merrill.

Morse, J M, Barrett, M, Mayan, M, Olson, K and Spiers, J (2002) *Verification Strategies for Establishing Reliability and Validity in Qualitative Research*. International Journal of Qualitative Methods, Vol. 1: pp. 1–19.

Moustakas, C (1994) *Phenomenological Research Methods*. Thousand Oaks, CA: Sage.

Munro, E (2008) *Effective Child Protection*. London: Sage.

Munro, E (2011) *The Munro Review of Child Protection. Interim Report: The Child's Journey*. London: Department for Education.

Murray, V M, Smith, E P and Hill, N E (2001) *Ethnicity and Culture in Studies of Families in Context*. Journal of Marriage and Family, Vol. 63: pp. 911–914.

Nadan, Y, Spilsbury, J C and Korbin, J E (2015) *Culture and Context in Understanding Child Maltreatment: Contributions of Intersectionality and Neighbourhood-Based Research*. Child Abuse and Neglect, Vol. 41: pp. 40–48.

Nandi, A and Platt, L (2013) *Britishness and Identity Assimilation among the UK's Minority and Majority Ethnic Groups*. Understanding Society Working Paper Series No. 2013. United Kingdom: University of Essex and London School of Economics and Politics.

O'Connor, T G and Scott, S (2007) *Parenting and Outcomes for Children*. York, UK: Joseph Rowntree Foundation.

Office for National Statistics (ONS) (2012) *Ethnicity and National Identity in England and Wales: 2011*. Office for National Statistics. London, United Kingdom.

Office for National Statistics (2019) *Overview of the UK Population: August 2019*. Office for National Statistics. London, United Kingdom.

Office for National Statistics (2020) *Child Abuse in England and Wales. Statistics and Research on Child Abuse in England and Wales. Bringing Together a Rage of Different Data Sources from across Government and the Voluntary Sector.* Cabinet Office. London, United Kingdom.

Ogbu, J U (1981) *Origins of Human Competence: A Cultural-Ecological Perspective.* Child Development, Vol. 52: pp. 413–429.

Okasha, S (2002) *Philosophy of Science: A Very Short Introduction.* New York: Oxford University Press.

Orb, A, Eisenhauer, L and Wynaden, D (2001) *Ethics in Qualitative Research.* Journal of Nursing Scholarship, Vol. 33 (1): pp. 93–96.

Owen, C and Statham, J (2009) *Disproportionality in Child Welfare: The Prevalence of Black and Minority Ethnic Children within the 'Looked After' and 'Child in Need' Populations and on Child Protection Registers in England.* London: Thomas Coram Research United, University of London.

Owen, M and Farmer, E (1995) *Child Protection Practice: Private Risks and Public Remedies. A Study of Decision-making, Intervention and Outcome in Child Protection Work.* London: HMSO.

Owen, M and Farmer, E (1996) *Child Protection in a Multi-Racial Context.* Policy and Politics, Vol. 24 (3).

Owen, E and Farmer, M (1996) *Child Protection in a Multi-racial Context.* Policy and Politics, Vol. 24: pp. 299–313.

Page, J and Whitting, G (2007) *Engaging Effectively with Black and Minority Ethnic Parents in Children's and Parental Services.* London: Department of Children, Schools and Families.

Page, J Whitting, G and McLean, C (2007) *Engaging Effectively with Black and Minority Ethnic Parents in Children's and Parental Services.* London, UK: Department for Children, Schools and Families.

Paiget, J (1955) *The Child's Construction of Reality.* London: Routledge and Kegan Paul.

Parekh, B (2000) *Rethinking Multiculturalism.* Basingstoke: Macmillan.

Parton, N (2003) *Rethinking Professional Practice: The Contributions of Social Constructionism and Feminist Ethics of Care.* British Journal of Social Work, Vol. 33 (1): pp. 1–16.

Parton, N (2010) *Child Protection and Safeguarding in England: Changing and Competing Conceptions of Risk and Their Implications for Social Work.* The British Journal of Social Work, Vol. 41 (5): pp. 854–875.

Parton, N (2014) *The Politics of Child Protection: Contemporary Developments and Future Directions.* Basingstoke: Palgrave MacMillan.

Patton, M Q (2002) *Two Decades of Developments in Qualitative Inquiry: A Personal, Experiential Perspective.* Qualitative Social Work, Vol. 1 (3): pp. 261–283.

Perks, R and Thomson, A (2006) *The Oral History Reader.* Second Edition. London: Routledge.

Peterson, G W and Hann, D (1999) *Socializing Parents and Children in Families.* In: M B Sussman, S K Steinmetz and G W Peterson (Eds.) *Handbook of Marriage and the Family* (pp. 327–370). New York: Plenum Press.

Phinney, J S and Chavira, V (1995) *Parental Socialisation and Adolescent Coping with Problems Related to Ethnicity.* Journal of Research on Adolescence, Vol. 5 (1): pp. 31–35.

Phoenix, A and Husain, F (2007) *Parenting and Ethnicity.* York, UK: Joseph Rowntree Foundation.

Phoenix, A and Pattynama, P (2006) *Intersectionality.* European Journal of Women's Studies, Vol. 13 (3): pp. 187–192.

Platt, D (2006) *Threshold Decisions: How Social Workers Prioritize Referrals of Child Concern.* Child Abuse Review, Vol. 15 (1): 4–18.

Platt, D (2011) *Assessments of Children and Families: Learning and Teaching the Skills of Analysis.* Social Work Education, Vol. 30 (2): pp. 157–169.

Platt, D and Turney, D (2014) *Making Threshold Decisions in Child Protection: A Conceptual Analysis.* The British Journal of Social Work, Vol. 44 (6): pp. 1472–1490.

Polkinghorne, D E (2005) *Language and Meaning: Data Collection in Qualitative Research.* Journal of Counselling Psychology, Vol. 52: pp. 137–145.

Prevention of Cruelty to Children Act (1889) https://www.legislation.gov.uk/ukpga/1889/44/contents/enacted

Prinstein, M J and Dodge, K A (Eds.) (2008) *Duke Series in Child Development and Public Policy. Understanding Peer Influence in Children and Adolescents.* New York: The Guilford Press.

Quah, S R (2003) *Ethnicity and Parenting Styles among Singapore Families.* Marriage and Family Review, Vol. 35 (3–4): pp. 63–83.

Quah, S R (2004) *Ethnicity and Parenting Styles among Singapore Families.* Marriage and Family Review, Vol. 35 (3): pp. 63–83.

Quintana, S M, Aboud, F E, Choa, R K, Contresas-Grau, J, Cross, W E, Hudley, C, Huges, D, Liben, L S, Nelson-Le Gall, S and Vietze, D L (2006) *Race, Ethnicity and Culture in Child Development: Contemporary Research and Future Directions.* Child Development, Vol. 77 (5): pp. 1129–1141.

Race Disparity Audit (2017) www.ethnicty-facts-figures.services.gov.uk, accessed 28th January 2020.

Radziszewska, B, Richardson, J L, Dent, C W and Brian, R F (1996) *Parenting Style and Adolescent Depressive Symptoms, Smoking, and Academic Achievement: Ethnic, Gender, and SES Differences.* Journal of Behavioural Medicine, Vol. 19: pp. 289–305.

Raj, S P and Raval, V V (2013) *Residential Child Care in Malaysia: An Exploratory Qualitative Study of Caregiver–Child Interactions.* International Perspectives in Psychology: Research, Practice, Consultation, Vol. 2 (3): pp. 194–206.

Rapmund, V and Moore, C (2000) *Women's Stories of Depression: A Constructivist Approach.* South African Journal of Psychology, Vol. 30 (2): pp. 20–30.

Reder, P, Duncan, S and Lucey, C (2003) *Studies in the Assessment of Parenting.* London: Routledge.

Reissman, C K (2008) Narrative Methods for the Human Sciences. *Adult Education Quarterly,* Vol. 59 (2): pp. 176–177.

Reupert, A, Maybery, D, Nicholson, J, Gopfert, M and Seeman, M V (2015) *Parental Psychiatric Disorder, Distressed Parents and Their Families.* Third Edition. Cambridge: Cambridge University Press.

Richman, A L, Miller, P M and LeVine, R A (1992) *Cultural and Educational Variations in Maternal Responsiveness.* Developmental Psychology, Vol. 28 (4): pp. 614–621.

Riessman, C K and Quinney, L (2005) *Narrative in Social Work: A Critical Review.* Qualitative Social Work, Vol. 4 (4): pp. 391–412.

Ritchie, J and Lewis, J (Eds.) (2003) *Qualitative Research Practice: A Guide for Social Science Students and Researchers.* London: Sage Publications.

Ritchie, J and Spencer, L (1994) *Qualitative Data Analysis for Applied Policy Research in Jane Ritchie and Liz Spencer.* In: Bryman, A and Burgess, R G (Eds.) *Analyzing Qualitative Data.* First Edition. England: Routledge.

Rodgers, B and Pryor, J (1998) *Divorce and Separation: The Outcomes for Children.* York, UK: Joseph Rowntree.

Rogowski, S (2015) *From Child Welfare to Child Protection/Safeguarding: A Critical Practitioner's View of Changing Conceptions, Policies and Practice.* Practice Social Work in Action, Vol. 27 (2): pp. 97–112.

Roopnarine, J L and Gielen, W P (2005) *Families in Global Perspective.* Boston: Allyn and Bacon.

Roopnarine, J L, Krishnakumar, A, Narture, L, Logre, C and Lape, M E (2014) *Relationship between Parenting Practices and Pre-Schoolers' Social Skills in African, Indo and Mixed Ethnic Families in Trinidad and Tobago: The Mediating Role of Ethnic Socialisation.* Journal for Cross Cultural Psychology, Vol. 45 (3): pp. 362–380.

Rousseau, J J (1762) *The Social Contract.* London: Penguin Books.

Royston, S and Rodrigues, L (2013) *Breaking Barriers: How to Help Children's Centres Reach Disadvantaged Children.* London: The Children's Society.

Rutter, M (1985) *Resilience in the Face of Adversity: Protective Factors and Resistance to Psychiatric Disorder.* British Journal of Psychiatry, Vol. 147: pp. 598–611.

Rutter, M (1999) *Psychosocial Adversity and Child Psychology.* British Journal of Psychiatry, Vol. 174: pp. 480–493.

Rutter, M, Yule, B, Quinton, D, Rowlands, O, Yule, W and Berger, M (1975) *Attainment and Adjustment in Two Geographical Areas: III. Some Factors Accounting for Area Differences.* The British Journal of Psychiatry, Vol. 126: pp. 520–533.

Saar-Heiman, Y and Gupta, A (2019) *The Poverty-Aware Paradigm for Child Protection: A Critical Framework for Policy and Practice.* British Journal of Social Work: pp. 1–18.

Saraswathi, T S and Pai, S (1997) *Socialisation in the Indian Context.* In: Kao, H S R and Sinha, D (Eds.) *Asian Perspectives in Psychology.* Cross-Cultural Research and Methodology Series, Vol. 19. New Delhi: Sage.

Sarna, J D (1978) *From Immigrants to Ethics: Towards a New Theory of Ethnicisation.* Ethnicity, Issue 5: pp. 370–378.

Sawrikar, P (2017) *Working with Ethnic Minorities and Across Cultures in Wester Child Protection Systems.* London: Routledge.

Schelling, T (1963) *The Strategy of Conflict.* New York: Cambridge University Press.

Schermerhorn, R (1996) *Ethnicity and Minority Groups.* In: Hutchinson, J and Smith, A D (Ed.) *Ethnicity.* Oxford: Oxford University Press.

Schön, D A (1987) *Jossey-Bass Higher Education Series. Educating the Reflective Practitioner: Toward a New Design for Teaching and Learning in the Professions.* San Francisco, CA: Jossey-Bass.

Schön, D A and Rein, M (1994) *Frame Reflection: Toward the Resolution of Intractable Policy Controversies.* New York: Basic Books.

Schön, R A and Silvén, M (2007) *Natural Parenting: Back to Basics in Infant Care.* Evolutionary Psychology, Vol. 5: pp. 102–183.

Scott, A, Shaw, M and Joughin, C (Eds.) (2001) *Finding the Evidence: A Gateway to the Literature in Child and Adolescent Mental Health.* Second Edition. London: Royal College of Psychiatrists.

Selwy, J, Saunders, H and Farmer, E (2010) *The Views of Children and Young People on Being Cared for by an Independent Foster Care Provider.* The British Journal of Social Work, Vol. 40 (3): pp. 696–713.

Serbin, L A and Karp, J (2004) *The Intergenerational Transfer of Psycho-social Risk: Mediators of Vulnerability and Resilience.* Annual Review of Psychology, Vol. 55: pp. 333–363.

Shaffer, A, Burt, K B, Obradovic, J, Herbers, J E and Masten, A S (2009) *Intergenerational Continuity in Parenting Quality: The Mediating Role of Social Competence.* Developmental Psychology, Vol. 45 (5): pp. 1227–1240.

Shaffer, D R (2008) *Social and Personality Development*. Belmont, CA: Wadsworth Publishing.

Shaw, I (2011) *Evaluating in Practice*. Surry, England: Ashgate Publishing.

Shaw, I and Gould, N (2001) *Qualitative Research in Social Work: Context and Method*. England: Sage Publications.

Sheppard, M (2009) *High Thresholds and Prevention in Children's Services – The Impact of Mothers' Coping Strategies on Outcome of Child and Parenting Problems: A Six-Month Follow-Up*. British Journal of Social Work, Vol. 39 (1): pp. 46–63.

Shumow, L, Vandell, D L and Posner, J K (1998) *Harsh, Firm and Permissive Parenting in Low Income Families: Relations to Children's Academic Achievement and Behavioural Adjustment*. Journal for Family Issues, Vol. 19 (5): pp. 483–507.

Sigle-Rushton W and McLanahan S (2000) *The Living Arrangements of New Unmarried Mothers*. Demography, Vol. 39 (3): pp. 415–433.

Simpson, G and Littlechild, B (2009) *International Aspects of Social Work with Children, Young People and Families*. In: Lawrence, S, Lyons, K, Simpson, G and Huegler, N (Eds.) *Introducing International Social Work*. Exeter: Learning Matters.

Skinner, B F (1953) *Science and Human Behaviour*. Boston: Pearson Education Inc.

Smesler, N J (Ed.) (1988) *Handbook of Modern Sociology*. Beverly Hills, CA: Sage Publications.

Smith, A (1996) *Nations and Their Pasts*. Nations and Nationalism, Vol. 2: pp. 358–365.

Smith, A (1998) *Nationalism and Modernism: A Critical Survey of Recent Theories of Nations and Nationalism*. London: Routledge.

Smith, C A and Farrington, D P (2004) *Continuities in Anti-social Behaviour and Parenting Across Three Generations*. Journal of Child Psychology and Psychiatry, Vol. 45, pp. 230–247.

Smith, J A (2004) *Reflecting on the Development of Interpretative Phenomenological Analysis and Its Contribution to Qualitative Research in Psychology*. Qualitative Research in Psychology, Vol. 1 (1): pp. 39–54.

Smith, R (2010) *Total Parenting*. Educational Theory, Vol. 60 (3): pp. 357–369.

Spera, C (2005) *A Review of the Relationship among Parenting Practices, Parenting Styles and Adolescent School Achievers*. Educational Psychology Review, Vol. 17 (2): pp. 125–146.

Spicer, P (2010) *Cultural Influences on Parenting*. Oklahoma: Zero to Three.

Spiegelberg, H (1982) *The Phenomenological Movement: A Historical Introduction*. Third Edition. Hague: Martinus Nijhoff.

Squire, C (2008) *Approaches to Narrative Research*. Southampton, England: National Centre for Research Methods.

Srouge, L A, Elicker, J and Englund, M (1992) *Predicting Peer Competence and Peer Relationships in Childhood from Early Parent–Child Relationships*. In: Parke, R D and Ladd, G W (Eds.) *Family–Peer Relationships: Modes of Linkage* (pp. 77–106). Lawrence Erlbaum Associates, Inc. New Jersey, USA.

Steinberg, L, Lamborn, S D, Dornbusch, S M and Darling, N (1992) *Impact of Parenting Practices on Adolescent Achievement: Authoritative Parenting, School Involvement, and Encouragement to Succeed*. Child Development, Vol. 63 (5): pp. 1266–1281.

Steinmetz, S K (1987) *Family Violence: Past, Present, and Future*. In: Sussman, M B and Steinmetz, S K (Eds.) *Handbook of Marriage and the Family*. New York, USA: Springer (pp. 725–765).

Stevenson, H W, Lee, S, Chen, C, Stigler, J W, Hsu, C and Kitamura, S (1990) *Contexts of Achievement*. Monographs of the Society for Research in Child Development, Issue 55.

Stevenson, O (2007) *Neglected Children and Their Families*. Oxford: Blackwell.

Stewart, S and Bond, M (2002) *A Critical Look at Parenting Research from the Main Stream: Problems Uncovered While Adapting Western Research to Non-Western Cultures*. British Journal of Developmental Psychology, Vol. 20 (2): pp. 379–392.

Stone, J (2003) *Max Weber on Race, Ethnicity and Nationalism*. In: Stone, J and Dennis, R *Race and Ethnicity: Comparative and Theoretical Approaches*. Oxford: Blackwell Publishers.

Suissa, J (2014) *Tough Love and Character Education: Reflections on Some Notions 'Good Parenting'*. Pedagogical Culture: pp. 115–132.

Super, C and Harkness, S (1997) *The Cultural Structuring of Child Development*. In: Berry, J, Dasen, P and Saraswathi, T (Eds.) *Handbook of Cross-Cultural Psychology: Basic Processes and Human Development*. Boston: Allyn and Bacon.

Super, C M and Harkness, S (2002) *Culture Structures the Environment for Development*. Human Development, Vol. 45 (4): pp. 270–274.

Super, M C, Giovanna, A, Harkness, S, Barbara, W, Piotr, O Z, Moises, R B, Sabrina, B, Parminder, P, Ughetta, M, Violett, K, Jesus, P and Harry, M (2007) *Culture, Temperament and the Difficult Child in Seven Western Cultures*. European Journal of Developmental Science, Vol. 2: pp. 136–157.

Swindler, J K (2008) *From Individual to Collective*. Journal of Social Philosophy, Vol. 3 (1): pp. 116–130.

Talbot, J (2009) *The Road to Positive Discipline: A Parent's Guide*. Los Angeles, CA: TNT Publishing.

Tashakkori, A and Teddie, C (2003) *Handbook of Mixed Methods in Social and Behavioural Research*. Sage. California, USA.

Taylor, B J (2006) *Risk Management Paradigms in Health and Social Services for Professional Decision Making on the Long-term Care of Older People*. British Journal of Social Work, Vol. 36 (8): pp. 1411–1429.

Teti, D M and Candelania, M (2002) *Parenting Competence*. In: Bornstein, M H (Ed.) *Handbook of Parenting*. Second Edition, Vol. 4: Social Conditions and Applied Parenting. Hillsdale, NJ: Lawrence Erlbaum Associates.

Teti, D M, Cole, P M, Cabrera, N, Goodman, S H and McLoyd, V M (2017) *Supporting Parents: How Six Decades of Parenting Research Can Inform Policy and Best Practice*. Research Practice Partnership: Building a Two-Way Street of Engagement, Vol. 30 (5).

Thelen, E and Smith, L B (1998) *Dynamic Systems Theories*. In: Damon, W and Lerner, R M (Eds.) *Handbook of Child Psychology: Theoretical Models of Human Development* (pp. 563–634). John Wiley and Sons Inc. New Jersey, USA.

Thoburn, J, Chand, A and Proctor, J (2005) *Review of Research on Child Welfare Services for Children of Minority Ethnic Origin and Their Families*. London: Jessica Kingsley Publishers.

Thoburn, J, Lewis, A and Shemmings, D (1995) *Paternalism or Partnership? Family Involvement in the Child Protection Process*. London: HMSO.

Thompson, A G (1992) *Teachers' Beliefs and Conceptions: A Synthesis of the Research*. In: D A Grouws (Ed.) *Handbook of Research on Mathematics Teaching and Learning: A Project of the National Council of Teachers of Mathematics*. New York, USA: Macmillan.

Torretti, R (1999) *The Philosophy of Physics*. Cambridge, UK: Cambridge University Press.

Triandis, H (2001) *Individualism, Collectivism and Personality*. Journal of Personality, Vol. 69 (6): pp. 907–924.

Tripp, J H and Cockett, M (1998) *Parents, Parenting and Family Breakdown*. Archives of Disease in Childhood, Vol. 78: pp. 104–108.

Tuli, M (2012) *Beliefs on Parenting and Childhood in India*. Journal of Comparative Family Studies, Vol. 43 (1): 81–92.

Turney, D, Platt, D, Selwyn, J and Farmer, E (2011) *Social Work Assessment of Children in Need. What Do We Know? Messages from Research*. Bristol: University of Bristol.

United Nations Convention on the Rights of the Child (1989) https://www.unicef.org/child-rights-convention/what-is-the-convention

Utting, D (2007) *Parenting and the Different Ways It Can Affect Children's Lives: Research Evidence*. York, UK: Joseph Rowntree Foundation.

Utting, D and Pugh, G (2004) *The Social Context of Parenting*. In: Hoghughi, M and Long, N (Eds.) *Handbook of Parenting: Theory and Research for Practice*. London: Sage Publications Limited.

Van den Berghe, P L (1981) *The Ethnic Phenomenon*. New York: Elsevier North-Holland.

Van Drenth, A, Knijn, T and Lewis, J (1999) *Sources of Income for Lone Mother Families: Policy Changes in Britain and the Netherlands and the Experiences of Divorced Women*. Journal of Social Policy, Vol. 28 (4): pp. 619–641.

Van Manen, M (1982) *Phenomenological Pedagogy*. Curriculum Inquiry, Vol. 12 (3): pp. 283–299.

Van Manen, M (1990) *Researching Lived Experience: Human Science for an Action Sensitive Pedagogy*. London, ON, Canada: Althouse Press.

Van Manen, M (2007) *Phenomenology of Practice*. Phenomenology and Practice, Vol. 1 (1): pp. 11–30.

Walton, F C and Caliendo, S M (2011) *Origins of the Concept of Race*. In: Caliendo, S M and McIlwain, C D (Eds.) *The Routledge Companion to Race and Ethnicity*. London: Routledge.

Ward, H, Brown R, Westlake D and Munro E (2010) *Infants Suffering, or Likely to Suffer, Significant Harm: A Prospective Longitudinal Study*. Research Brief DFE-RB053. London: Department for Education.

Ward, H and Rose, W (Eds.) (2002) *Approaches to Needs Assessment in Children's Services*. London: Jessica Kingsley.

Waylen, A and Stewart-Brown, S (2008) *Parenting in Ordinary Families: Diversity, Complexity and Change*. York, UK: Joseph Rowntree Foundation.

Waylen, A and Stewart-Brown, S L (2010) *Factors Influencing Parenting in Early Childhood: A Prospective Longitudinal Study Focusing on Change*. Child: Care, Health and Development, Vol. 36 (2): pp. 198–207.

Weisner, T S (2002) *Ecocultural Understanding of Children's Developmental Pathways*. Human Development, Vol. 45 (4): pp. 275–281.

Weiss, L H and Schwarz, J C (1996) *The Relationship Between Parenting Styles and Older Adolescents' Personality, Academic Achievement, Adjustment and Substance Misuse*. Child Development, Vol. 67 (5): pp. 2101–2114.

Welbourne, P (2002) *Culture, Children's Rights and Child Protection*. Child Abuse Review, Vol. 11 (16): pp. 345–358.

Wengraf, T (2001) *Qualitative Social Interviewing: Biographic Narrative and Semi-Structured Methods*. London: Sage Publications.

Wengraf, T (2002) *Historicising the Socio, Theory, and the Constant Comparative Method*. In: Chamberlayne, P, Rustin, M and Wengraf, T (Eds.) *Biography and Social Policy in Europe: Experiences and Life Journeys*. Bristol, England: The Policy Press.

Wentzel, K R (1998) *Parents' Aspirations for Children's Educational Attainments: Relations to Parental Belief Systems and Social Address Variables*. Merrill-Palmber, Vol. 44: pp. 20–37.

Wheeldon, J and Åhlberg, M K (2012) *Visualizing Social Science Research*. In: Wheeldon, J and Åhlberg, M K (Eds.) *Visualizing Social Science Research: Maps, Methods, and Meaning*. Thousand Oaks, CA: Sage.

White, A (2005) *Assessments of Parenting Capacity: Literature Review*. Australia: Centre for Parenting and Research Development of Community Services.

White, M and Epston, D (1990) *Narrative Means to Therapeutic Ends*. New York: W. W. Norton.

White, S, Wastell, D, Broadhurst, K and Hall, C (2010) *When Policy Overleaps Itself: The Tragic Tale of the Integrated Children's System*. Critical Social Policy, Vol. 30 (3): pp. 405–429.

Whiteside-Mansell, L, Bradley, R H, Little, T D, Corwyn, R F and Spiker, D (2001) *An Examination of Cross-Racial Comparability of Mother-Child Interaction among African American and Anglo-American Families*. Journal of Marriage and the Family, Vol. 63 (3): pp. 767–778.

Whiting, J W M and Child, I L (1953) *Child Training and Personality: A Cross-Cultural Study*. London: Yale University Press.

Wildman, S M and Davis, A D (1997) *Making Systems of Privilege Visible*. In: Delgado, R and Stefancic, J S (Eds.) *Critical White Studies: Looking Behind the Mirror* (pp. 314–319). Philadelphia, PA: Temple University Press.

Wiles, R, Heath, S, Crow, G and Charles, V (2005) *Informed Consent in Social Research: A Literature Review*. ESRC National Centre for Research Methods. Southampton, United Kingdom.

Wilkinson, S (1998) *Focus Groups in Feminist Research. Power, Interaction and Co-Construction of Meaning*. Women's Forum, Vol. 21 (1): pp. 111–112.

Williams, C and Soydan, H (2005) *When and How Does Ethnicity Matter? A Cross-National Study of Social Work Responses to Ethnicity in Child Protection Cases*. The British Journal of Social Work, Vol. 35 (6): pp. 901–920.

Williams, F and Churchill, H (2006) *Empowering Parents in Sure Start Local Programmes*. London: DfES.

Winnicott, D W (1965) *The Maturation Process and the Facilitative Environment*. New York: International Universities Press.

Winnicott, D W (1973) *The Child, the Family and the Outside World*. London, United Kingdom: Penguin (republication).

Winter, P (2011) *David Cameron Unveils 458m Plan to Help "Problem Families"*. www.guardian.co.uk/politics/2011/dec/15/david-cameon-plan-problem-familie, accessed 23rd December 2011.

Woodcock, J (2003) *The Social Work Assessment of Parenting: An Exploration*. British Journal of Social Work, Vol. 33: pp. 87–106.

Yancey, W, Eriksen, E and Juliani, R (1976) *Emergent Ethnicity: A Review and Reformulation*. American Sociological Review, Vol. 41, pp. 391–403.

Zaman, R M (2014) *Parenting in Pakistan: An Overview*. In: Selin, H (Ed.) *Parenting across Cultures. Science across Cultures: The History of Non-Western Science* (Vol. 7). Dordrecht: Springer.

Zimmerman, T S (Ed.) (2002) *Integrating Gender and Culture in Parenting*. New York: Routledge.

Index

Note: Page numbers in *italics* indicate a figure and page numbers in **bold** indicate a table on the corresponding page.

Lightning Source UK Ltd.
Milton Keynes UK
UKHW020430070922
408454UK00004B/57

9 780367 543853